Dear Reader:

The book you are about to read is the latest bestseller from the St. Martin's True Crime Library, the imprint *The New York Times* calls "the leader in true crime!" Each month, we offer you a fascinating account of the latest, most sensational crime that has captured the national attention. St. Martin's is the publisher of Tina Dirmann's VANISHED AT SEA, the story of a former child actor who posed as a yacht buyer in order to lure an older couple out to sea, then robbed them and threw them overboard to their deaths. John Glatt's riveting and horrifying SECRETS IN THE CELLAR shines a light on the man who shocked the world when it was revealed that he had kept his daughter locked in his hidden basement for 24 years. In the Edgar-nominated WRITTEN IN BLOOD, Diane Fanning looks at Michael Petersen, a Marine-turned-novelist found guilty of beating his wife to death and pushing her down the stairs of their home—only to reveal another similar death from his past. In the book you now hold, THE GOOD SON, Stella Sands examines a case of youthful rebellion gone horribly wrong.

St. Martin's True Crime Library gives you the stories behind the headlines. Our authors take you right to the scene of the crime and into the minds of the most notorious murderers to show you what really makes them tick. St. Martin's True Crime Library paperbacks are better than the most terrifying thriller, because it's all true! The next time you want a crackling good read, make sure it's got the St. Martin's True Crime Library logo on the spine—you'll be up all night!

Charles E. Spicer, Jr.
Executive Editor, St. Martin's True Crime Library

The
Good Son

STELLA SANDS

St. Martin's Paperbacks

THE GOOD SON

Copyright © 2011 by Stella Sands.

Cover design and photo of houses by Kirk DuPonce. Mug shot courtesy Mansfield Jail.

For information address St. Martin's Press, 175 Fifth Avenue, New York, NY 10010.

EAN: 978-0-312-58646-1

Printed in the United States of America

St. Martin's Paperbacks edition / February 2011

St. Martin's Paperbacks are published by St. Martin's Press, 175 Fifth Avenue, New York, NY 10010.

10 9 8 7 6 5 4 3 2 1

For Sass, always.

Acknowledgments

I was indeed privileged to have had many generous and knowledgeable people willing to help me with this book. Attorneys first. I would like to thank Larry M. Moore, David Pearson, Bob Ford, Tim Moore, and Ray Hall, Jr., for supplying me with legal information, background, and personal beliefs about the case. For sharing insights and facts, I would like to thank Detective Ralph Standefer.

For opening my eyes to the case and for her constant support, I would like to thank my dear friend Jennifer Dixon; for being a source of comfort and encouragement, a thank you to Marjorie Frank; and for her insightful comments on the manuscript, a deep dept of gratitude to Margaret Mittelbach.

Heartfelt thank yous to my agent, Giles Anderson; to my discerning, funny, and always right-on editor at St. Martin's, Allison Caplin Strobel; to Charlie Spicer for giving me another wonderful opportunity to write for St. Martin's; and to copy-editor Katherine Pradt, who made certain that no participle dangled.

And as always, I'd like to say a special thank you to Jess and AF, for always being there.

Chapter One

Deck the halls with boughs of holly,
Fa la la la la, la la la la.
'Tis the season to be jolly . . .

Suzy Wamsley hummed along to her favorite holiday tune as she put the finishing touches on her family's sparkling Christmas tree. The Christmas season was always a jolly time for the Wamsleys. Their home—a sprawling two-story mansion in the Walnut Estates neighborhood of Mansfield, Texas, just south of Arlington—was a veritable Santa's workshop. In truth, the house at 820 Turnberry Drive seemed to have been constructed with Christmas lights in mind—the eaves purposely built to display the hundreds of twinkling white lights that Rick Wamsley painstakingly hung each year; the fireplace expressly fashioned to show off the colorful Christmas stockings; the front lawn perfectly suited to the Santa and sleigh that were brightly lit by a spotlight in the flowerbeds.

Rick and Suzy, both 46 years of age, had spent the day basking in the holiday spirit. Although it was only December 10, they always gave themselves plenty of time to get things just right. Neither wanted the headache of rushing around in the last few days before Christmas. With the tree meticulously decorated, presents beautifully wrapped, and trayloads of cookies baked and placed in the freezer, the couple took a moment to stand back and admire their work. Everything looked festive and cheery. After moving tinsel from one branch to another and rearranging some of the glittering ornaments, Suzy remembered that the brownies she had been baking especially for her son Andrew were ready to come out of the oven, and she dashed to the kitchen. Rick stayed in the living room and repositioned the presents for their children, Andrew and Sarah, and their beloved granddaughter, Brittany.

When everything was exactly as it should be, the couple headed for bed—exhausted. In just a few days, their neighbors the Clarkes and the Leggs would be coming over for their traditional holiday get-together to exchange gifts, enjoy a scrumptious meal, and toast another year of good health and good cheer. This year, it was the Wamsleys' turn to host the party, and Suzy and Rick wanted to make sure that they maintained their five-star rating as fabulous hosts. Then, just a few days after the get-together with the neighbors, the extended Wamsley family would converge on 820 Turnberry to celebrate the holiday, as they did every year. Life was good. Sweet dreams would surely flow easily. It was just before midnight.

Rick and Suzy got undressed and slipped into their king-size bed in the first-floor master bedroom. Rick fell right to sleep. But Suzy was restless. Instead of waking her husband, she shuffled sleepily into the living room, turned on the TV, and stretched out on the plush sofa. Wearing her usual bedtime garb—just a T-shirt and panties—and with a warm blanket pulled up tight to her chin, Suzy eventually fell into a deep sleep.

Sing we joyous, all together
Fa la la la la, la la la la.
Heedless of the wind and weather
Fa la la la la, la la la la.

* * *

At 3 a.m., a car inched along the deserted streets of Walnut Estates and turned onto Turnberry Drive. The vehicle entered the driveway at number 820, and the male driver turned off the engine. After a few moments, he got out of the car, walked through a gate on the side of the house that led to the backyard, and stealthily entered the house through a back door. Slowly and cautiously, he checked out the rooms and made mental notes of the inhabitants' whereabouts. After a few minutes, he returned to the car and gave his report to the two female passengers: one male asleep in the master bedroom; one female asleep on the living room couch.

With that information, all three silently exited the car and entered the house via the same clandestine route. Inside, everything was dark and silent. They crept down a hallway, past the laundry room, and into the kitchen. The male intruder stopped there, and waved on his accomplices. The two females furtively continued into the formal dining room, where they stood stone still, backs against the wall.

"You can do it," whispered one to the other.

"Okay," she replied.

"The sooner you do it, the faster we can go home."

"Yeah."

"I believe in you."

"I can do it."

"Do it quickly!"

There was a moment of tense silence. . . . "No, I can't."

"You have to. We're gonna have to do it tonight."

"I can't."

"Yes, you can!"

"No."

"Yes!"

"Yes, I can!"

"Go!" demanded the encouraging female as she pushed her reluctant companion around the corner and into the living room. "Do it!" she urged.

Stumbling into the living room where the unlit Christmas

tree stood sentinel, the female stopped between a coffee table and the fireplace—within five feet of the couch. With a
gun in her gloved hand and without heeding the gifts and
tinsel, she took aim, and fired. *Bang!* The bullet struck the
sleeping woman on the left side of her head.

With adrenaline coursing through her body, the gun-
wielding female continued toward the bedroom, all the time
hearing the words "The male is in the master bedroom" and
"You can do it!" As she got to the door, she saw the man sitting straight up, a startled expression on his face. She headed
toward him, firing once, twice—but missed him both times.
The man charged out of bed to tackle his assailant as she
kept firing, again and again and again. Finally, she hit him
directly above the right eyebrow.

But the bullet didn't stop Rick Wamsley. He lunged forward, rushed toward her, and grabbed her. The two struggled
out of the bedroom and into the living room, where they
ended up in a heap by the fireplace. Despite having been
shot, Rick fought back. He seized his attacker's hair and
pulled as hard as he could. He punched her and pushed her,
finally pinning her down by putting the entire weight of his
body on top of hers. As they wrestled, the gun came loose
from his attacker's hand and lay on the rug by the hearth, a
few feet away.

Hearing the sounds of this frantic struggle, the male intruder, who had been waiting in the kitchen, raced into the
living room. There, he desperately tried to pull Rick Wamsley
off the female shooter. But the bleeding man—summoning
all his waning strength—wouldn't let go. The three struggled
toward the front door. As they did, Rick managed to grab the
gun. He lifted it high above his head and brought it down,
bashing the male intruder in the head.

Seeing that her friends were now in serious trouble, the
third intruder, who had been waiting in the dining room,
dashed into the kitchen, grabbed two sharp knives, and ran
to the front door. She handed one knife to the male intruder,

and with the other knife, she began to stab the victim. Raising his hands against each blow, Rick successfully defended himself time and time again, receiving only superficial wounds to his hands. Realizing that her strategy wasn't working, the female handed her knife off to her girlfriend.

"Go stab the lady," she ordered. "Finish her off! Make sure she's dead!"

Doing as she was told, the original gun-wielding female picked herself off the floor and returned to the living room, seven-inch-long knife in hand. She began stabbing the woman on the couch in a sustained frenzy—one time, two times, three times, four times, five times, six times—sixteen times, seventeen times, eighteen times.

Bang! A shot rang out from the entryway by the front door. Rick had taken a bullet to his back. The bullet exited underneath his shoulder—yet somehow he was still alive. Although he kept fighting, trying as hard as he could not to lose consciousness, Rick's sense of reality was slowly fading.

"Why?" he gasped, looking at his attackers.

"Because I'm pregnant," blurted out the female.

"We can help you," Rick said weakly.

"Shut up, or I'll shoot you," she replied.

Hearing the conversation and realizing that the male still wasn't dead, the knife-wielding female returned to the entryway, and with Rick now facedown by the front door, she began stabbing him in the back—one time, two times, three times . . . nineteen, twenty, twenty-one times.

Then there was quiet. Neither Rick nor Suzy moved—or breathed. The three perpetrators stood still for a moment, catching their breaths and surveying the situation. When they felt certain both of their victims were dead, they took one last look around, gathered the knives and gun, and made their way through the formal dining room, into the kitchen, down the hallway, and out a door leading into the garage. Passing a white Jeep Cherokee and an Acura, they continued on to the driveway. There, after popping the trunk to their car, they grabbed a white trash bag they had put there earlier and began shedding their outer clothes. They tossed in sweatshirts, shoes, the knives, and the shooter's gloves. The male closed the trunk, settled into the driver's seat, and started up the engine. One female sat next to him; the other sat in back behind the passenger seat. And just as they had come in— slowly, quietly, stealthily—they drove out, down Turnberry Drive, turning left onto Muirfield, and then out of swanky Walnut Estates.

The driver took back roads, stopping just once to clean the blood that was running down his face. As they drove through the darkness, the three reviewed the events that had just taken place.

"I'm real proud of you," said the female in the front seat to the female in the back seat, who had used the gun on Suzy.

"Congratulations," said the male driver.

"I knew you could do it. You did a great job. Now, we're gonna go home," said the female in the front seat.

"Finally," replied the exhausted female in the back seat.

As they meandered through the silent, unlit streets, past the Christmas decorations adorning darkened homes, the female in the front seat remembered something and grabbed the other female's cell phone. She made a call. "I got in some trouble," she said into the phone. "I need an alibi."

After just fourteen miles, the car pulled up to the home where both females lived, and one female went inside and got soapy water and a rag. All three assailants had some blood on them, so they began cleaning themselves up. When they felt satisfied that they had washed away all traces of their brutal exploits, they entered the house. The female who had originally wielded the gun took a shower in the back room. The male went into the front bathroom to take a bath, and the other female, whose house it was, put a load of clothing into the washing machine —including bloody T-shirts and jeans. She then carried the white garbage bag from the trunk of the car to a container and placed it outside to be carted away the next day.

Around forty minutes later, they were ready for bed. They soon fell asleep, worn out from their frenzied fury.

'Tis the season to be jolly,
Fa la la la la, la la la la

Later that morning, after only a few hours sleep, the female who had shot Suzy Wamsley was awakened by an alarm clock. She crawled sleepily out of bed, got dressed, and set off for high school. She attended her six classes—acting as if nothing unusual had taken place. When she returned to the house, where the other two had lounged the morning away, the three worked together to remove everything from the car and to vacuum it thoroughly. Using Formula 409, they scrubbed anything they thought they had touched, inside and out. They then tackled the trunk, vacuuming and wiping down every inch of it. After that, the original gun-wielding female cleaned the gun, placed it in a bag, sealed it, and buried it in the flower garden.

At around 9 p.m. that evening, December 11, 2003, the Wamsleys' neighbor Patty Clarke arrived home from a dinner and was surprised that the Wamsleys' Christmas lights were not on. They had been shining brightly for the past few days, lighting up the neighborhood, as well as everyone's spirits. Clarke thought it was odd that the house was dark, but she assumed Suzy and Rick had gone out for the evening and had forgotten to turn the lights on.

Later that night, the male and one female got back into the car and returned to Turnberry Drive. The female went into the kitchen and picked up the phone and dialed 911. When the operator came on the line, the intruder said nothing, but laid the phone down, off the hook, on the kitchen counter. She then returned to the car and the two drove back home.

Nearly twenty hours after the murders, the two dead bodies in the living room had yet to be discovered.

Chapter Two

At 11:41 p.m. on December 11, 2003, a 911 operator in Mansfield received a call. "Can I help you?" she asked. She received no response. "Hello. Is anyone there?" Still, no one responded. Within seconds, she contacted the Mansfield police. "Open line," she said. "Phone off the hook at 820 Turnberry Drive. Check it out."

Officer Patrick Knotts of the Mansfield Police Department was the first to arrive. While waiting for backup, he stationed himself at the open garage door. He kept vigil, making sure that no one entered or exited 820 Turnberry without his knowledge.

A few minutes later Officer Jeff Ambreit of the Mansfield Police Department, along with Reserve Officer Michael Omlor, pulled into the driveway in a marked car. On the manicured lawn, the two saw a lit Santa and sleigh.

"Merry Christmas," said Ambriet.

"Let's hope," replied Omlor.

The newly arrived officers left Knotts by the garage and walked to the front door. As they passed the windows, they peered in. A spectacularly ornamented Christmas tree along with other holiday decorations filled the room. *How festive!* they thought. *Someone's going to have a merry Christmas.* When they got to the front door, they began knocking. There was no response. Then the officers rang the doorbell. Still, no response. *Strange,* they thought, *a 911 call and no respondent.* The men were soon joined by a fourth representative from the Mansfield Police Department, Officer Gilbert Martinez. *This was turning into a real party.*

After walking around the outside of the house and peering in all the windows, Knotts, Ambriet, and Martinez decided to check out the inside. Omlor remained stationed at the front door. With guns drawn and flashlights shining, the three entered the house from the door inside the garage. They first passed a small laundry room before coming to the kitchen. A lovely breakfast nook lay off to the side. There, on the kitchen counter, a telephone lay off the hook. The men proceeded into the living room area, making sure not to touch anything.

Ambriet's eyes immediately rested on the couch, and he gasped. There, he saw the body of a female—reclining and unmoving. Blood covered her chest. Continuing to scan the room, he looked to the right, into the foyer area, and saw a male lying facedown in a pool of blood near the front door. Numerous puncture wounds dotted the man's back. Wasting no time, the officers called the Mansfield Fire Department and asked them to dispatch an EMT to assess both victims and see if any treatment was possible.

As the officers continued to scan the living room, they saw a large amount of blood soaked into the beige carpet in front of the fireplace. Near that, next to a narrow area rug, they saw two bloody handprints marking the floor. Another large pool of blood was visible on the carpet by the formal dining area. And within that pool of blood, the officers saw a blade, with no handle attached.

Stunned and speechless, Knotts and Ambreit began to check the rest of the house. *Could there be other victims? Was a killer—or killers—lurking in a closet?* Cautiously, they entered the master bedroom. Small woodchips were scattered on the bed. The officers looked at the headboard and observed what appeared to be a bullet hole. As they searched each room, the officers examined the windows and outer doors. No windows were broken; no door appeared to have been pried open; and no items, such as TVs or computers, were obviously missing.

When they were satisfied that no one was hiding in the house and there were no other victims, the officers went back out the way they came in. As they passed the refrigerator, they noted a college schedule. *Perhaps someone besides the two victims lived in the house*—but they couldn't be certain.

At 12:17 a.m., a few minutes after the police had completed "clearing the house," the fire department arrived. An EMT rushed inside and checked the two victims to see if either had a pulse. In practically no time, he reported what the police officers had already surmised: two deceased.

The officers called into their commander to report their findings. Then they set up a crime scene tape and waited for the forensics specialists and detectives to arrive.

At approximately 12:40 a.m. on December 12, 2003, Commander Julie Bain of the Mansfield Police Department telephoned Max Courtney, owner of Forensic Consultant Services in Fort Worth, and requested his assistance at a crime scene. Courtney had an arrangement with the Mansfield Police Department to assist in crime scene investigation and to do lab analyses on major cases. As soon as Courtney received the call, he got dressed, grabbed a cup of coffee, and headed for his lab to gather his equipment. He then drove to the address Bain provided—820 Turnberry in Mansfield—and arrived at approximately 2 a.m.

When Bain paged Sergeant Mark Kelly of the Mansfield Police Department, Kelly was deep in sleep, but after hearing that he was needed to videotape a bloody crime scene in Mansfield, he immediately got dressed and headed down to the police department to pick up his crime scene equipment. He then drove to 820 Turnberry, arriving soon after Courtney.

At approximately 1 a.m., Ralph Standefer's alpha pager went off. Standefer, a detective with the Mansfield Police Department for nineteen years and a licensed police officer for twenty-one years, was the detective on call that week and would be the lead investigator. He had been fast asleep, but the words streaming across his pager woke him up quickly: "Two deceased of apparent gunshot and stab wounds. Extremely bloody scene. Eight-twenty Turnberry Drive." Right away, Standefer got out of bed and put on a pair of jeans, a Mansfield police golf shirt, and a ball cap. All of his gear—jacket, gloves, bulletproof vests, ammo, bug spray, rubber gloves, flashlights, department-issued shotgun—were in his unmarked take-home truck. After strapping on his pistol, a Glock .40 caliber, he backed out of his driveway.

When he pulled up to 820 Turnberry, Standefer spoke to the responding officers to get up to speed. Then he entered the home with Courtney and another law enforcement official, Texas Ranger Keith Denning, who had also been called to the scene. They proceeded to do a brief walk-through. Using flashlights, gloves, and plastic booties to protect the crime scene from new footwear impressions, they spent about seven minutes surveying the house. But it took only a few seconds to see the horror. Standefer immediately called the Crime Scene Unit and secured a search warrant.

As soon as the warrant was issued, at 4:30 a.m., Standefer and Courtney entered the house again, this time to do a thorough search. They went in through the larger of two garage doors—one was a double door, the other a single—and walked around the two cars parked inside. A motion-sensitive light in the garage went on. Once in the house, they passed a utility room before coming to the kitchen, where, they noted, overhead lights were on, as was the light inside the pantry. In the kitchen, they saw a mini Christmas tree and an AT&T telephone attached to the wall. The phone was off the hook, and the receiver was lying on the counter.

The two men then proceeded into the living room, where,

according to Standefer, "it looked as if one hell of a fight had taken place." Lamps were knocked over, tables were overturned, and blood was everywhere.

Standefer and Courtney saw the body of a deceased white male in his underwear lying in the entryway, head to the south wall, feet to the north. They also saw a deceased white female lying on the couch in the living room, where she had apparently been sleeping. Near the couch, the officers saw several different Christmas items, suggesting that the deceased woman had been working on holiday decorations.

As they scanned the living room carpet, they saw a bullet, two pieces of a blue plastic hair-comb clip, and another piece of plastic on the floor nearby. Blood spatter dotted one of the two easy chairs in the living room, and a significant amount of blood was on the chair itself.

Moving on to the master bedroom, they noted that the bed appeared to have been slept in. Courtney noticed two bullet holes in the wall and a bullet hole through the headboard of the bed, which aligned with one of the holes in the wall. He noted that there were no bloodstains in the room.

While Courtney and Standefer were examining the scene, Sergeant Kelly was taking videos and Daniel Jordan Sherwin of the Mansfield Police Department was taking 35-mm photographs of every room.

Many items in the house, such as bills and letters, as well as the newspaper on the front lawn, indicated the identity of the deceased. The police determined that the two victims were Rick and Suzy Wamsley. By the look of things, it appeared that one other person lived in the house as well.

Much later, when Standefer was asked about his reaction to the scene, he reflected, "I don't know that you can ever call one of these scenes 'run of the mill.' My experience has been that there are some scenes that are just average and there are ones that you automatically know you will forever carry with you. This was one of those—one I automatically knew I would never forget."

* * *

At 7:30 a.m., December 12, a neighbor named Keith Cowand, who shared a back fence with the Wamsleys, got up to play golf. As he left his house, he saw police cars and a news truck with cameras outside. Cowand assumed that a local TV station was doing a human-interest story on the holiday decorations in their neighborhood. After all, the houses looked spectacular and nothing nefarious ever took place in the tony Walnut Estates section of Mansfield.

When he finished playing his golf game, Cowand headed home. The streets in the neighborhood were now lined with cop cars. After he parked his car, Cowand went into his backyard and looked over the fence. Something serious seemed to be taking place at the Wamsleys'. Officers were combing the yard and police vehicles filled the Wamsley driveway.

One police officer, who was searching the backyard for evidence, saw Cowand and went up to him.

"Can I help you, sir?"

"Just wondering what's going on," said Cowand. "A lot of action over here."

"Did you hear anything last night?" the officer asked.

"Not last night but the night before," Cowand replied.

"Oh? What did you hear?"

"It sounded like multiple gunshots. Blam, blam, blam."

"What time was that?"

"I remember exactly what time it was because I looked at my clock," said Cowand. "It was 3:23 a.m."

"Ever hear anything like that before?"

"Never. Not in this neighborhood. But I know the sound. Used to live in Oak Cliff, Dallas. Guns went off all time of night and day."

"You do anything about it?"

"Figured it must've been a bad dream. Turned over. Went back to sleep."

The officer asked him how long he stayed awake after the shots.

"I heard them, sat up, looked at my bedside clock, and then I wondered what to do. I just didn't do anything. Just went back to sleep. Can't say how many seconds or minutes." Then, after a pause, Cowand asked, "Something serious happen, officer?"

Around the same time that Cowand left for his golf game, the Wamsleys' neighbor Patty Clarke was drinking a cup of coffee in her kitchen when one of her son's friends showed up at her house.

"What's going on next door?" he asked.

Clarke had no idea that anything was going on. She went to the window and saw several squad cars—their lights still spinning—in front of the Wamsleys' house. Quickly, she got dressed and went outside to speak to the police.

"Did you hear anything last night?" they asked.

"No. Nothing at all," she replied. "Something happen?"

Chapter Three

As word spread throughout upscale Walnut Estates that the lovely couple at 820 Turnberry had been murdered, the residents were shocked. *It was simply unbelievable! Shot and stabbed?! Here? How could that be?*

Questions abounded: *Had the Wamsleys come upon a burglary in progress? Were the robbers attempting to steal Christmas bounty? Was a madman roaming the streets? Had a murder/suicide taken place? Were the Wamsleys involved in some kind of drug deal gone bad? Did they owe huge sums of money to someone—who got impatient? What was going on?*

Fear and paranoia engulfed the neighborhood, which bordered the Walnut Creek Country Club and was considered *the* place to live in Mansfield, according to the *Dallas Observer.* With perfectly manicured lawns, large two-story brick-and-stone homes, and residents riding their own golf carts, all that was missing was a huge banner saying: Welcome to Mansfield: Home of the Good Life.

The Mansfield police tried to keep the community calm. They assured the residents that they were doing everything possible and with some lucky breaks and good investigative work, they would most likely apprehend the killers very soon. But they offered few details, so rumors continued to circulate.

* * *

A little after 4 a.m. on December 12, Texas Ranger Keith Denning knocked on Sarah Wamsley's apartment door in Arlington. Surprised at having a visitor so early in the morning, Sarah's roommate hesitatingly went to see who was there. The gentleman, dressed in officer's clothing, said he wanted to speak to Sarah Wamsley. The roommate called to Sarah and said that a police officer wanted to see her.

Sarah was surprised. She knew she'd done nothing wrong, and immediately thought something must have happened to her ex-boyfriend.

After identifying himself, Denning walked with Sarah into the living room.

"I think you'd better sit down," he said.

Sarah took a seat, and as sensitively as he could, Denning told her the dreadful news—both her mother and father had been killed. Stunned, she seemed unable to comprehend what he had said. She asked him to repeat it. He did, and assured her that no mistake was made. Sarah broke down, sobbing, shaking, and unable to speak. After a while, she gathered herself together and told Denning that she wanted to call her grandparents, her father's parents. But when she started to dial, she realized she couldn't think straight and had no idea what their number was. Denning dialed 411 and asked for the number of a Lewis and Marjean Wamsley in Bartlesville, Oklahoma. He then called Sarah's grandparents and handed her the phone.

At 4:50 a.m., the phone rang at the Wamsley home in Bartlesville. They had been sleeping soundly, but immediately awakened at the sound of the phone. Their first thought was that someone was hurt.

Marjean picked up the phone by the bed, but because it was so unusual to get a call at that hour, Lewis picked up an extension. A hysterical and incoherent Sarah was on the other end. Neither Marjean nor Lewis could understand what she was saying.

"What is it, honey? What's the matter?" asked Marjean.

After many attempts at getting out the words, Sarah finally said, "Mom and Dad are gone." Then, through tears and gasps, she said, "Come as fast as you can. Get a plane and get down here just as fast as you can." Sarah was unable to continue speaking, so Denning took the phone and explained as delicately as he could what had happened. He asked them if they would be able to come to Texas; Sarah needed them.

Of course they would come! But could it be true? Their son and daughter-in-law dead? Stunned, Marjean and Lewis stared at each other, before both broke down in tears.

After Sarah had calmed down, Denning asked her if she would be able to go down to the Mansfield police station and give a statement. Although deeply distressed, Sarah said she would. It was arranged that she would meet with the police later in the day.

At 8:30 a.m., December 12, Andrew Wamsley was watching the news on TV with his girlfriend, Chelsea Richardson, at her house.

"Breaking story," stated the newscaster. "This, just in. A horrific incident has taken place in the Walnut Estates area. Mr. Rick Wamsley and his wife Suzy were shot and stabbed to death. More information will follow as soon as it comes in."

Andrew and Chelsea looked at each other, unable to utter a word. *What? Why didn't anyone notify them personally? What was going on!*

As soon as they could get themselves together, the two got into Andrew's Mustang and drove directly to Turnberry Drive. When they arrived, the street was cordoned off beginning three houses down from 820. Officer Mary Moore, stationed at the traffic post, stopped the Mustang and asked the driver who he was. "I live at 820, over there. I'm Andrew Wamsley."

Moore immediately contacted Standefer, who hurried over to Andrew's car. Without giving him any details, Standefer asked Andrew and his companion to follow him to the police station. They arrived around five minutes after they left.

Chelsea Richardson's mother Celia slept in on December 12—her day off—only to be awakened around noon when the telephone rang. It was her friend Peter Nguyen. He told her that something dire had happened to Andrew's parents and that she should turn on the TV. Immediately, she woke up her son James and together, they put on the news to find out what had happened. Upon hearing that Mr. and Mrs. Wamsley were dead, they were shocked. *In the fancy neighborhood where the Wamsleys lived? Impossible!*

Not knowing where Chelsea and Andrew were—the teens had slept in the living room the night before but were gone now—they decided to go to the police station to find out exactly what was going on.

Celia and James arrived at the Mansfield station at around 1:30 p.m. As soon as they walked through the door, Celia saw her daughter, and the two hugged each other. Then they sat down and talked. Chelsea filled in her mother on all that she knew. She told her that she had been interviewed briefly by Detective Danny Sullivan, and then released. She said Andrew was still being interviewed. Celia, Chelsea, and James then went outside to wait for Andrew.

Lead investigator Detective Standefer, along with Sergeant Stan Davis, took Andrew into Commander Julie Bain's office, because at that time, the station was overcrowded and the interview room was already occupied. Although the Mansfield Police Department had no specific rule regarding how many officers must be in during an interview, usually two people were present just in case one officer missed something. Plus, having two interviewers allowed one interviewer to collect his or her thoughts while the other was asking questions.

During the interview, Andrew, nineteen, nearly six feet

tall, weighing around 220 pounds, and wearing a hooded
sweatshirt and jeans, was calm and collected—even meek.
When Standefer told him he was sorry about the death of his
parents, Andrew looked down at the floor, tears falling from
his eyes. They asked Andrew when he had last seen his parents. After thinking for a moment, he said that on December
9, he had asked his parents for permission to go on a camping trip. He reported that permission was given, but cold
weather had forced them to change plans and, instead, he
had stayed at Chelsea's house. When asked how he had
spent the evening of December 11, he said he was at Chelsea's house, where they had watched a movie, then gone to
Putt-Putt golf, and ended up visiting a friend, Jeremy Lavender, and hanging out at Jeremy's house for hours.

Standefer asked him to show him his hands, thinking
that whoever had committed the murders would most likely
have injuries from the stabbing. (Often assailants cut themselves when stabbing another person—particularly when
multiple stab wounds are involved.) Standefer noticed only
one four-inch scratch on Andrew's hand, which wasn't very
old or very deep. Did it mean anything? Maybe. On the other
hand, the teen could have gotten it anywhere.

After around forty-five minutes, the interviewers decided
they had all they needed. As Andrew was leaving, Standefer
asked if he would sign a Consent-to-Search form for his
Mustang. Without hesitation, he agreed. Standefer assigned
a crime scene technician to conduct the search of the vehicle.

Andrew also voluntarily agreed to be fingerprinted, and
was told he was free to go.

Meanwhile, Andrew's sister Sarah had arrived and was waiting in another room, so when Standefer was free, he began his
interview with her.

During the interview, Sarah, 25, was open, but extremely
upset; cooperative, but clearly distraught. When asked if she

could think of anyone who might have committed the murder and why, Sarah stated that her parents had no enemies and, as far as she knew, they owed no one any money or had any outstanding debts. She did, however, recall an incident that had taken place about a month earlier, on November 9, 2003. She thought this incident might be important.

That day, she stated, she and her parents were driving in her dad's Jeep Grand Cherokee to the town of Joshua, to ride their horse, Toby, who was being trained there. The three left the Wamsleys' home at around 10 a.m., and after they exercised Toby for a few hours, they got back in the Jeep to return home. On their way, as they were going north on I-35 through Burleson, they decided to look for a place to stop for lunch.

While they were driving along, Sarah told the investigators, all of a sudden there was a huge boom that shook the car. Sarah and her parents were unnerved and scared. No one knew exactly what had happened. Their first thought was that an enormous rock had somehow hit the Jeep. As soon as he safely could, Rick pulled over, at a Chili's, and everyone got out. They looked at the car. Something had definitely hit the Jeep, but it wasn't a rock. In fact, the point of impact looked eerily like a bullet hole.

Suzy immediately grabbed Rick's cell phone and called Andrew. She left a message on his machine, telling him where they were and what had happened. Then, she called 911, and the stunned family waited for the Burleson police to arrive.

Within minutes, a squad car pulled into the Chili's parking lot. The officer went up to the Wamsleys and asked what had happened. He then examined the Jeep. Immediately he saw a bullet in the left rear panel of the car, just outside of where Sarah had been sitting. The officer called for back-up, and soon several cops arrived. Sarah and her mother were so shaken—*had somebody tried to kill them?*—that they could hardly stand up. Two officers escorted them inside Chili's and tried to calm them down. The officers outside extracted the bullet and bagged it as evidence.

As Sarah continued telling her story to the Mansfield police, the investigators asked her if anyone had been arrested after the shooting incident. She said that no one was. They asked her if she suspected anyone at the time. Of course, she said, it could have been just a random shooting—kids just having some "fun"—but she also thought it could have been her ex-boyfriend, Todd Cleveland, the father of her daughter, Brittany. She told the detectives that on the night before the shooting, November 8, she, her parents, and Brittany were at the Wamsleys' home in the living room playing Candy Land. At one point, Sarah said, she went into her father's office and made a call to Child Protective Services (CPS), to file a report against Cleveland. She suspected that while Brittany was in Cleveland's care, the little girl may have been harmed. The shooting the next day could have been a coincidence, Sarah said, but it had also crossed her mind that Cleveland could have been retaliating.

Before the interview was over, Standefer asked Sarah if she would be willing to submit to a polygraph test. Without hesitation, she said she would. He told her that they would be fingerprinting her. "It's routine," she was informed. "Family members have to be ruled out first."

After Andrew had finished his interview, he had asked the detectives where Sarah was. They had told him she was being interviewed and would soon be out. Andrew had decided to wait for his sister so they could be together and have some time to reflect on what had taken place. After all, they hadn't even had a chance to see each other since their parents were murdered!

When Sarah came out of the office, Andrew asked her how her interview had gone. Through tears, she told him it went okay, but she simply couldn't believe what had happened.

Andrew agreed. It was like a bad dream. It was unreal. *How could we no longer have our parents?*

After a few moments, Sarah asked Andrew how his interview had gone.

Clearly upset, Andrew responded, "They'll probably end up finding blood of Mom and Dad in my car."

Taken aback, Sarah asked why.

"Mom cut her finger and then drove my car around the block," said Andrew.

"Oh. And what about Dad?"

"Dad worked on the car with me. When he got in to see if it worked properly, some of his blood was most likely in the car."

"I'm sure they'll get to the bottom of this," said Sarah.

After the siblings said goodbye to each other, Andrew walked out of the station and saw Celia, Chelsea, and James waiting in the parking lot. Andrew looked distraught. "They took the car," he told them.

"It doesn't matter," said Celia. "Let's go. They'll call you when they're ready."

Chapter Four

On the same day that Sarah and Andrew Wamsley were interviewed by the police, the bodies of Rick and Suzy Wamsley were transported to the Tarrant County Medical Examiner's office in Fort Worth to await further examination and autopsy.

Kelly Belcher was a trace analyst with the Tarrant County Medical Examiner's office and a member of the American Academy of Forensic Sciences. As a trace examiner, her job was to perform head-to-toe analyses of decedents prior to autopsy in an attempt to recover small or microscopic materials that could be lost with continued handling of the body. She was to retain any evidence for future examination. Usually, the items she recovered included hairs, fibers, paint scrapings, and gunshot residue.

When Belcher arrived at the office, she was directed to Rick Wamsley's body. In examining the corpse, she saw that the hands were bagged—this was to prevent any materials that may have adhered to the hands from being lost when the body was transported from the crime scene to the medical examiner's office. And something, in fact, had adhered. Belcher observed what appeared to be hairs on Rick's left hand and wrist area, as well as on the right hand. She removed the hairs with tweezers, placed them in small pieces of white paper, made pharmaceutical folds to seal them in, put everything inside a small manila envelope, and labeled the envelope as evidence.

On December 13, 2003, Dr. Daniel J. Konzelmann, a deputy medical examiner for the Tarrant County Medical Examiner's office, was called in to perform an autopsy on Rick Wamsley to determine the exact cause of death—accident, homicide, suicide, or natural event.

As the doctor carried out his duties, he made copious notes.

The decedent "arrived at the medical examiner's office wearing only underwear. His hands were bagged and he was wrapped in a white sheet and lay in a body bag. His height was 73 inches—6 feet one inch—and his weight was 240 pounds."

Konzelmann noted "a tremendous amount of blood on the body surface, especially on the face and in the neck area." Wet blood, he wrote, as well as thick crusted and congealed blood, covered a large part of his body. The deceased "suffered a number of different types of injury," including gunshot and stab wounds, cuts, and blunt force trauma.

The deputy medical examiner documented a gunshot wound, which "entered the right forehead above the eyebrow and passed through the skin and underlying tissues through the open sinuses that surround the nose, through the soft tissues of the skull, and came to rest next to the left inner jaw, where a large-caliber bullet was recovered." Konzelmann noted that the entry wound was circular and had powder stippling around it, suggesting that the bullet was fired at an intermediate range, probably less than three feet away. The wound was potentially fatal, but "by itself, it was not the fatal gunshot wound."

Konzelmann noted a "gunshot wound of the back, which entered the left midback toward the midline and passed through the skin and underlying tissues, the muscles of the back, the back eighth rib, left lower lung lobe, left upper lung lobe, then passed through the fourth rib toward the side on the left, and exited the front of the axilla." After the bullet emerged, it started to re-enter the upper arm but did not have enough energy left, and so "it caused a small laceration or skin tear and dropped back out." The entry wound for this bullet also was circular, measuring about three-sixteenths of an inch in diameter, with gunpowder embedded, or stippled, around the edges, suggesting again that this was a shot fired at an intermediate range. The exit wound was "localized in the front portion of the deceased's left chest right in front of his armpit."

The examiner also noted multiple stab wounds in clusters. Five stab wounds were located on the left upper chest: "Two of the wounds entered the left upper lung lobe . . . and entered . . . the main artery to the lungs. One penetrated his chest cavity and severed his superior vena cava" (a large blood vessel that leads to the right upper chamber of the heart and brings blood back from the upper extremities and the head). There was a stab wound on the left side of his body, a stab wound on his left mid-back, and a stab wound on his right mid-back. The examiner noted a large stab and cut wound of the midline of the chin going down to the neck area.

In all, Konzelmann noted, Rick Wamsley "had 21 entry stab wounds." Of those, five were potentially fatal. There were thirteen stab wounds to the back. They were deep and they bled a lot, but they were not the direct cause of death.

Because there was bleeding in the soft tissues around the paths of the stab wounds, bleeding in both sides of the chest cavity, bleeding within the sac surrounding the heart, and bleeding in the soft tissues of the lung itself, the deputy medical examiner surmised that there had to have been at least a little blood pressure in the surrounding capillaries and arteries when these wounds were inflicted. That meant the deceased was still alive when he was being stabbed.

Konzelmann documented that the deceased also had numerous wounds to his neck, but they did not appear to "cross any vital structures."

There were wounds to the right palm and fingers, which were consistent with "someone grasping a knife and having it pulled out and causing those cuts." Konzelmann noted thirteen individual sharp-force wounds to the hands and arms. He also noted cuts and/or bruises on both hands, although most were on the palm of the right hand. There were also several cuts to the left thumb and on the three middle fingers on the left hand.

The final statement on the autopsy report asked for the cause and manner of death. Konzelmann listed the cause of death as "multiple gunshot wounds and sharp-force wounds." Later, when asked why he had cited multiple reasons as the cause of death, Konzelmann responded, "Because any wound can be potentially life-threatening if untreated. Several of the stab wounds would have been sufficient to cause death in and of themselves, and the gunshot wound from the back was also sufficient to cause death in and of itself."

As to the manner of death, Konzelmann noted on the autopsy report, it was "homicide."

On December 13, 2003, Dr. Gary L. Sisler, a deputy medical examiner for Tarrant County, was asked to perform an autopsy on Suzy Wamsley.

In his report, Sisler noted that the deceased had paper bags on her hands, placed there to preserve trace evidence. He noted that she had suffered "a gunshot wound to the left ear, which entered the front of the ear, exited the back of the ear, and then re-entered the left parietal bone." Sisler recovered the bullet from her head.

All in all, the examiner noted eighteen stab wounds, including seven stab wounds to the left chest and breast area, several to the right chest, four stab wounds to the left front of the neck, a single cut wound over the left jaw, and a smaller wound below that. There was no subcutaneous hemorrhaging in the tracks of the stab wounds, indicating to Sisler that the decedent had no blood pressure when she was stabbed. In other words, her heart had already stopped beating and she was dead when the stab wounds were inflicted. Apparently, the frenzied stabbing of Suzy Wamsley had been overkill.

In the official autopsy report, Sisler wrote that the cause of death was "a gunshot wound of the head." The manner of death: "Homicide."

No one who had been to the scene of the crime on Turnberry Drive would have been surprised by the conclusions about the Wamsleys' manner of death. But the motive? The identities of the perpetrators? Those remained anyone's guess.

Chapter Five

Rick Wamsley grew up in Bartlesville, Oklahoma, a town of about thirty thousand people that was located forty-five miles north of Tulsa. By all accounts, he was a happy and well-adjusted kid, who loved playing with his friends and his two younger sisters and older brother. Rick was known to be tenacious when he wanted something badly enough—and he badly wanted to make the junior high school football team. Although he was just an average kid athletically, he worked hard to improve his strength and skills before trying out for the lineup. And his dedication paid off. He made the squad. But after playing several games, just being on the team wasn't enough. He wanted to be the best. To excel, he rededicated himself to becoming faster and stronger, and that paid off, too. During his senior year at Sooner High School, he was the only football player who played both offense and defense.

After graduating from high school, Rick enrolled at Oklahoma State University in Stillwater, around sixty miles west of Tulsa. It was a new experience for him to be away from home and not one that he embraced easily. However, after a while, he settled into the life of a college student and successfully completed his freshman year. At the end of the term, he returned home for the summer and worked odd jobs, enjoying the luxury of some peace and quiet and not having to study late into the night.

In September, he returned to Oklahoma State for his sophomore year. But by the weekend before Thanksgiving, he had had enough of book learning and campus life—and he decided to drop out of college. He packed his belongings and headed for home. When he arrived, he told his surprised parents that he had quit. He wanted some real-life experiences. Although not thrilled with this decision, Rick's parents welcomed him back home. They also told him he'd better find a job.

For a time, he lived at home and did menial work, including building fences and working a shift at Wal-Mart, but soon, he landed a job with Phillips Petroleum Company as a member of a magnetic tower survey crew. At first, he enjoyed the new job, but in time, the long hours outdoors and the hands-on, dirty work became too much for him. One day, after a particularly long and difficult stint, he told his dad, "I don't know what I want to do, but I sure as hell don't want to do this the rest of my life. I'm going back to school."

That summer, before he returned to college, Rick renewed his acquaintance with a high school friend from Bartlesville, Suzy, who was studying art at Oklahoma Christian College. They started dating and soon fell in love. They were a stunning couple—tall, handsome, dark-haired Rick and lanky, beautiful, redheaded Suzy. In 1978, two years after Suzy's high school graduation, they decided to get married. Seven months later, on Valentine's Day, Suzy and Rick had their first child, a healthy baby girl. They named her Sarah.

With Suzy's input and support, Rick stuck it out and graduated from college. Soon after that, he was offered a job in the accounting department of Shell Oil Company in Houston. It was a terrific opportunity, and Rick didn't hesitate to take it. The young family moved all the way to the big city in Texas. Although it was a new experience for them, the Wamsleys soon got used to Houston, going to the Livestock Show and Rodeo, the aquarium and zoo, and wandering around Market

Square. They liked city life, but still managed to go back home to Oklahoma whenever they could.

While living in Houston, Suzy gave birth to another child, Andrew, in 1984. Their family was growing, and so, too, were Rick's ambitions. After all, now he was responsible for the lives of two young children as well as his wife. He wanted to move up the professional ladder and the economic one as well.

While Rick was working for Shell in Houston, UTEX—a small company outside Salt Lake City, Utah—gave him an offer that was too good to refuse. UTEX asked him if he would join the company in the position of comptroller, and he grabbed it. The job was well-paying and challenging, so once again, the Wamsleys picked up and moved to a new state.

The family loved living near Utah's national parks and visiting the nearby ski slopes but, in time, Rick received a lucrative offer from Meridian Oil in Fort Worth, Texas, to work in their accounting department. Once again, the family packed up and hit the road, ready to start life anew. While at Meridian, Rick went back to school and completed his degree in accounting, becoming a certified public accountant.

At that time, the Wamsleys lived at the Wind Castle Apartments in Arlington, approximately twelve miles east of Fort Worth. By 1995, they had acquired enough money to move to their dream house on Turnberry Drive in Mansfield. Life was good. The Wamsleys could afford pretty much anything they wanted. They lived in a lovely community and their kids were going to great schools. As the months and years went on and his children were growing up, Rick felt he wanted to spend more time with them. Plus, he loved working around the house and fixing up the yard. So, he took a chance. He decided to quit his job and open a home office. After all, hadn't he worked for others long enough? It was a huge gamble, and he wondered if he could succeed in business for himself. He thought he could, but he knew he would never know for sure unless he tried.

As was the case whenever Rick set his mind to anything, he soon succeeded. In practically no time, he became a highly successful auditor, specializing in oil and gas litigation. And he was totally enjoying being at home, playing with the kids, and tinkering around the house. He even found time to build a tiered fountain in the backyard and a flagstone patio. Things couldn't have been better. Rick loved watching football games, Coke in hand and chips nearby. His favorite team was the Dallas Cowboys, of course.

While Rick stayed at home, Suzy worked at various jobs, including selling antiques at a booth she leased at a local mall. But in time, she, too, decided that she wanted to spend more time with her children, so she gave up working outside the home and returned to being a full-time mother. The one thing that could get her out of the house, however, at any time and on any day, was shopping. It was her passion. A self-described "professional shopper," she could always find something among the racks and shelves that she wanted or needed. But that was not a problem. Rick could always stay with the kids, and he was doing so well that money was no object. Suzy loved to decorate and do any kind of arts and crafts projects, as well as gardening, so staying at home was a joy for her.

By all accounts, the Wamsleys' marriage was a happy one. On Rick's fortieth birthday, Suzy invited their next-door neighbors as well as Rick's parents from Bartlesville to come to their home to celebrate. What Suzy didn't tell Rick was that she had planned a surprise. While the six of them were having drinks and enjoying hors d'oeuvres, a well-dressed gentleman knocked on their door and told them he would be taking them out for a ride—in a stretch limousine—to one of the most expensive and well-known restaurants in Fort Worth. Rick was flabbergasted—and thrilled.

Not to be outdone by Suzy, Rick planned a surprise for Suzy's fortieth birthday. He flew an old friend of Suzy's, whom she hadn't seen for years, from Virginia to Mansfield for a get-together. When Suzy first saw her friend, she was speechless. However, within minutes, the two former best friends were chatting as if they had been in contact every day for the past decade. They spent a fantastic weekend together.

Suzy was a superb cook, but if one of the kids or Rick didn't like what she had prepared for dinner, she would quickly and effortlessly whip up an alternative. She always had plenty of Andrew's favorite brownies on hand and made a habit of ordering pizza for his friends when they came over to play video games. Suzy was also known to be a wonderful homemaker. The Wamsleys' house was always spotless and beautifully decorated.

According to neighbors, the Wamsleys liked everybody and everybody seemed to like them. To Suzy and Rick, family and friends came first. Rick was not only an adoring husband, but he was also a caring and thoughtful son. Every year on his father's birthday, December 7, Pearl Harbor Day, Rick sent his dad a birthday card. When the Wamsleys' neighbors the Clarkes needed a ride home after a car accident sent them to the emergency room, Rick came to the rescue, even though it was almost midnight. Suzy was just as kind and caring. In December 2003, Suzy surprised her elderly neighbor, who was moving into an assisted living facility, with a set of gorgeous towels. If anyone in the neighborhood suffered a death in the family, Suzy would show up with a pie and a full serving of heartfelt condolences.

Yes, Rick and Suzy appeared as happy and loving as they had when they first met. In fact, they had celebrated their twenty-fifth wedding anniversary in July 2003—and they would have celebrated their twenty-fifth Christmas together that same year. But it was not to be.

The Wamsleys seemed to have had a wonderful relationship with each other. But their relationship with their children was less clear-cut. Their two children, Sarah and Andrew, and Sarah's daughter, Brittany, had brought Rick and Suzy enormous amounts of pleasure. However, as with most families, it was not always smooth sailing.

Pretty and perky, Sarah had been a cheerleader at Mansfield High School. Without doubt, her biggest fan was her mother, who went to all the pep rallies to take pictures of her beautiful dark-haired daughter. But by Sarah's own account, she was not always the easiest teen to be with. She described herself as a "wild child"—rebellious and a know-it-all. Starting around age thirteen and continuing for many years after, she was often at odds with her parents. She dated older men; she drank a lot; she partied whenever she could. When she was sixteen, after Rick and Suzy had tried for months to quell what they thought was reckless behavior, they sent her to Millwood, a mental health facility in Arlington, hoping that the professionals there could help her settle down. However, the situation didn't really improve. Finally, Rick and Suzy had had enough, and only weeks before she was to graduate from high school, in March 1997, they kicked their daughter out of the house, tossing her belongings onto their front yard. They felt like a dose of harsh reality, *really* tough love, might bring her to her senses.

But it seemed to have just the opposite effect. Sarah gathered her belongings and moved in with Todd Cleveland, a Mansfield Community College student she had met at a party, dated briefly, and fallen for. The two forged a loving relationship and in 1999, when Sarah was nineteen, she got pregnant. Her parents were extremely upset. After all, Sarah was so young and, besides, she hardly even knew the man. Regardless what her parents thought, Sarah and Cleveland became the proud, young parents of a baby girl, Brittany.

For a time, Cleveland and Sarah got along well and enjoyed their new responsibilities, but soon, according to Sarah, Cleveland became abusive, telling her that she was stupid and berating her for "not knowing anything." Sarah became upset and depressed and went to counseling back at Millwood to try to sort things out. The counselors there put her on antidepressant medication. After many therapy sessions in which she discussed her relationship with Cleveland, she realized she needed to get away from him. But knowing what she should do and actually doing it were two different things. Even though she understood she'd be better off without Cleveland, she couldn't find the strength to leave him.

When Sarah was twenty-two, things became so bad that she voluntarily went into Millwood as an inpatient and stayed there for a couple of weeks in April 2001. When she got out, she continued her counseling, but found herself unable to stay away from Cleveland. She moved back in with him and negativity and self-doubt overtook her. She started to sink, but before she hit rock bottom, she returned to Millwood, in June.

It took her a full year of therapy to finally bring herself to leave Cleveland, and when she did, she gave him custody of Brittany. At that time, she didn't feel she could be a good mother and believed that Brittany would be in better hands with him. Sarah did, however, retain visiting rights.

According to friends, after Sarah and Cleveland split up, Sarah still suffered from depression. She struggled with alcohol, even as she worked as a teller at a finance company. Several co-workers reported that Sarah had told them she was going to "hurt herself."

On one occasion, she swallowed a handful of antidepressants and was rushed to a hospital, where she had to have her stomach pumped. One psychiatrist described her as suffering from depression and "possible emotional abuse by her mother" and "minimal support from her family"—the latter two pronouncements Sarah later denied. Another psychiatrist diagnosed her as bipolar, a personality disorder characterized by extreme mood swings.

On March 29, 2002, Sarah was arrested after plowing her car into a fence and trying to flee from police. She pleaded no contest to DWI, driving while intoxicated. But that incident seemed to have had a profound effect on her. She began to take herself and her life more seriously and started to get herself together.

In late 2002, she felt she had gotten her priorities in order and that she could now be a good mother to her daughter. To that end, she filed a lawsuit to regain custody of Brittany. The custody battle that then began became contentious and acrimonious, but the one thing she could count on unconditionally was her parents' support—both emotionally and financially. Finally, when the court case was over, Sarah was awarded custody of her daughter.

Sarah and her parents had been healing old wounds—and Brittany was the balm in all of their lives. Rick and Suzy adored and doted on their granddaughter. So when Brittany announced that she wanted a horse "more than anything in the world," Rick and Suzy decided to buy one. Rick had never owned a horse, but he and Suzy had always wanted one, and after all they had the money and time to spend training it. This was one of the best decisions the Wamsleys ever made. Rick, Suzy, Sarah, and Brittany loved that horse. On Wednesdays, Rick and Suzy would pick up Brittany after school and go to Joshua to ride and groom Toby. After that, they would drive home and wait for Sarah to get off work. Then they would all have dinner together and spend the evening playing a game—often Candy Land. Most weekends, too, the four of them spent the days riding Toby.

It looked like the tumultuous years—and the battles between Sarah and her parents—had become a distant memory.

Andrew's early years seemed to be happy ones. He was a well-adjusted kid who got good grades in school and stayed out of trouble. Suzy often went fishing with her son, and they always had a great time, spending hours talking and waiting for the fish to bite. Usually, they were more successful at having fruitful discussions than they were at catching fish. Rick sometimes found the time to toss the ball around the yard with Andrew, but mostly Andrew liked playing video games and spending time reading and listening to music in his room. This sometimes annoyed his parents, who wanted him to be more involved with the family goings-on. Andrew's best friend was Klint Atchley. The two met when they were only three years old and remained close throughout grammar and high school, even after they moved apart. The two would spend practically every weekend together, but when the Atchleys would go away for a weekend or on a vacation, Andrew missed them so much that he would call and leave many, many messages on their answering machine, asking if they were home yet.

As with Sarah, when adolescence kicked in, not all was smooth sailing. According to one family acquaintance speaking with the *Dallas Observer*, "Andrew seemed impulsive and immature." The acquaintance reported that once, when the family went out for dinner to celebrate Rick's birthday, Andrew threw a bowl of *queso* dip across the room because his father wouldn't order another bowl.

"He's a jackass," stated a neighbor who was about the same age as Andrew. "Andrew used to always say how he hated his dad," he told the *Dallas Observer*. A friend further reported to Glenna Whitley and Andrea Grimes of the *Dallas Observer* that he was at the Wamsley home one time when Rick and Andrew quarreled over an overdue video. At first Andrew stubbornly continued watching the video, even though Rick said he wanted to return it. Finally, Andrew hurled the video at his father in anger. It hit him in the head, causing him to bleed. Another confrontation at the Wamsley house caused the police to pay them a visit on a domestic disturbance call. However, no arrests were made.

Co-workers at Putt-Putt golf, where Andrew worked as a shift manager, talked about the difficulties they encountered with him. "He's kind of a jerk, actually, very arrogant," said former co-worker Jonathan Aston. "He thought highly of himself. He was one of those managers that nobody wanted to work on his shift."

By most accounts, Andrew's relationship with his sister was rocky, too. The word was that they didn't get along and fought constantly. One altercation got so rough that Andrew told a friend that Sarah slammed his head into a water heater. Andrew also told the friend that he had serious conflicts with his parents. Behind the Wamsleys' smooth façade, the friend said, there was deep turmoil. According to an article in the *Dallas Observer* printed weeks after the murders, several family friends reported that the Wamsleys were "controlling and suspicious of outsiders." According to the same article, a boyfriend of Sarah's said that both children felt that people were friends with the Wamsleys only because they "wanted something" from them.

These characterizations of the Wamsleys suggested there was trouble in paradise. But despite any family conflicts, the Wamsleys were generous with their children financially—though the money sometimes had strings attached. More than anything else, they wanted their children to graduate from college. Rick and Suzy made an agreement with Sarah and Andrew—they could live in the Wamsley home as long as they attended college. In fact, the Wamsleys told them, they would pay for their cars and insurance, and give them cash for spending, but they had to stay in school.

When Sarah decided that college was not for her, all their hopes rested on Andrew, and for a time, things went along smoothly. After graduating from Mansfield High School in May 2002, Andrew began attending Tarrant County College. True to their word, the Wamsleys gave their son a 1998 white Mustang—but they stopped short of giving him the title. Andrew told them he wanted to soup it up, and they were leery of that. They felt the car was fast enough.

By the fall of 2003, Andrew decided he had had enough of school and dropped out of college, but he didn't tell his parents. And for some time, they were unaware of his decision. However, when they found out, they felt betrayed—and disappointed. They felt their only alternative was to cut him off financially, which they did. They no longer paid for his car—gas, registration, insurance—nor did they give him spending money. Although they didn't kick him out of the house, they gave him a strict curfew.

Andrew had met Chelsea Richardson through Chelsea's brother James in late 2002. At the time, Chelsea was attending Everman Joe C. Bean High School in the blue-collar town of Everman, which abuts Arlington. In the middle of her senior year, Chelsea started going to an IHOP with James, where Andrew and James loved to play Yu-Gi-Oh!, a Japanese collectable card game that they could play for eight hours straight, often until six in the morning. "It's a lot safer than drugs," said one of Andrew's friends. In time, the IHOP became their home away from home.

By January 2003, Chelsea and Andrew began dating and soon became inseparable. They saw each other every day, usually at Chelsea's house, where they watched movies and played video games. However, at that time, Andrew was still living with his parents, so he would leave the Richardsons' and go home every night. In June, Chelsea graduated from high school, and Andrew attended the event along with James, Chelsea's mother, Celia, and her sister Brenna. It was a proud day for them all, and Chelsea had plans to go on to college, although she wasn't certain what career path she wanted to pursue. Becoming a nurse or a lawyer were two of her thoughts. Although Celia seemed to have taken immediately to Andrew, the same could not be said of the Wamsleys' feelings towards Chelsea. Friends of the Wamsleys later reported that they thought Chelsea was "white trash."

Celia Richardson and her husband had moved into their small tract house at 7417 Lea Place in July 1998. Thaddeus "Tank" Richardson, Celia's husband and Chelsea's father, was an ironworker and former Marine. In May 1999, about a year after the Richardsons moved to Lea Place, Tank had a massive heart attack and passed away. Tank was in his forties, and the close-knit family was devastated. Tank was their rock. Plus, it was all the more shocking because he had been in perfect health, or so they thought.

Now, Celia had to figure out how to make ends meet without the salary that Tank brought in. With no time for self-pity, she began working several jobs. Within a short time, however, Chelsea was having such a hard time adjusting to her dad's death, that she asked her mother if she could stay home and spend time with her. Without hesitation, Celia did just that and gave up one of her three jobs.

Growing up, Chelsea was outgoing and bubbly. From time to time, her mother would take her to her job, and the employees all remarked on how adorable and friendly Chelsea was. She never made a nuisance of herself or acted out in a manner that would cause her mother to have to reprimand her. Chelsea made friends easily. In fact, one close friend remarked that she could make friends with the devil himself. She particularly enjoyed helping the elderly and would often spend hours talking with older neighbors and shopping for them, bringing them necessities if they were homebound. In school, she earned good grades, and her teachers remarked that she was diligent and helpful. She was named to the yearbook committee, an honor given only to those who did outstanding schoolwork. Never lacking for boyfriends, Chelsea always seemed to have an adoring male by her side—and in 2002, this became Andrew Wamsley.

After graduating, Chelsea had even more time to spend with Andrew. Although from the outside, they may have looked like an unlikely couple with wildly different home lives, upbringings, and economic means, they nevertheless seemed to have found a connection that went beyond the superficial. They shared their most private thoughts and even made plans for the future—how they would one day live in a nice house with a lovely lawn and plenty of cars, one for each to drive and then some for Andrew to work on. They would spend their days chilling with friends.

But exactly how they could make that happen—Chelsea was not working or attending college and Andrew had dropped out of college and was working for minimum wage at Putt-Putt—was a topic that they gave plenty of time and thought to.

Chapter Six

On December 12, 2003, while Detective Standefer was interviewing Andrew at the Mansfield Police station, the detective heard something that piqued his interest. Andrew stated that he and Chelsea had been at the home of a person named Jeremy Lavender on the night of the murder.

Following up on all leads that came their way, the Mansfield Police Department sent a female police officer to Jeremy's home, where he lived with his parents, on December 14. When she arrived, Jeremy and the officer went into his living room and began talking. The officer asked Jeremy how he knew Andrew and Chelsea. He told her that he had known Chelsea for about four years, since he was around fourteen. He recounted that he had met her at the movies in "just a chance encounter." According to Jeremy, after the movies, Chelsea asked him if he wanted to go out, and he told her that he'd give it a try. After discovering that they enjoyed each other's company and had lots to talk about, they soon became close friends. For Jeremy, the relationship was the most important one in his life. After several years of friendship, they decided to push the relationship up a notch and became boyfriend/girlfriend. However, a few months later, Chelsea told him she was going to California. When she returned, she called to tell him she had a new boyfriend, who turned out to be Andrew Wamsley.

When Chelsea told Jeremy she was breaking up with

him, he told the officer, he was extremely upset. He told Chelsea he wanted to still be her boyfriend, but Chelsea was adamant: They could remain friends but could not be boyfriend and girlfriend. When the officer asked Jeremy how Chelsea treated him, he said she always treated him well, even after they had split up.

When asked what he was doing on the night of December 11, Jeremy stated that Chelsea, Andrew, and a friend of theirs, Susana, had come to his house and hung out there for a long while before they left for home.

"Last name?" the officer asked.

"Toledano," he replied and then continued with his story. After the other three drove off, he said, Chelsea had called him and they talked on the phone for a couple of hours, as they often did.

At the end of the interview, the officer asked him if he would write a statement detailing what he had told her about his actions on the night of the murder. He said he would. The officer handed him some paper and a pen. After Jeremy finished writing his statement, the officer thanked him and told him that he was free to come and go as he wished. He was not a person of interest at that time.

As it turned out, neither was Susana. No police officer contacted her until two months later.

Chapter Seven

Susana Alexandria Toledano was born on September 28, 1984, in Prospect Heights, Illinois, a northern suburb of Chicago. She attended school there, taking classes in Spanish until she was around eight. Spanish was her first language, because her mother, grandmother, and everyone else in her home spoke only Spanish. In the fourth grade, she began taking classes in English.

Life for Susana in Prospect Heights was fun, happy, and carefree. She was in the Girl Scouts for four years and enjoyed the camaraderie of a close set of friends. Although shy, she had friends from all different ethnic and social groups and was able to adapt to just about anyone.

Susana was close with her grandmother, who adored her. After all, Susana was her first grandbaby and a girl to boot. Home life with her mother, Angela, sister Jessica, and brother David was always hectic, with everyone coming and going at all times of night and day. Her happiest childhood memory was when her father took her to a father-daughter dance when she was in elementary school. She thought she looked lovely in her frilly dress and matching bow. Her saddest memory was when her father moved out not long after that. One of her favorite pastimes growing up was riding her bike, which she did practically every day. She loved visiting friends and exploring places in her neighborhood.

However, Susana's idyllic life abruptly came to an end

just after she finished middle school in 1999. Her mother wanted a warmer climate and a drastic change of scenery, so she got the family together, including Susana's grandmother and her grandmother's boyfriend, and the whole group moved to Texas. Susana hated the idea of leaving behind everyone and everything she knew and loved, but she had no choice. After all, she was only fifteen and had no way of being on her own.

The day she set foot in Fort Worth, Susana knew she'd hate it. First of all, the heat was oppressive. She loved the cold weather in Illinois, especially the snow. Second, no one rode bikes; everyone drove in cars. And third, she didn't know a soul and was terrified of going to a new school as a freshman. Once easygoing and carefree, Susana felt herself almost overnight become a sullen and depressed teen.

Susana's first day at Everman Joe C. Bean High School—called Everman for short—was stressful and lonely, just as she knew it would be. No one spoke to her or even acknowledged her existence—until the last class of the day. That's when a bubbly blonde came up to her and introduced herself.

"Hi. I'm Chelsea. What's your name?"

Susana almost broke down crying. Here was this cool person coming up to *her* and saying hi! Maybe she wasn't invisible after all. The two started talking and found they had a lot in common. They spent the rest of the afternoon together, and when evening came, Susana reluctantly went home. The next day, the two met up in school and Chelsea included Susana in everything she did. Susana was overwhelmed, and grateful. In time, the two started spending all their spare time together. Susana started thinking that maybe her new life wouldn't be so bad. She vowed that Chelsea would be her BFF and became increasingly more dependent on her for friendship, support, social interaction, and even help with her schoolwork.

School was hard for Susana. Growing up, she spoke

"Spanglish," but she never really felt totally comfortable speaking in either Spanish or English. In her first year at Everman, she failed most of her six classes. But Chelsea tutored her and helped her any way she could, and finally Susana was able to just barely get by.

Around two years after Susana and Chelsea met, in late November 2002, Susana was having problems at home with her mother. They couldn't agree on anything and were always at each other's throats. Finally, after Susana and Chelsea talked over the situation, Chelsea suggested that Susana should move in with her family. She told Susana that she had asked her mother and Celia had said Susana could come live with them in their house. Chelsea also pointed out that Susana didn't legally have to live at home anymore since she was already eighteen. So, after some further discussion and planning, Susana moved into 7417 Lea Place.

At that time, Susana did not have a car, but she did have a job. After school, she worked at the Jack in the Box, a quick-serve hamburger restaurant in Arlington, off of Little Road and Pleasant Ridge, for anywhere from twenty-five to forty hours a week at seven dollars per hour. An average check every two weeks was almost $380. She paid some of the expenses at the Richardsons', and in exchange, got room and board and a ride to work every day.

While living with Chelsea, Susana's routine would be to get up early, get dressed and go to the bus stop, ride the bus to school, attend classes, and then leave school at either 11:50 or 12:30 depending on whether or not she stayed for lunch. Then Brenna, Chelsea's older sister, or someone else from the Richardsons', would pick her up and take her back home, where she would do chores, get dressed for work, and be driven to Jack in the Box.

One day, while Chelsea was driving her mother's car with Susana and three other passengers, they got into an accident. Susana's arm was broken, and as a result, she received a

$6,000 insurance settlement. Susana used the money to buy a black 1988 Mustang GT, paying for it in cash. Susana tried to drive it once, but it stalled and she never tried again.

Susana and Chelsea took out a page in the Everman High School yearbook in 2003, the year Chelsea graduated, and placed photos of the two of them together, along with cartoon drawings of sexy females. They added the words "Naughty & Nice," "Smile Now, Cry Later," and "Up to No Good." Chelsea wrote a poem, "Friends are Forever," which she also included on the page: "Who hold[s] my hand in tragedy," it begins, will see that "Morals . . . and sticking to you" is the kind of friend Chelsea is.

With Chelsea's help and support, Susana had begun to like her life in Texas. It was where she belonged. And she felt totally at home.

Chapter Eight

In the early days of the police investigation—the days following December 11, 2003—Todd Cleveland was a person of interest. During Sarah's interview with detectives, she had mentioned that Cleveland might have been responsible for the shooting of the Wamsleys' Jeep; plus, he was involved in the acrimonious custody battle over Brittany, in which Rick and Suzy were heavily invested. He seemed like the most likely suspect.

But Cleveland wasn't the only person of interest to the police. Sarah and Andrew were also under consideration, not because of any evidence the police had found linking them to the murders, but because family members are always suspects in murders that take place in the home. Plus, in this case, the Wamsley children stood to gain over $100,000 in cash, a $1.65 million home, and $1 million from a life insurance policy. Surely, they had the motive.

However, nearly two months after the horrific murders, no blood or bullets could be linked to any of the suspects, and the case was quickly going cold. Residents of Walnut Estates were becoming increasingly anxious and angry. *How could it take the police so long to find a crazed killer? What was the Mansfield Police Department doing anyway?*

"We're worried about our safety," said Rob Brown, a resident of Walnut Estates who traveled for business and worried about leaving his family alone. "The tension level in the neighborhood is pretty high. I would like to be able to put my family at ease."

In response to the growing apprehension, Thad Penkala, a police spokesperson, said, "We can't always release all the details because it might jeopardize our investigation and eventually the prosecution of a case. But we are making some progress."

That was small comfort to the residents of Mansfield, a city that typically averaged one killing a year.

In early February 2004, the police ratcheted up their investigation. They decided to convene a grand jury in an attempt to discover some new information that might lead them to a suspect. Susana Toledano and Jeremy Lavender were the first to be subpoenaed.

On February 17, 2004, Susana was called to testify in front of the Tarrant County Grand Jury. At that time, she was no longer living at the Richardsons' home but had moved back in with her mother "to get away from everything that was going around."

Tarrant County assistant district attorney Michael D. Parrish questioned her and, under oath, she told the jury where she was on the night of the murder. She stated that she, along with Andrew and Chelsea, were at Jeremy Lavender's home for several hours. Afterward, they returned to the Richardsons' house and soon went to bed. When asked if she had any idea who had committed the killings, she replied that she did not.

After Susana finished testifying, Parrish asked her if she would voluntarily give the police a sample of her DNA. The only reason she was being asked, he told her, was because she was living with Chelsea and both of their hair was dyed, as were some strands of hair found in Rick Wamsley's hand.

Surprised at the request, Susana told him she wanted to think about it and talk it over with her friends. After leaving the courtroom, Andrew and Chelsea picked her up, and together they all went to the office of a lawyer Chelsea's mother had recommended.

Susana told the lawyer what had just taken place in front of the grand jury and, after discussing with her whether or not to give a DNA sample, Susana decided to go back and give it. When she returned to the courthouse, she was asked to give a signed statement saying that she was giving permission for her mouth to be swabbed. According to Susana, they swabbed "one [Q-tip] on each side and stuck it back on two different envelopes and I signed it."

About a week later, on February 23, 2004, Jeremy Lavender was subpoenaed to appear before the grand jury. Again, Parrish was the questioner. He asked Jeremy what he knew about the night of the murders of Mr. and Mrs. Wamsley. Jeremy's story matched exactly with that of Susana's: Andrew, Chelsea, and Susana had spent the evening at his house.

Around a month later, on March 26, 2004, Susana left Tarrant County to visit her uncle, meet her uncle's girlfriend, and see their new baby in Addison, Illinois. She was excited about the trip, not only because she would be going back to her childhood home, but also because she would be getting away from the pall that had descended over her world after the Wamsleys' murder.

Chapter Nine

Nearly four months after the murders, theories still abounded as to who might have committed the killings and why. The police had been following several leads, but they all ended up being dead ends, and they had been unable to make any arrests.

But then, in early April, some startling information came to light and, all of a sudden, the dominoes started to fall.

"We've got a match," said a person from the medical examiner's office to Detective Standefer at the Mansfield Police Department. "The DNA on the hair in Rick Wamsley's hand—we've got a match!"

"No way!" responded a stunned Standefer.

"And to the broken hair clip."

"I will never forget that phone call," said Standefer later. "I knew we were finally there, and things were fixing to start falling in place." But, he admitted, he was surprised when he heard the name of the match.

Earlier, Standefer had issued a "pen register" warrant for several of the potential suspects' cell phones—Andrew, Chelsea, Sarah, Susana, Celia, James—even several of the Wamsleys' neighbors. That meant he could track their phones' locations—he was certain that they would never be far from their phones—and he assumed this information would come in handy one day, as soon as the investigation led in a specific direction. And it was now leading straight to one of them: the best friend of the girlfriend of the boy whose parents were murdered—Susana Toledano. According to the medical examiner's office, Susana's DNA was a match to the hair found in Rick Wamsley's hand and to the hair clip found on the floor at the crime scene.

This was huge!

Standefer tracked Susana all the way to the Chicago area, from cell phone tower to cell phone tower. From the most recent calls she made, he discovered that she was still there. Standefer immediately telephoned the Illinois State Police and "was lucky enough to get transferred to Bob Hunt." Standefer explained the case to Hunt and told him that he would be coming up to interview a murder suspect and asked if Hunt could help him out. "Wow," said Standefer later. "Bob latched on like a bulldog and started to gather all the information he could prior to my arrival."

On April 4, 2004, Standefer, along with Texas Ranger Keith Denning and Detective Barbara Slayton-Bell, flew to Chicago's O'Hare Airport. Standefer had a warrant for Susana's arrest, but he had no idea how easy—or hard—it would be to locate her once his team arrived. In fact, the Mansfield-based crew didn't even book return flights; they knew they would have to stay as long as it took.

When they arrived in Chicago, Officer Hunt and his partner, Romero "Ram" Montes, picked them up at the airport. They went out for lunch so they could talk over the details. When they finished, they checked the location of Susana's phone again. With the assistance of the U.S. Marshals Service and its computer tracking equipment, the detectives learned the location of the apartment complex where Susana was staying.

After deciding on a strategy, they drove to the address. Hunt went to the apartment manager's office, showed his badge, and got a key to the apartment where Susana had been traced. Hunt and the others approached the apartment and, under the guise of being a maintenance worker, Hunt knocked on the door. Standefer had described to Hunt what Susana looked like, so when she opened the door, Hunt knew it was her. Standefer was standing around the corner, where Susana couldn't see him—at first. Then, after getting the sign from Hunt, Standefer stepped out and said, "Do you remember me?"

According to Standefer, Susana turned pale white, with a typical "deer in the headlights" look. He asked her what she knew about the Wamsley murder. Trying to keep her composure, she repeated the story she had told previously, about spending the evening at Jeremy Lavender's house. But after they talked for a while and she kept sticking to her story, the officers told her that they had some evidence to connect her to the murder. "You can't get out of it. We know it's you."

Susana was shocked. *Evidence? How could that be?* She said they must be wrong.

"Do you want to come clean?" they asked.

"I don't know what you mean," she responded.

Then they became even more specific. "We have your DNA."

Susana knew they had her DNA—she had given it to the police department two months prior. *But what did that prove?* "I know," she said.

The officers then told her that some of her hairs were found in the hand of Mr. Wamsley. They repeated, "We know it's you."

Susana took a deep breath. She sensed she was in trouble. After trying to figure out the best angle to take, she started telling a story that was far different from the one she had told the grand jury on February 17.

"It was Hilario Cardenas who did it," Susana said. "He did it."

"Who?" asked Standefer.

"Hilario Cardenas. Night manager at the IHOP."

Hilario Cardenas? That's a new one! thought Standefer.

Susana reluctantly began to fill in the details. She stated

that she was at the Wamsleys' house the day the couple was murdered, but she was not the murderer. She was just an accomplice, she said. She and Hilario had gone to the Wamsleys just to rob them, and while she was outside and Hilario was inside, she had heard shots.

After the interview, because Susana had implicated herself as an accomplice, Standefer arrested her and she was taken to the Addison, Illinois, police department. On the way there, Standefer sent word to the Mansfield Police Department to check out a potential suspect: Hilario Cardenas. "You just might have a killer on your hands," he warned.

Soon after Susana arrived at the police station, a marathon interview began. Seven hours later, at 10:12 p.m., she gave the police a signed statement in her own handwriting telling her revised version of the murder.

Susana stayed in the DuPage County Jail in Addison for two weeks before being extradited by plane to Tarrant County Jail. A day or so later on April 20, she went to the courthouse and received a court-appointed lawyer.

Chapter Ten

Once the Mansfield police located Hilario Cardenas, they went to the IHOP at the Arlington Mall and began to interview him. Hilario stated that he was twenty-four years old, the night manager at the IHOP, and married with a four-year-old daughter. Asked if he knew Chelsea Richardson, Andrew Wamsley, or Susana Toledano, Hilario replied that he did. He said that Chelsea, Andrew, and Susana, along with Chelsea's brother, would come to the IHOP practically every night and stay for hours playing Yu-Gi-Oh!. The group would hang out in a big booth, often until six in the morning, and battle with the cards.

To break up the monotony of the early morning hours when the restaurant was practically empty, Hilario said he would spend time talking to the teens about Yu-Gi-Oh! tactics, as well as another of his interests, tropical fish.

When asked about the murder of the Wamsleys, he seemed surprised. He said he didn't know that the Wamsleys had been murdered. When asked if anything out of the ordinary had ever taken place during his friendship with the group, Hilario recalled that one night just before Halloween, Andrew had asked him if he could get him a gun. Hilario said he was shocked by the request and had asked Andrew why he wanted one. Andrew had told him that he, Chelsea, and Susana wanted to learn to shoot and planned to do target practice at a house owned by a friend of Chelsea's mother, Ruth Brustrom.

Asked if he supplied Andrew with a gun, Hilario stated that he did. He said he bought it off the street and brought it to Andrew, who paid him $200 for it. Hilario said he never went to Ruth Brustrom's place, where the group supposedly did target shooting, and he didn't know anything about what they actually did with the gun.

The officers decided to ask Hilario if he would voluntarily submit to a polygraph test. He agreed, so they took him down to the station. Although the results of polygraphs are typically not admissible as evidence in court, they are frequently used to evaluate the truthfulness of suspects and witnesses. After being interviewed for hours, Hilario was given the polygraph, and he failed. The test suggested he was lying about his story. However, after being given some time to rest, he was given another polygraph, and he passed. This time, the results indicated he was telling the truth.

Hilario was let go and told he could go home.

But the detectives had gotten something out of the interviews. Their interest had been piqued after hearing a new name once again. They decided to contact Ruth Brustrom right away.

Chapter Eleven

In November 2003, Ruth Brustrom, thirty-seven, with freckles and curly red hair, stood in the sprinkling rain and watched as Andrew Wamsley and Susana Toledano shot rounds of bullets from a handgun at a target in her pond. A few days earlier, Andrew had called her and asked if he, Chelsea, and their friend Susana could come by and do some target practice. Brustrom said that they could, as long as they shot directly into the water so stray bullets wouldn't hit any of her neighbors.

Brustrom had known Chelsea since she was around nine years old, when Chelsea's father and Brustrom's husband had worked together in a power plant. When Chelsea's father died, Brustrom's husband, Ray, took over the role of father to the Richardson kids. But not long after, Ray, who worked construction and raised fighting roosters, passed away, too. That was in August 2002. Brustrom, however, remained close to Chelsea's mother and the Richardson kids.

The Brustrom family lived on a five-acre spread that included a mobile home, several barn-red outbuildings, some junked cars, and a high-flying Confederate flag. Laid-back and easygoing, Brustrom was a favorite of Andrew and Chelsea. They could sit and talk with her for hours. With a large tattoo of a rose surrounded by the words "In Loving Memory of Ray" on her right arm, Brustrom served as both a surrogate mother and loyal friend to the teens.

During the early part of November 2003, Andrew, Chelsea, and Susana came often to visit Brustrom, and each time, they practiced their shooting, aiming the bullets into her pond. Brustrom got to know Andrew pretty well and really liked him. She felt that he was by far the best boyfriend Chelsea had ever brought around—intelligent, kind, and even-tempered.

But at one point in early December, the visits abruptly stopped and Brustrom became concerned. After several attempts to reach the teens, she finally got Andrew on his cell phone. He didn't say much, and immediately handed the phone to Chelsea. She was crying hysterically. Between tears, Chelsea told Brustrom that Andrew's parents had been murdered a few days earlier. Brustrom recalled having heard something about a Mansfield slaying on TV, but hadn't connected Andrew's family with the murders. In fact, she didn't even know Andrew's last name.

"He can't wait to come out," Chelsea said to Brustrom. "We need to get away."

Brustrom told them they were more than welcome to come anytime at all. She felt terrible for Andrew, losing his parents that way. *It was unimaginable!*

One evening around Christmas, Chelsea and Andrew came to Brustrom's house. She tried to make the visit as festive as possible—and succeeded. Although his parents had recently been murdered, Andrew enjoyed himself, laughing and singing along as everyone belted out some off-key holiday tunes.

At one point during the evening, Andrew said to Brustrom, "Don't say anything to anyone about the gun." Brustrom thought that was odd, but she figured that maybe he was paranoid about being tapped as a suspect just because he was doing target practice. After all, everyone knew that immediate family members are the first to be scrutinized in murder cases.

More than a month passed before Brustrom saw them again. It was February, and one night, the couple showed up at her door. They said that Andrew's probate lawyer suggested that they get away and go on a vacation, so they wondered if they could move in with her and chill out. Brustrom took them into her home without a moment's hesitation.

In practically no time, the three fell into a comfortable routine. Andrew was a good cook, so he prepared all the meals. Chelsea washed the dishes and helped Brustrom take care of her kids. Both Andrew and Chelsea kept the house clean and tidy. One evening while they were chatting after dinner, Chelsea told Brustrom that she and Andrew planned to take a long vacation somewhere far away after they were cleared as suspects. Eventually, she added, they planned to get married. Ruth was thrilled. "If your daddy was still alive, I know he'd be happy," she told Chelsea.

However, as the days wore on, Chelsea and Andrew's relationship started unraveling. Being under suspicion was stressful for both of them. At first, Andrew had participated in all their discussions and activities, but then he began to withdraw and become easily agitated. The once cheerful and bubbly Chelsea would often break down crying in the middle of a sentence. Tension between the two began to escalate and their roughhousing started getting out of control. Angry arguments flared up practically every day, sometimes more than once a day. Brustrom told them she couldn't deal with their fighting and they'd better get themselves together. When after several weeks they were still unable to control themselves, Brustrom told them she had had enough. They had to leave.

Reluctantly, the couple moved back to Chelsea's mother's house in early March. At first, things remained dicey between them, but as the weeks passed and it seemed that the investigation was winding down, they found themselves less stressed and more able to relax. They even started to enjoy being with each other again. One thing they especially liked doing was setting up the aquarium that Andrew had brought from his parents' home and watching and feeding the fish.

In April 2004, Chelsea and Andrew once again started spending time with Brustrom. She was thrilled that they seemed to be getting back to their old selves. One day, as she was shopping with the two, Chelsea received a call on her cell phone. After she hung up, Brustrom noticed that Chelsea was "upset, nervous." She asked her what was wrong.

"Susana got arrested," Chelsea said. Then she added, "If she had went to Mexico, this wouldn't have happened."

Brustrom was shocked to hear that Susana had been arrested and wondered what she had done. *Maybe she was dealing drugs? Could she be involved in prostitution? Perhaps she'd robbed someone?* Knowing Chelsea as she did, Brustrom knew she would fill her in on all the details in due time.

Chapter Twelve

On April 6, police felt they had enough probable cause to make a second arrest—Hilario Cardenas. Susana Toledano had implicated him in the killings. She told the Addison, Illinois, police that Hilario had committed the crimes. As a result, Hilario was charged with capital murder.

But then on April 7, a stunned Mansfield heard some *truly* shocking news. In the parking lot outside a Chicken Express near Chelsea Richardson's home, Mansfield police arrested Chelsea along with her boyfriend, Andrew. That was Andrew *Wamsley*, the nineteen-year-old son of Suzy and Rick. The two were charged with solicitation of capital murder, based on circumstantial evidence, including Hilario's claim that he was solicited by Chelsea and Andrew to kill the Wamsleys—but which he vehemently denied doing.

Andrew, Chelsea, and Hilario were all being held at the Mansfield Law Enforcement Center in lieu of $1 million bail. Susana was being held there too on an additional $5 million fugitive bail, which had been set by the state of Illinois.

On April 9, an NBC 5 News report announced that the Wamsley killings were the result of a murder-for-hire scheme. Andrew Wamsley and Chelsea Richardson did the hiring. Susana Toledano and Hilario Cardenas were the killers.

But then on April 19, an even bigger shock came. The

complaint against Andrew was amended to say that he—
Andrew—and not Hilario, was the person who shot and
stabbed Suzy and Rick Wamsley to death. *Andrew* was being charged with capital murder.

The motive, police claimed, was the Wamsleys' $1 mil-
lion life insurance policy and other assets.

Chapter Thirteen

Finally, it seemed, the frightened people in the Walnut Estates section of Mansfield could breathe a sigh of relief. "We have told the citizens of Mansfield that we believed this was an isolated incident, and we still believe that to this day," said Officer Thad Penkala of the Mansfield Police Department.

But who actually did the killings? Who pulled the trigger and who stabbed with the knife? So many different versions of what occurred on December 11 had been told to the police that one needed a scorecard to keep track.

On May 19, 2004, Jeremy Lavender was re-subpoenaed to appear before the Tarrant County grand jury. Assistant District Attorney Parrish stated that he had some new information that made Jeremy's previous testimony suspect. Jeremy was stunned. He thought his involvement with grand juries and the murders was over. It had been five months since the deaths of Rick and Suzy Wamsley and nearly three months since he had been in front of the grand jury. *What new information could they possibly have?*

In front of the grand jury, Parrish said to Jeremy, "We have your phone records from the night of the murder, from both your cell and your landline. Those are your numbers, aren't they?"

"Yes," responded Jeremy shakily.

Parrish told him that the records showed that he and

Chelsea did not talk for hours on the night of December 11 after Chelsea had left his house, as he had told the grand jury in February. As a matter of fact, stated Parrish, the records clearly showed that Chelsea called him five times on his cell and four times on his landline—indicating that Chelsea was not even at his house, as he had reported. *What did he think about that?*

"Obviously," Parrish stated, "your previous testimony that Chelsea and Andrew were at your house the night of the murder is suspect. And your testimony that you and Richardson spoke for hours after she left were downright lies."

Jeremy sat motionless. Chelsea had told him what to say and he had done exactly as she asked. Everything had seemed just fine—at least for a while. *Now what was he supposed to do?*

Parrish took a few moments to explain to Jeremy what was at stake. He stated that if he told the truth, he would not be prosecuted for perjury—a crime, Parrish said, that was punishable by a prison sentence of up to five years.

After processing these new details, Jeremy considered what might be the best thing for him to do. *I don't have much choice*, he thought. Jeremy then renounced his previous testimony and said he wanted to come clean and tell the truth—his version of the truth, anyway.

The young man admitted that he had lied when he previously appeared in front of the grand jury. He stated that at that time, he had no idea what he was covering up. No one had told him anything about a murder. He also stated that he had no idea where either Andrew or Chelsea was on the night of the murder, or whether or not they spent the evening together.

In recounting a new version of what took place that evening, Jeremy stated that he was home all night and had gone to bed around 11 p.m. He said he had received a call from Chelsea very early in the morning and had been extremely angry about it. "Nobody has ever called me that early when

I'm asleep," he commented. He also said that when Chelsea called, she asked him to be her alibi. He asked her what she needed an alibi for and she told him it didn't matter. Jeremy assumed it had something to do with a curfew, so he had no reservations about offering up an excuse. He said that Chelsea told him that if the police asked him anything about the night of the 11th of December, he was supposed to tell them that he had planned to meet her at Putt-Putt golf, but because he didn't have any gas, Chelsea, Andrew, and Susana had come to his house instead. "Say we visited for a while," Chelsea told Jeremy on the phone, "and then say we left." After that, he was supposed to tell the police that he and Chelsea talked on the phone for hours, into the early hours of the morning.

Jeremy said that was all he knew. Honest. That was the whole truth, and nothing but the truth.

Chapter Fourteen

While incarcerated in Texas after her arrest, Susana eventually told detectives about the months leading up to the murders and the plans that Chelsea and Andrew had hatched in order to get money from the Wamsleys.

It all began in October 2003. Andrew and Chelsea seemed to have decided that Andrew's parents had to die so they could get the proceeds of a $1 million life insurance policy and the family's estate.

Susana said she was told that because she was living rent-free at Chelsea's and that either Chelsea or Andrew drove her to work every day, she owed them something—big time. Hilario, she said, was convinced to join in the scheme with the promise of money and a horse for his daughter to ride.

Over time, Susana told the investigators, they discussed several different plans, and even tried them out.

The first plan was to cut the brakes in the family car and make it look like an accident. Hilario was tapped as the best one to do it because he knew cars inside and out. However, according to Susana, he "chickened out," and that meant they had to come up with another scheme. According to Hilario, when it came to actually doing the job, he realized that he simply didn't have it in him to hurt anyone.

The second plan was to shoot at the family car's gas tank while the car was in motion so that the car would explode and everyone in it would die. They had seen that done dozens of times on TV, so they figured it must work. In this plot, Susana was tapped as the shooter and Andrew as the driver. After some planning, the two decided to do it on I-35 in Burleson, after Rick, Suzy, and Sarah were on their way home from Joshua and riding Toby. On November 9, Andrew and Susana got in Andrew's Mustang and waited until they saw the Jeep go by. Then they drove right by them, and Susana took aim and fired. However, she missed the gas tank. After that, Susana told investigators, Chelsea and Andrew were furious with her because she had failed miserably. Now, they told her, she "owed" them one.

According to Susana, a third plot was to cause Sarah to have a car accident by putting Drano in balloons and then placing them in her gas tank. Susana admitted that she and Chelsea poured the Drano into the balloons, but she never saw whether or not the balloons were placed in Sarah's gas tank. Later, Chelsea told her that they were, but once again, the plotters failed in their attempts to harm the Wamsley family.

Another scheme, according to Susana, was to sneak into the Wamsleys' home, kill both Wamsleys, remove an item or two to make it look like a robbery, and then, for added effect, shoot Andrew in the arm so it would look like he was trying to save his family. According to Susana, Hilario was never a part of that plan. She, Chelsea, and Andrew attempted to carry out that plot in late November 2003. The three snuck into the Wamsley house while the parents were asleep. Andrew and Chelsea had told Susana that since she "screwed up, it was her job to fix it." Susana went into Andrew's bedroom and hid in the closet for around half an hour, sitting on the floor. From time to time, Chelsea and Andrew would come in and give her pep talks. However, Susana was too scared and told them she didn't think she could do it. They snuck out of the house in the dark of night and returned to Chelsea's.

Susana said that because she had screwed up shooting at

the car and chickened out in the house, she was under great pressure to make it right. "They kept on and they kept on and they kept on," she said.

According to Susana, Hilario was interested in participating in the plots—at first. At the IHOP, he would sit and discuss the plans with the others for hours. But then, after he provided them with a gun, he began to distance himself and would not return phone calls or show up to execute his part in any of the plans. It soon became clear to the others that he was a no-show and that it would be up to them to do the job.

Chapter Fifteen

While Susana was incarcerated in Texas in early July 2004, Assistant DA Parrish offered her a plea deal. In return for writing her full and complete version of the truth and for giving truthful testimony in court, if called upon, she would be given a life sentence with the possibility of parole after 30 years. Parrish pointed out that if she did not agree to these conditions, she could be facing a trial and the possibility of death.

After carefully considering the offer with her court-appointed lawyer, Tim Moore, Susana felt that since the police had DNA evidence linking her to the killings, her best bet would be to accept the plea agreement. Moore was a 1985 graduate of South Texas College of Law, where he received his JD degree, and a member of the Texas Criminal Defense Lawyers Association. On July 13, Susana gave a full written account of the murders, and in exchange, she was permitted to plead guilty to murder—not capital murder—for killing one person, as the plea agreement stated.

Hilario Cardenas was represented by Ray Hall, Jr. While in law school, Hall had ridden bareback in the International Professional Rodeo Association, which might explain his style: Western clothes, or boots and a suit. Sometimes, Hall donned a hat and black jeans. Bailiffs called him "cowboy." Hall and the assistant district attorney worked out an agreement that

Hilario would provide what information he could about the murders, and Hilario would be indicted for conspiracy to commit capital murder—not capital murder itself. While the charge was less, the severity of Hilario's punishment remained an open question. And he would not be asked to testify in court against any of his co-conspirators.

On July 29, 2004, nearly four months after Chelsea and Andrew were arrested, the state of Texas, represented by Michael Parrish, filed a written notice of a plea offer for them as well. The plea offered life to both Chelsea and Andrew in exchange for guilty pleas to the offense of capital murder. If Chelsea and Andrew agreed to plead guilty, they would avoid a trial and the possibility of being sentenced to the death penalty.

On September 24, 2004, Chelsea appeared before the Honorable Leo Everett Young in Fort Worth, Tarrant County, Texas. Chelsea's lawyer, Mike Maloney, stated that the plea offer had been tendered to his client and that he and Chelsea were requesting that the offer be kept open until October 1, 2004, when they would state their decision.

Andrew's lawyer, Larry M. Moore, graduated from Texas Law School in 1977. In late 1984, he was made director of the criminal division of the DA's office, and at the age of thirty-two, he was supervising more than a hundred trial lawyers in that office.

Moore spoke to Andrew about the offer. His advice was that if he "did it [the crime], he should take the deal." Moore also requested that the offer be kept open until October 1.

Judge Young granted the requests. A time of 1:30 p.m. for Andrew and 2:30 p.m. for Chelsea on October 1 was established to hear their responses to the plea offers.

On October 1, 2004, at 2:43 p.m., Chelsea was sworn in before Judge Young first. She stated her full name: Chelsea Lea Richardson. Her lawyer, Mike Maloney, then asked her if he had conveyed to her an offer he had received from the state for her to enter a plea of life to capital murder as opposed to having a death penalty trial.

"Is that correct?" asked Maloney.

"Yes, sir," answered Chelsea.

"Did I explain all the ramifications of the offer to you?" asked Maloney.

"Yes, sir," Chelsea responded.

"Do you wish to accept the plea?" asked Maloney.

Without hesitation, Chelsea stated, "No."

"Can you afford counsel or hired counsel for a capital murder trial?"

"No, sir."

"Are you asking for a court appointed counsel?" asked Maloney.

"Yes," stated Chelsea.

The judge then questioned Chelsea about her assets. In response, she stated that she did not have a bank account or an automobile and that she did not own anything of value. The court declared that new counsel would be appointed and that she would face a trial.

The judge then said to Chelsea, "You understand that if I allow Mr. Maloney to withdraw and appoint new counsel for you, that you're looking at a trial?"

"Yes," Chelsea replied.

"Where the death penalty would be an issue," the judge stated. "Do you understand that?"

"Yes."

After the judge was certain that Chelsea understood she was now looking at a death penalty trial, ADA Parrish addressed the judge and said, "We'll be asking you for two months next year to give her a death trial."

The judge then said once more, "And Ms. Richardson, I'm gonna establish again that you're not doing this and requesting new counsel in order to—or in the hopes that— you might secure a better deal, is that right?"

"Yes," said Chelsea.

The judge then summed up the hearing. "At this time," he said, "the court has considered the defendant's request for appointed counsel along with financial statement, and the court is gonna find that the defendant is indigent, not able to hire counsel. At this point, this being the case—where the state may seek the death penalty—the court is going to appoint as lead counsel Mr. J. Warren St. John." St. John soon after asked Terry Barlow to assist him, as second chair.

Maloney was then relieved of any further obligation, except to cooperate with any new counsel, and Chelsea was led away in handcuffs.

When Andrew appeared before the judge, he wore leg shackles and the county uniform. His lawyer, Larry Moore, asked the same questions Maloney did to Chelsea and the same recitation took place. The judge asked Andrew if he was, in fact, Andrew Wamsley, to which Andrew replied yes. The judge then asked if Moore had told him about the plea offer and what it meant, and Andrew again answered yes. Then the judge asked Moore if Andrew accepted the plea, and Moore said no. The judge asked Andrew if that was correct, and Andrew responded that it was. Just as he had with Chelsea, the judge explained the ramifications of that decision. Andrew stated that he understood them and "recognized he was looking at a death penalty trial." Moore was then appointed first chair in Andrew's case.

In Texas, each administrative judicial district of the state appointed a committee to draft the standards for appointment to the defense of death penalty cases in that region, and also formulated a list of lawyers qualified to serve as lead counsel or as second chair in cases within the region. The qualifications for each are based on the number of years of experience, the number of cases tried, and other experiential details. Lawyers are classified as qualified to serve as lead counsel, as second chair, or as both. Moore specifically asked for David

Pearson IV to be appointed as second chair. According to Moore, "David is an outstanding lawyer. He works very hard, and I knew that he would be a good choice for this case." Pearson, like Moore, specialized in criminal cases, including many death penalty cases. Also, although Pearson was qualified to serve as lead counsel, at that time, according to Moore, he wanted to be second chair "as he did not want to be the person primarily responsible for the defense of a death penalty case."

Andrew and Chelsea would be tried separately. Defendants are tried separately for a number of reasons, including the following: if there is a reasonable expectation that evidence would be admissible against only one or the other of the defendants; if each defendant blames the other so that a joint trial would not allow for a fair trial; and if tried jointly, evidence used against one might be considered by jurors in their overall verdict, even if the judge instructs jurors not to consider evidence used against one in the other's case. In that scenario, "both tend to get smeared with the same brush," said Martin B. Margulies, a professor at Quinnipiac University School of Law. "And limited instruction by the judge isn't going to empty the minds of the jury." It seemed to the lawyers that all three reasons might apply to Chelsea and Andrew, and therefore, they felt it would be best to try them separately.

Chapter Sixteen

May 18, 2005, was a sunny, warm seventy-two-degree day in Fort Worth as Justice Everett Young called the court to order. All of the approximately seventy-five seats in the room were taken. The lightwood benches were filled with family and friends of the Wamsleys and the Richardsons, as well as lawyers interested in hearing a capital case, hoping to garner some tips for when they would have their day in court in a death penalty case.

"Okay. Let's go ahead and bring the jury in, please," said Young. Looking at the courtroom from the back, the jury and witness stands were on the left, as was the prosecution table. On the right were the defense table, the bailiff's desk, and in the front, out of view, the holding cells.

Fort Worth was riveted by the trial. Newspapers and radio and TV shows covered all the lurid details, from teens gone adrift to the atrocities of the actual murder. There was a lot at stake in this case. After all, *if,* and that "if" was a very big word, *if* Chelsea Richardson was found guilty and *if* the jurors felt the death penalty was appropriate, Chelsea would become the first woman in Tarrant County *ever* to receive the death penalty.

Selecting the jury turned out to be easier than many anticipated, considering all the pretrial publicity. The pool from which the lawyers selected the jurors was large, and each person swore he or she could hear the testimony without being biased one way or the other ahead of time. Twelve jurors—eight women and four men—and one alternate took their seats, raised their right hands, and were sworn in. Judge Young then laid out the order of the trial to the jury. The state, as represented by Michael D. Parrish and Catherine Page Simpson, known as Page, would read the indictment, and the defendant would enter her plea. The state would then make an opening statement, outlining its case. "At the conclusion," continued the judge, "the defense has the right to make an opening statement. Afterwards, both sides get to introduce evidence. At the conclusion of all the evidence, the attorneys will make their closing arguments. . . . It is your duty to determine the facts and determine them from the evidence and the reasonable inferences arising from evidence, and in doing so you must not indulge in guesswork or speculation."

After the judge's statements, the indictment was read. Chelsea, wearing a light blue blouse and skirt, glasses, and with her blond hair down and straight and described by a courtroom spectator as "having big breasts, no bootie, and pale," was asked how she pled.

"Not guilty, Your Honor," she stated forcefully.

Simpson rose first to present the state's opening argument. Strong and elegant, she was an all-business, no-nonsense lawyer. Since graduating law school in 2001, Simpson's reputation grew to that of a determined, confident, and resolute attorney. She walked directly over to the jury. Scanning each face, Simpson said, "My first question is this. What would you do for one million dollars?" She then paused to allow the jurors time to contemplate. "That's what this case is about. This case is about how far four people would go for a million dollars—what money and greed does to a person."

Simpson then gave the jurors a synopsis of what they would soon hear in full. "Rick and Suzy Wamsley are the victims in this case. The Wamsleys were hard-working people who were fortunate to have been able to put away a little for retirement. They enjoyed the things that they had and they tried to provide a nice home for Andrew, who still lived with them in their house.

"When the defendant, Chelsea Richardson, met Andrew Wamsley in 2002," Simpson continued, "she thought she hit the jackpot. . . . He had a nice car, he had a nice house."

Simpson went on to say that the Wamsleys also had a life insurance policy worth $1 million, and, she stated emphatically, "Andrew stood to inherit half. But why stop at half when you can have the whole thing?" asked Simpson. "At that point, the plan evolves to include killing Sarah Wamsley, Andrew's sister, so there would be no one else to inherit the estate."

However, Simpson stated, Chelsea "didn't have the stomach for the dirty work. But luckily, because she was so controlling and manipulative, she had already surrounded herself with people that would do whatever she asked. No questions."

First, there was Susana Toledano. Susana, Simpson pointed out, had already taken responsibility, and in return for her truthful testimony, "she's gonna take a life sentence to murder." And then there was Jeremy Lavender. Jeremy, she stated, had been convinced to provide a false alibi for Chelsea. A third person was Hilario Cardenas, whom Chelsea "ripped into this scheme to kill the Wamsleys. Chelsea even convinced Hilario to get them a gun, all on the promise of living in a nice house and allowing Hilario's daughter to ride their horse."

After outlining the horrific details of the night of the murder, Simpson told the jurors that Chelsea was the mastermind, the manipulator, the person who put Susana up to killing the Wamsleys. "That's the case you have in front of you," she told the jurors. "I'll stand up at the end of this case," she said, "and ask you to find the defendant guilty of capital murder, because she is guilty. Thank you."

Throughout Simpson's statement, the jurors were spellbound. After all, they were hearing for the first time that four young people were involved in the murder of one of their parents. And, they were looking straight at a bespectacled young woman who was being accused as the mastermind—and could face the death penalty.

After Simpson took her seat, the judge asked if the defense attorneys had an opening statement.

"Briefly, Judge," responded Warren St. John.

St. John, a 1984 graduate of South Texas College of Law, where he received a J.D. degree, was a highly respected lawyer in area state and federal courts. Strong and solid, with light colored hair, he was fearless in court, taking charge of any case in which he was involved. After thanking the jurors for their time and patience, St. John immediately got to the point. He began by saying that they would be hearing testimony from Susana Toledano, "who went inside the Wamsleys' house, took a gun she got from Hilario Cardenas, and shot and killed Mr. and Mrs. Wamsley. So, you're gonna see a killer testify in this trial."

He paused to allow the jurors to think about that. *A killer, and a woman besides!*

Mocking the prosecutors, he dismissed the idea that his client, Chelsea Richardson, was so controlling a nineteen-year-old—this "brand-new baby high school graduate"—that she would be able to control what Hilario Cardenas did, what Susana Toledano did, and what Andrew Wamsley did. "That's just absurd," he said. On the other hand, "Andrew has the motivation," stated St. John forcefully, "to get the money. . . . He knows what estate his parents had, what assets they had."

St. John's version of the killings, which he laid out clearly and succinctly for the jurors, was that "after Andrew showed Hilario how to use the garage door opener in his Mustang, Susana and Hilario went to the Wamsley home and killed Andrew's parents. Chelsea did not go there. She was not there, and there's no physical evidence that she was there."

Then, continued St. John, after Susana was extradited to Texas, she knew from speaking to authorities and from the evidence they had, that she could face death for killing two people. "So, she says in her own mind, how can I save my own life?" According to St. John, the answer that she and her lawyers came up with was "that [it was that] little girl's idea over there, the nineteen-year-old back in December of oh three, that little girl. It was her idea, she's the mastermind, knowing that she [Susana] could be put to death."

What role did Chelsea play in the murder? pondered St. John aloud. "The evidence will establish that Chelsea Richardson had nothing to do with this case . . . the motivation to get the money ultimately rested with Susana and Hilario."

St. John concluded by saying, "After you've looked at the evidence, your correct decision will be not guilty."

And with that, he took his seat.

Having heard two different versions of the night the Wamsleys were murdered, the jurors knew they would have a tough case ahead of them: Who was telling the truth?

Assistant DA Parrish stood up to call his first witness. Parrish was tall and slim with salt-and-pepper hair, a tailored suit, and glasses. He knew how to work the room, walking up close to the jury at times, close to the defense table at other times.

Lewis C. Wamsley was sworn in. He stated that he was seventy-one years old, married to Marjean, and lived in Bartlesville, Oklahoma. When asked by Parrish how many children he had, he responded: "Rodney Allen Wamsley, the oldest; Rick Kendall Wamsley, deceased"—and then he paused, to collect himself before continuing. "Krista Kay Peters, the eldest daughter; and Kendra Sue Otta [phonetic], my youngest daughter." Lewis went on to give details about Rick's childhood, including how hard he worked to achieve the success he did in life. He also said that Suzy and Rick were a great match. They got along beautifully and seemed to have a good time whatever they did. When asked how he learned of his son's death, he described the telephone call from Sarah and said that he and his wife, Marjean, were in "shock, disbelief . . . words cannot describe." When asked whether or not Rick had a life insurance policy, he stated that he did, in the amount of $1 million. He said that an estimate of the value of their estate was approximately $1,650,000. When Parrish asked Lewis if Rick was a "thoughtful, caring son," Lewis responded, trying to keep his voice even as tears welled up in his eyes, that Rick was all that and more. "He was the best son a father could ever have."

Susana Toledano was called next. Around five feet, seven inches tall, blondish hair, fair skin and wearing "the county suit in navy blue," she was sworn in. Courtroom watchers strained their necks to get a good look at her. After all, she admitted to having killed Suzy Wamsley, so they were only feet away from an admitted murderer. Many no doubt thought, *Is this what a killer looks like? Could've fooled me!*

Asked her name, Susana stated softly, "Susana Alexandria Toledano." When asked her age, she said she was twenty.

"Back in December 2003, how old were you?" asked Parrish.

"Nineteen."

Parrish then asked, "For your testimony in this case, what are you receiving?"

"A life sentence," Susana replied in a quiet voice.

"To the murder of?"

"Suzanna Wamsley," she replied.

Susana stated that the life sentence was negotiated by her attorney, Tim Moore.

When asked about her relationship with Chelsea, Susana stated that they had met at Everman High School. "Chelsea was the opposite of me," she said. "I'm not one to just go up to her and introduce myself like formally or informally." She told the court that the two of them soon became best friends and that, in time, she moved in with Chelsea.

When asked when and where she first heard anything about harming the Wamsleys, she said that it was in October at the IHOP in Arlington. Chelsea and Andrew, Susana reported, were talking about "getting rid of them so he can get the insurance money." When asked what specific plans were discussed, she said that one was to "get rid of the sister first by putting chemicals in her gas tank." They were "gonna pour Drano in balloon bags and then put it down her gas tank . . . so she would have a car wreck." Susana said that she and Chelsea were "doing the pouring and the holding of the balloons," but that she did not see whether the balloons were ever placed in Sarah Wamsley's gas tank. Chelsea, Susana told the court, later told her that she had placed the balloons in Sarah's gas tank while Susana was at work.

Parrish then asked Susana when was the first time she had heard mention of a gun. She responded that after the balloon incident, sometime in November 2003, the discussion came up while she, Andrew, and Chelsea were at the IHOP. Susana said that at first, Hilario Cardenas, a night manager at the IHOP, was just their friend. Then, after a while, Hilario became involved in these discussions. "Once Hilario came into the picture . . . other plots to get rid of the Wamsleys were discussed . . . [including] cutting of the brakes [on the Jeep and having them have an accident] and then afterwards like the shooting of the car . . . after the shooting of the car, there was the robbery thing."

After further questioning, Susana mentioned that in "the robbery thing," Hilario was to go with Susana and Andrew to the Wamsley house, while Chelsea stayed at her home. Hilario was to shoot the mom and dad, then shoot Andrew in the arm. Chelsea's role, stated Susana, was the alibi.

Susana mentioned that she got a revolver from Hilario and she, Chelsea, and Andrew decided to practice shooting the gun to see who was the best shot. In order to practice, the three went to the home of a friend of Chelsea's, Ruth

Brustrom, on whose property was a large pond into which
they could shoot their gun. When asked why they were prac-
ticing shooting, Susana said that the plan was to drive up
behind Rick Wamsley's Jeep and shoot the gas tank and then
have the car explode. Asked if the plan ever went into effect,
Susana replied, "Yes, Andrew had come over early one
morning. Me and Andrew got in the car and we went to some
street out of Burleson and waited. When the Jeep drove by,
like in the highway, is when I had shot the car."

"When you fired the shot and nothing happened, what
did Andrew say?" asked Parrish.

"He said 'shit' and didn't say anything all the way back
to Chelsea's house."

"And what happened then?"

"[Chelsea] bitched me out . . . for a good ten, fifteen minutes," Susana said, adding that Chelsea was extremely angry
about the failed attempt. Susana said that she told Chelsea
she was sorry and tried to apologize. When Andrew spoke
to his parents later, calling them from home and making it
sound like he had been there all along, they told him he was
grounded. His parents didn't know for sure who had shot at
their car, but his mother knew it was someone in a white
Mustang—although at the time, she didn't mention that to
Sarah. Sarah thought her mother was calling Andrew "simply" because someone had shot at them—not to check on his
whereabouts.

Susana then told the court that after that failed attempt,
they came up with the plan that she—Susana—would shoot
Andrew's parents. "I was the one that messed up when I shot
the car and I missed. Chelsea told me that I had fucked up
and that we were gonna have to take everything in our hands
and I was gonna do it."

When asked if Hilario was still part of the group, Susana
said that he was distancing himself and had stopped answering Chelsea's calls. Susana reported that Hilario did, however,

get them the gun each time they needed it. But other than that, Hilario was out of the picture. Susana said that Hilario "was just talk" in terms of actually participating in the murders.

Susana then told the court that around two weeks after the Jeep incident, she, Andrew, and Chelsea drove to the Wamsley house and entered it through the garage. Both Andrew and Chelsea made her understand that since she had "messed up" and got Andrew in trouble, that she was the one who had to fix it. They went through the kitchen to the formal dining room and then into Andrew's room. Susana stated that she stayed in the closet for a while, trying to get up the courage to do the shooting. After approximately forty minutes in the closet, Susana told Chelsea and Andrew she couldn't do it and they "were like okay. So we snuck out of the house again and drove home." Chelsea told her that "we're gonna have to do it anyway soon."

"If the Wamsleys were killed, what were you gonna get out of this?" asked Parrish.

"We were gonna fix up my Mustang and then I was gonna switch cars with Andrew and then I wouldn't have to go to work." Susana stated that Chelsea and Andrew were going to get a house, and the plan was that she would live with them and they would "just chill." Susana explained that she had her own Mustang, even though she couldn't drive, that she had bought with insurance money from a car wreck she was in while Chelsea was driving. Her Mustang sat idle in the back of the Richardsons' house, she stated.

Parrish then asked, "On the night that the murders actually happened, how were you first told?"

Susana stated she got a text message at school from Chelsea. It said, "We're gonna do it tonight." Many hours later, after Susana had gone home and changed her clothes, Andrew picked up both her and Chelsea in his Mustang and they drove to Turnberry Drive. They parked in front of the house "by the garage in the little driveway thing." Susana said that Andrew went inside to scope out the house. Then, the three went inside, but, Susana stated, she still wasn't sure she could do it. She said that Andrew and Chelsea gave her pep talks, telling her to "do it soon and . . . go for it."

She said that the mom was on the couch with the TV on. Chelsea, Susana stated, encouraged her, saying, "I know you can do it. I believe in you" and "the sooner we get it over with, the sooner we can go home" and "you don't have to worry about anything." Chelsea then pushed her in the back and "I had to run and I shot the mom." She said that she then ran into the master bedroom and started shooting at the dad. "He got out of bed real quick and charged at me." As he got to her, they backed up into the living room, and Susana fell with Rick landing on top of her. "He was a big man," she commented.

Then, Susana stated, she and Rick Wamsley wrestled into the living room area near the fireplace. At that time, she was "very scared and nervous." She explained that Andrew came in to help and grabbed Rick. While the three of them wrestled, pulled, and tugged on each other, she lost the gun. She stated that after that, she never fired the gun again in that home, that night.

When asked about shooting Rick, Susana stated that every time she shot him, it was in the front of his body: when he was sitting up in bed, when he was charging at her, and when he grabbed her. Then, according to Susana, Rick got hold of the gun and hit Andrew in the head with it. By this time, Susana stated, Chelsea was at the front door, along with Andrew. Rick was sitting on the floor.

"Does Rick Wamsley say anything at that time?" asked Parrish.

"He asked why, and that's when Chelsea said because she's pregnant."

"And what did the dad say then?"

" 'We can help you,' " Susana reported.

Chelsea had two knives with her and with one, she began to stab Rick Wamsley. Susana reported that Mr. Wamsley tried to block the knife with his left hand, and Chelsea was successful only in stabbing him in the hand. So, stated Susana, "me and Chelsea switched," and I took her knife and she grabbed the gun.

"Okay. After she gives you the knife and she takes the gun, does she say something to Rick Wamsley?"

" 'Shut up, or I'll shoot you.' And I turned around and I told her that there was no more bullets, and she said, 'Shhhh, he doesn't know that.' "

With the knife in hand, Susana reported, she started stabbing the dad in the hand, finishing up what Chelsea was unable to do, but then Chelsea screamed at her "to go stab the mom." She said she did what she was told. Then, she said, she went back to the area by the front door and saw the dad was face down on his tummy. Later, Susana stated, she learned Rick had been shot in the back. While he was face down, "I stabbed him in the back," she reported. At that time, Susana said, Chelsea still had the gun.

"After you stabbed the dad in the back, what did the three of you do?"

"We left and went to the car." In the car, Susana testified, Chelsea used her cell phone to call someone directly after the murders.

Then Susana detailed how they got rid of their clothes, drove to Chelsea's, and washed off because she had blood all over her arms and Andrew was bleeding on his arms and head and Chelsea had a little bit of blood on her. Susana said Chelsea told her she was "very proud of me, and that she knew I could do it, and that I did a great job and that we're gonna go home." Susana reported that once at the Richardson house, they all cleaned up and did some laundry. Then, Andrew remembered that he had left some things back at his house, so he and Susana got back into the Mustang, drove to Turnberry Drive, and Susana went inside and got the jeans, the shirt, and the CD case from on top of the dinette table.

That morning, Susana testified, she went to school and returned home around noon. She stated that at that time, she cleaned the "very sticky and bloody" gun and put it in the same pouch she had gotten from Hilario and placed it in the corner of the flowerbed in the front of the house—the agreed-upon place where Hilario would drop off and pick up the gun, when advised to do so. The three of them began to vacuum the Mustang, she reported, "clean the windows and everything inside, and the trunk as well." After that, Susana stated, she went to work at Jack in the Box.

Parrish asked her, "How did you learn that the bodies were discovered?"

"Chelsea called me at Jack in the Box," Susana replied, late on the night of the 11th "and told me that she and Andrew had gone by the [Wamsley] house and that she had used the phone to dial the [911] number." Susana said Chelsea and Andrew were coming by to pick her up and told her that she should act as normal as possible if anyone spoke about the murders. "Just make it seem like nothing happened and just be me."

After the murders, Susana reported, Andrew began living at Chelsea's and she lived there too until February 2004. During those months, she stated, no police officer ever came and questioned her. Then, she told the court, she was subpoenaed to go before the grand jury on February 17, 2004, after she had moved back home with her mother "to get away from everything that was going around and not to cause any suspicions towards me."

Susana stated that Parrish, the man who was questioning her now, was the one who questioned her in front of the grand jury on February 17. She stated that she gave her DNA that day.

On March 26, 2004, Susana told the court, she went to Illinois to see her uncle and to meet her uncle's girlfriend and to see their new baby. Then, on April 5, 2004, Susana reported, she was arrested in Illinois for capital murder.

Susana admitted that the statement she gave the police then was "part lie and part truth."

"Who was the first person that you actually told the truth to about what happened?"

"Cathy Minick," Susana stated. "I told her the truth after I was extradited to Texas. Mr. Moore was assigned as my lawyer." Minick, she stated, was Mr. Moore's private investigator.

"In early July of 2004," stated Parrish, "did we come to an agreement through Mr. Moore about what your sentence would be?"

"Yes."

"And that was the life sentence we've already talked about?"

"Yes," replied Susana.

"Part of that agreement was you would sit down and give a full and complete statement."

"Yes."

Parrish then offered State's Exhibit 112 into evidence. Susana stated that she recognized Chelsea's handwriting on the letter.

The bailiff then handed the jurors aids, which were direct copies of State's 112 so they could read along as the letter was read into the record. Parrish then asked Susana to read the document aloud.

"It says, 'Alex [a nickname Chelsea used for Susana, based on Susana's middle name, Alexandria]. Given a chance we'll all be—all three be together and free by Christmas. I'd never leave you. We'll go to El Salvador. . . . I've been trying to write you but they won't let me. I ain't said nothing. Neither has Drew [Andrew Wamsley's nickname]. Well, do you remember Kev. Well, yeah, well, it happened again except with Drew and we are calling it little Alex. But girl, we need you to save us. . . . All you have to do is write a letter and mail it to Mike [Mike Maloney, Chelsea's lawyer] and I'll clear—it will clear me and Drew so he can get money and we can bust you out with Mario's help, but we can't help you unless you get us out. They only offer death penalty to me and Drew. . . . Drew has been getting beat up in here. Susana, please, save me, Drew and the baby. Just write a statement saying we had nothing to do with it, only you and Hilario. . . . You gotta help us so we can help you get out. Girl, my mom is sick, my uncle Bill is dying. . . . All you have to do is tell them we had nothing to do with any of it and Hilario needed money so he robbed Drew's family. . . . If not for me, do it for the baby so it has a life, a chance, a mommy and daddy and an aunt Susana. . . . Always love, Bubbles [a nickname for Chelsea]. Please don't kill me, Drew, and the baby. Friends forever. Save us so we can bust you out and save you with the money. Come on girl."

After Susana finished reading the letter, Parrish asked if the reference to a baby in this letter was true or not.

"It was not true. I believe it was an attempt to manipulate me."

Parrish asked Susana, "How do you feel about what y'all did?"

"Very bad."

"How bad?"

"Severely. Like there's not one day that passes by that I cannot have like not a flashback from it. Not one day that I [don't] blame myself for this, mostly because I was the one that did most of it. I was the one that was—the one that was mainly involved in this, even though it wasn't—I wasn't the one to begin with like to plan this and all at the beginning."

"Had you ever shot anybody before?" asked Parrish.

"No."

"Stabbed anybody before?"

"No."

"Ever been arrested by the police for one single thing before?"

"No."

"Then how could Chelsea and Andrew get you do to this?"

After a long pause, Susana said in her customary soft voice, "I don't fully know."

Parrish waited a long moment and then said, "Pass the witness."

Susana never once glanced at Chelsea during her testimony. Chelsea, on the other hand, stared straight at Susana, a pronounced snarl on her face. If the jurors looked over at Chelsea, they might have seen a young girl who blatantly didn't believe a word her former friend was saying.

The court stated that the Defense could now begin to cross-examine the witness. St. John rose and took center stage. He began by speaking directly to Susana, reminding her that he represented Chelsea Richardson and that in exchange for her, Susana's, testimony, she was offered a life sentence for killing Suzy Wamsley. "Now that's not a life sentence to capital murder, that's a life sentence to murder, is that correct?" St. John asked.

"Yes," responded Susana.

"Now you have just testified for about two hours that you killed two people?"

"Right."

"But your agreement with the state is that you get to have a life sentence to killing only one person, is that correct?" asked St. John.

"Yes."

St. John asked her if her attorney, she, and the state of Texas signed a written plea agreement. Susana stated that she did sign it.

St. John walked right up to the jury and reiterated that Susana knew, based on her cooperation, that she would not be sentenced to death but would spend the rest of her life in prison.

St. John then stated that when Susana was arrested on

April 5, 2004, she told a Texas Ranger, the Mansfield Police Department, and the Illinois State Police, "I was picked up by Hilario to get something to eat . . . walked up to the house and the garage . . . and heard some gunshots."

"It's all a lie," said Susana.

"And so you're just telling those police officers up there a lie, right? . . . So Hilario never was at the house according to the truth you're telling today?"

"Right."

Then St. John asked if she ever wrote Chelsea's mother a letter from jail, to which she firmly responded no. St. John asked again, "Never sent her a letter on May the twentieth or twenty first of two oh oh four."

"No."

St. John then showed her a letter and envelope, Defendant's 3 and 4, postmarked May 19, and asked her if she recognized her writing on either. Susana responded that she did not recognize the letter or envelope. "You never wrote this letter?" Parrish asked. Susana responded again that she did not.

St. John then asked how well she knew "these folks," the Wamsleys.

"None whatsoever."

"You didn't even know them?"

"No."

"Did you know there was a life insurance policy?"

"Yes."

"Well, how much money did you get out of this thing?"

"Nothing."

"Not a dime?"

"No."

"So you made no money and you're going to prison for the rest of your life?"

"Yes," said Susana softly with her head down.

"What did they ever do to you, ma'am?"

"Nothing."

Then St. John showed the jury some pictures of Chelsea as a child. He pointed out that she was a good student; that she was active in school, especially on the yearbook committee; and that she "was liked at school, had a lot of friends in school, had a good personality, that's why they called her Bubbles." St. John asked Susana if what he had just said about Chelsea was true.

"Yes."

"And you were thankful that Chelsea Richardson's mom helped you have a place to live when you were having tough times, is that fair?"

"Yes."

St. John asked if she killed two people because she wanted "to prove her friendship to Richardson."

"Yes," replied Susana.

"Was [Chelsea Richardson] in the Mustang when you were trying to kill the folks in [the Jeep in] Burleson?"

"No."

He then wondered aloud why she didn't call the police if there was a plot to kill some people. "Why didn't you say, 'Man, I can't do that, that's crazy'?" A month or a month and a half went by and she "felt compelled because you're such good friends with Chelsea that you go ahead and kill two fine folks, right? . . . You could have called the authorities at any time and stopped these person's families from being killed . . . if you wanted to, but you chose not to do that. It's your fault. You are the one that killed them. You could have stopped it, but you didn't do it. Nobody made you kill anybody, if you didn't want to do that?"

"No," said Susana softly.

Much later, after the trial had ended, Susana admitted that she was close to breaking down during this part of the testimony, but tried as hard as she could not to show it. "I wanted to appear strong."

Disgusted, St. John said, "No further questions."

*   *   *

By then, it was around four o'clock and the judge ordered a short recess. After fifteen minutes, the jury returned and ADA Simpson called the state's next witness, Special Agent Ann-Margaret Hinkle. Hinkle stated she was a specialist with the FBI and her area of expertise was as a crime scene specialist and coordinator for the evidence response team for the Dallas division of the FBI. She stated that previously she had worked on the Polly Klaas kidnapping case in 1993; the Oklahoma City Bombing; the Centennial Park bombing; the Unabomber cabin investigation; the New York Twin Towers terrorist attack; and the Pentagon terrorist attack, among other cases.

Hinkle said she was asked by the Mansfield Police Department on May 12, 2004, to assist in draining a pond in Ruth Brustrom's yard and search for evidence in relation to the Wamsley case. After a group of people, including volunteer firefighters and a public utilities person, pumped all the water out of the pond, which she estimated as being a quarter of an acre, she and eight members of her team used metal detectors "to locate metal targets in the mud." Specifically, they were to find "expended rounds." When asked how many bullets they recovered, she stated, "somewhere around five, six."

Officer Jeff Ambreit of the Mansfield Police Department was called next. He told the court that on December 11, 2003, at approximately 11:41 p.m., he was dispatched to 820 Turnberry in Tarrant County. Ambreit stated that he and Reserve Officer Omlor went to the front door, knocked and rang the bell, but got no response. Together they made the decision to check on the "safety of anyone who might be inside the residence." Before they entered the house, they called out "Mansfield Police," just in case there might be someone sleeping, but they got no response.

Ambreit stated that he went inside with officers Martinez

and Knotts and saw an apparently deceased female on the couch and an apparently deceased male face down in the foyer area in front of the front door. He stated that they checked "under the beds, inside the closets, in all the bedrooms, throughout the entire house"—but located no one else. He stated that the fire department soon arrived and a paramedic determined that neither person in the house was alive. He stated that the phone was off the hook. He told the court that in the dining room area there appeared to be "some type of blade of some sort inside that pool of blood there."

And with Ambreit's testimony, the first day of trial was over.

The jury had gotten to hear from the attorneys what the case was about. They had gotten a chance to see the young, blonde defendant who was on trial for her life and who looked, according to one spectator, "serious, pissed off, angry, threatening, and straight-faced" and according to another, "angelic and sweet." They had heard testimony from her former best friend, who admitted to having killed Suzy Wamsley and playing a role in the death of Rick Wamsley.

The jurors had to be wondering: *How could two young people have gotten themselves into such dire circumstances?* And, they had to be asking themselves: *Will I be able to carry out, if necessary, the vows I made when selected for the jury—that if the state proved its case beyond a reasonable doubt, I would be able to send a nineteen-year-old to death by lethal injection—and live with myself for the rest of my life?*

Chapter Seventeen

The first day had been a heavy day of testimony. The prosecution felt it had scored points. Susana seemed to be a credible witness. She seemed honest. She gave details implicating herself in no uncertain terms, and she took full responsibility for carrying out the murders. In her testimony, she tapped Chelsea as the mastermind of the killings: Chelsea was the one who manipulated her; Chelsea was the one who got everyone to carry out her own selfish plans; Chelsea was the one who pushed her to kill. Surely, the prosecution felt, the jury could see that Chelsea was culpable.

St. John also felt he had scored points with the jurors. He had shown them that Susana was a liar and should not be trusted. She had changed her story several times to fit her needs. He reminded them of her motivation—life, not death. He mocked the prosecution's statements that Chelsea could have been behind the whole ordeal, this "brand-new baby high school graduate."

But what did the jurors think? It was only the beginning of the trial, and many more days of testimony would come before they had to make up their minds.

May 19, 2005, was the second day of the trial. Max Courtney was the first witness. He stated that he was the lab director and owner of Forensic Consultant Services of Fort Worth. On December 12, 2003, he was called to 820 Turnberry

Drive, and after the search warrant arrived, at 4:38 a.m., he began his examination. Checking his notes, he stated that he had examined blood spatter; found a bullet in the bedroom which he later took out of the wall behind a hole in the headboard; saw a knife blade on the dining room floor; found a fired bullet on the dining room floor; and sprayed Luminol in many areas of the house in an effort to uncover hidden bloodstains.

On December 16, he testified, he had seen Chelsea Richardson in a briefing room at the Mansfield Police Department. She was there for the purpose of taking some DNA swabs from her cheek, some scalp hairs, and some inked palm prints. He recalled that Chelsea was cheerful and friendly and had told him, "I should have your job. I would be very good at it." Courtney thought her comment was "unusual."

On cross-examination, Courtney told St. John that he compared latent prints (print impressions left at a crime scene that remain invisible until chemically treated) with a set of known prints, including Chelsea's. "They were compared, but we made no identification," stated Courtney.

The defense seemed to have scored a point. No physical evidence had been found to link Chelsea to the murder scene. A slight smile crossed Chelsea's face. She believed that the jurors would have to take this fact into consideration in their deliberations.

The next witness was Daniel Jordan Sherwin. He stated that he was a patrol officer, a crime scene officer, and a team leader of the hostage negotiation unit with the Mansfield Police Department. In the early hours of December 12, he was called to the scene, where he photographed every room in the house. Subsequently, on December 13 he was called back and collected some cash, around $14,000 and also some foreign currency, which was located "in one of the upper drawers on the left side of a dresser that had a mirror attached to it in the master bedroom." In case the jury had its doubts, robbery did not appear to have been a motive for the murders.

Sergeant Mark Kelly was sworn in next. He stated that while he was doing investigative work at 820 Turnberry, Detective Standefer called and asked him to stop what he was doing and return to the police station. When Kelly met with Standefer, the detective showed him a consent-to-search form that Andrew Wamsley had signed. Standefer then directed him to a white Mustang with Texas license number C23 YDH in the police department parking lot, gave him the key, and asked him to search the vehicle.

During the initial search, Kelly said, he recovered a shirt in the back seat on the driver's side on the floorboard, which had some hairs and fibers on it; "a white latex glove," which he seized; and several receipts—one from Best Buy, three from Putt-Putt golf, and one from Petco. All were dated December 10, 2003, except the one from Petco, which was dated December 11, 2003, at 5:56 p.m. The Best Buy purchase, he reported, was a rap CD called *Hit the Jackpot*. Kelly sprayed Luminol on surfaces throughout the vehicle in an effort to uncover any unseen traces of blood. (When Luminol is sprayed on blood, a chemical reaction causes the bloodstains to glow bluish green.) By far, Kelly stated, the strongest responses to the Luminol were in the back seat area: on the headrest, midway down the back seat and at the very bottom of the seat, and on the leading edge of the back seat—basically on the back of the passenger's seat. There was also a faint glow of luminescence on the driver's seat. He stated that he cut these areas out of the vehicle on December 17 so they could be taken for analysis. However, according to Kelly, the seats had been thoroughly cleaned, and as a result, the blood could not be identified as belonging to any one person because it was so compromised by the cleaning process.

Kelly stated that on February 5 he went back to the Mustang to search it more intensely. He removed a foam cushion on the bottom of the passenger's seat and also went to the very back part of the back seat and cut out a portion there. He also removed some carpet along with a cotton ball from under the seat. As it turned out, none of these samples could be identified either because of the cleaning process that had previously taken place.

Keith Cowand, who lived one block away from Turnberry, was called to testify next. He stated that he was a retired principal. He said that he was awakened by gunshots at 3:23 a.m. on December 11, but decided he must have been dreaming and went back to sleep. He stated that he didn't know exactly how many shots he heard, but it was more than two. "It was just blam, blam, blam, and I, you know . . . I was just trying to get my senses about me." He said he did not recall anything else being out of the ordinary on that day or the day after.

Jeremy Michael Lavender was the next witness. Chelsea had tried to get Jeremy to provide her with an alibi—but the plan had backfired. Now he was a key witness against her. Jeremy stated that sometime before the Wamsley murders, Chelsea had asked him to get her a gun, saying she had something to take care of. Jeremy said that he refused. "I'm like no, I'm not gonna get you a gun to go out and commit a crime. I'll go down for it." After that, she had told him never mind, "I don't need it no more."

Jeremy stated that on December 11 at 3:42 a.m., he received a call on his cell phone from Chelsea; then another at 3:43 a.m.; another at 3:45 a.m.; one at 3:46 a.m.; and a final one at 4:02 a.m. When asked if he had gotten any other calls that day from Chelsea, he responded that she had also called him three or four times on his landline. He said she had asked him to be an alibi for her. She told him she had gotten into some trouble, but couldn't tell him what it was. She told him that if he was asked, he should tell the police that she, Andrew, and Susana came over to his house, stayed for a little while, and then left to go home. After they got home, Jeremy was to say, he and Chelsea spoke on the phone for a couple of hours.

Jeremy stated that when a female police officer came to his house on December 14, he told her the story that Chelsea had asked him to tell. He admitted he also wrote down the story in his own handwriting for the police officer. He went on to say that on February 23, 2004, the first time he was called in front of the grand jury, he also told them the same story—just what Chelsea told him to say.

"Was any of that true?" asked Parrish.

"No, it was not," Jeremy replied.

Parrish then reminded Jeremy that on May 19, 2004, he was re-subpoenaed to the grand jury and was told that they now had his phone records, which they did not have in February. "At that time," said Parrish, "what did I tell you before you testified?"

"Told me that if I tell the truth that I won't be prosecuted for perjury."

"And on that day, on May the nineteenth of two oh oh four, did you renounce your previous testimony and tell the truth?"

"Yes, I did," stated Jeremy.

Parrish then passed the witness to the defense for cross-examination.

Defense attorney Terry Barlow then took over for St. John. Barlow, who obtained his law degree from the University of Houston Law Center in 1985, began his criminal law career in the Tarrant County District Attorney's Office in 1987, where he served in various positions—as chief of the Tarrant County Narcotics Task Force, chief of the Gang Unit, and chief of the Juvenile Division. He entered private practice in 2000, specializing in criminal offenses.

Barlow asked Jeremy his age and where he went to school. Jeremy stated that he was twenty-one and graduated from Northside High School in May 2002. When asked how he knew Chelsea, he said that Chelsea had been his girlfriend for a few months and then "she said I gotta break up because I got to go to L.A." He said that when Chelsea came back, she said she had a new boyfriend, whom he later learned was Andrew. "And you're upset at Andrew—you were upset because Andrew had kind of taken your place?"

"Right."

Barlow ascertained that both Chelsea and Andrew treated Jeremy like a friend, unlike Susana, whom he had met about a year after he met Chelsea. Jeremy said that Susana was mean to him. "She would like cuss me out sometimes and call me bad names. I couldn't handle it. . . . Just kind of out of the blue she'd just go off on you." In contrast, he said, Chelsea always treated him nicely, even after they split up.

Barlow asked Jeremy if he had been scared when the prosecution came and talked to him about the telephone records. Jeremy admitted that he was afraid to go to the penitentiary for perjury.

He asked Jeremy if he remembered who asked him questions at the grand jury. Jeremy responded that he didn't remember. Barlow asked him if he had some memory problems. Jeremy admitted that he had a learning disability and had been a client of the office of MHMR: Mental Health and Mental Retardation. He stated that he began going to the agency when he was about twelve or thirteen. He wasn't taking any medication currently, he said, but back in 2003 at the time of the murders, he was taking Prozac for depression and to calm his nerves.

The defense hoped to show that Jeremy—with his shaky memory and history of mental problems—was not a reliable witness. But they may have succeeded only in demonstrating that he was an easy target for Chelsea's machinations.

Detective John R. Brackett of the Burleson Police Department was called next. He testified that on November 9, 2003, at 2:30 p.m., he went to the Chili's parking lot in the 1000 block of Northeast Burleson Boulevard to examine damage to a white Jeep. He observed a bullet and dent in the back side of the car and placed the bullet in Burleson

Police Department evidence. He stated that when he asked the Wamsleys if they recalled any vehicle going in the same direction that passed them at the same time as the shot, "They advised me that they remember[ed] seeing a white Mustang pass them."

About a month after that incident, Brackett said, he read about the Wamsleys' murder and immediately advised the Mansfield Police Department of the situation that had occurred with the Jeep. He made the bullet available to the Mansfield Police Department for comparison.

When Barlow cross-examined the detective, he asked him, "Did [the Wamsleys] mention to you at all that, hey, our son has a white Mustang?"

"No," he responded.

Apparently, Rick and Suzy Wamsley never dreamed their son would harm them—let alone shoot them. Or if they did suspect it, they were keeping it to themselves.

Andrew Wamsley's sister, Sarah Elizabeth Wamsley, was the next to testify. She introduced herself as the daughter of Rick and Suzy Wamsley. She spoke softly and appeared very upset. She stated that she was twenty-six years old and had one daughter, Brittany. She recounted what happened on November 11, when the Jeep was hit. She stated that her mother "immediately asked my father for his cell phone, and she ended up calling Andrew." About three minutes later, her mother made a 911 call.

When asked what her mother said to Andrew, Sarah replied, "She said Andrew, where the F are you? We're at the Chili's." She gave the location and she asked him to meet us there. Sarah stated that her mother made two calls to Andrew's cell phone and then two calls to the Wamsleys' home phone. But Andrew didn't answer.

Under cross-examination, Sarah mentioned that her father was a CPA and made a pretty good living. Tears welled up in her eyes as she spoke. "Were you named in his will to your knowledge?" St. John asked.

"Before [the deaths], I didn't know anything about the will," Sarah replied. "My family, my mom, dad, both, never talked anything about any life policy." Sobbing, Sarah left the stand.

Ruth Brustrom was called next. First, ADA Simpson established that Chelsea, Andrew, and Susana had gone to Brustrom's house and done some target practice in her pond, with her permission. Then Simpson asked her, "Of the two, Andrew and Chelsea, who was the more dominant?"

"Chelsea," she replied.

"Who was more dominant between Susana and Chelsea?" she asked.

"Chelsea," replied Brustrom again.

Brustrom admitted the three came to visit "just about every week in the fall of 2003."

On cross-examination, St. John asked Brustrom when she had seen Chelsea for the first time after December 12, 2003. She replied it was two or three weeks later.

"Did you notice any marks or anything, cuts on her hands, bruises, contusions, any injury to her body whatsoever?"

"No," Brustrom replied.

"And you never saw Chelsea shoot the gun, period?"

"No."

On redirect examination, Simpson asked, "Did you testify before a grand jury on May 12, 2004?"

"Yes."

"When you were asked the question, 'Who did you see shoot the gun?' do you recall what your answer was?"

"I said Andrew, Chelsea, and Susana."

"Fair to say that you've known [Chelsea] a long time . . . Don't want to see anything bad happen to her?"

Brustrom responded that indeed, she didn't want to see anything bad happen to Chelsea.

Simpson continued by asking Brustrom about the day Chelsea learned Susana was arrested. Brustrom stated that she, Chelsea, and Andrew were shopping at Wal-Mart, in April of 2004, when Chelsea got a call on her cell phone. After that, Brustrom said, both Chelsea and Andrew appeared upset and nervous. Simpson asked if Chelsea said anything about Susana.

"She said that if she had went to Mexico, this wouldn't have happened."

After Simpson passed the witness back to St. John, he asked her, "When you were testifying in front of the grand jury, were you nervous or something?"

She said she was. "When they asked [who had fired the gun], all three names came out. And later when I realized what I had done I went back—two or three days later after I calmed down, I told [the assistant district attorneys] that I had made a mistake, that Chelsea did not fire the gun."

On redirect, Simpson asked Brustrom if she was there the whole time the teens were shooting. She said that she wasn't. She stated that she was in the house and could hear the gun being fired. When pressed, she admitted that she didn't know for sure who was shooting.

Detective Mark Malcom of the Mansfield Police Department was called next. He testified that on May 12, 2004, he went to Burleson and assisted in the recovery effort in Ruth Brustrom's pond.

On cross, Barlow asked, "Besides looking for bullets, you participated in the investigation of this case beyond just being out at the pond?"

"Yes," he responded.

". . . you had a series of conversations with Hilario Cardenas?"

"That's correct," replied Malcom.

"Would it be fair to say that you developed information that led you to believe and suspect that Hilario Cardenas was a capital murder suspect in the murder of Rick and Suzanna Wamsley?"

"Yes, sir."

"And along with other officers, caused an arrest warrant for capital murder to be prepared for Hilario Cardenas?"

"Yes, sir," replied the officer.

In an attempt to bolster the theory that Hilario was the killer—not Chelsea—the defense continued, going on to reveal details of Hilario's arrest and subsequent interviews. Malcom stated that the warrant for Hilario Cardenas was executed on April 6, 2004, and that Hilario was arrested in Arlington and taken to Mansfield. In the evening hours, Malcom conducted videotaped interviews with Hilario, with another detective present, Detective Barry Moore. Malcom talked to Hilario for several hours on April 6, and again on April 7. Malcom said that Hilario waived his right to counsel during these conversations. "Each time we talked to Hilario," said Malcom, "we felt that we obtained some more truthful information from him, but I didn't believe he was being one hundred percent truthful." Malcom stated that on April 7, he obtained a written statement from Hilario. At that time, Malcom said, Susana and Hilario were still the leading suspects.

Dr. Gary L. Sisler, a deputy medical examiner for Tarrant, Parker, and Denton counties, was called to the stand next. He stated that his job was to determine the cause of death in homicides, suicides, and natural deaths. On December 13, 2003, he performed an autopsy on Suzanna Wamsley. He then told the jury what he found: a gunshot wound to the left ear; several stab wounds over the right and left chest areas as well as to the front of the left neck; and a cut wound over the left jaw. Going into greater detail, he stated that there were "a cluster of seven stab wounds in an area [of the right chest] measuring five inches by five inches; four stab wounds over the left anterior neck; three stab wounds over the left chest and breast area; and a single cut wound along with a smaller wound over the left jaw." He said that he didn't "find any evidence of hemorrhage on the surface or in the wound tracks . . . which indicates to forensic pathologists that the decedent had no blood pressure at that time and we refer to the wounds as being made perimortal, either at the time or near the time of death." He stated that he listed the cause of death as a gunshot wound of the head. The manner of death was homicide.

Several members of the Wamsley family were in tears upon hearing the testimony of Dr. Sisler. Imagining what Suzy had gone through was too much for them to bear.

After being treated to the gruesome details of Suzy Wamsley's murder, the jury was dismissed for the day.

Chapter Eighteen

On May 20, the trial continued. Dr. Nizam Peerwani was sworn in first. "I am a medical doctor and I work as the chief medical examiner for several counties, including Tarrant." Best known as medical examiner in the David Koresh–Mount Carmel incident in Waco, Texas—where more than seventy-two cult members died in the Branch Davidian compound either by gunshot wounds or fire—he was also well-known within the international human rights community, having worked as a forensic pathologist in numerous countries, including Iraq, Afghanistan, Indonesia, Guatemala, and El Salvador, in organizations such as Physicians for Human Rights, giving voice to those who died unjustly.

Peerwani stated that when an autopsy is performed, "our office requires that any case that is a result of violent means, especially homicides, the case is reviewed by all the doctors . . . and these are then signed by each and every doctor approving the cause and manner of death." He stated that he signed off on the autopsy performed by Dr. Daniel J. Konzelmann on Rick Wamsley in December 2003 and on the manner of death: homicide. When asked to describe for the jury how Rick Wamsley arrived at the medical examiner's office, Peerwani said, "He was in a body bag. . . . Upon first inspection, it was revealed that he had a tremendous amount of blood on his body surface, especially on his face and neck area." Peerwani then detailed the gunshot wounds:

to the right side of his forehead just above the right eyebrow, and to the mid-back, slightly to the left of the midline, with the exit wound in the front part of his left chest right in front of the armpit. He then stated that there were "multiple stab wounds, and there was a lot of clustering of the stab wounds. There were five stab wounds within a very small area of the left upper chest; nine stab wounds" clustered in another area of the chest; and "thirteen similarly clustered stab wounds of his left upper back. He had a stab wound of his left flank . . . he had a stab wound of his left mid-back and a stab wound of his right mid-back. So in all he had twenty-one entry stab wounds." Peerwani also detailed "a very large complex wound, a stab and cut wound of his chin, the midline of the chin going down to the neck area."

When asked which wounds were determined to be fatal stab wounds, Peerwani said, "Of the five stab wounds of the left upper chest, one of them penetrated his chest cavity and severed his superior vena cava, which is a very large blood vessel that comes to the right upper chamber of the heart and brings blood back from the upper extremities and the head. So this certainly was a fatal stab wound. In addition, he had two stabs of his left upper lobe of the lung and three of his right upper lobe, so they were all potentially fatal stab wounds, but certainly one of them was clearly a fatal stab wound."

Patricia Eddings was called to the stand next. Eddings said she was a senior trace analyst with the Tarrant County Medical Examiner's Office (and trace analyst Kelly Belcher's supervisor). "In that capacity, I examine evidence dealing with things that are small and microscopic in size . . . things such as hairs, fibers, paint, glass, gunshot residues . . . and sometimes foot impressions." Simpson asked Eddings if she examined the hairs found at the crime scene in Rick Wamsley's left hand. She replied that her office had performed microscopic comparisons of the hair with that of Rick Wamsley, Suzanna Wamsley, Sarah Wamsley, Andrew Wamsley and Chelsea

Richardson. However, none of the hairs was a match, except for a single strand that had the microscopic characteristics of the hair of Suzanna Wamsley.

On cross-examination, Barlow asked her if any of the "hairs that were removed from Rick Wamsley's hand and wrist area exhibited similar characteristics to Chelsea Richardson."

"Not at a microscopic level," Eddings responded.

Carolyn Van Winkle was called next. Van Winkle stated that she worked in the DNA section of the crime lab in the Tarrant County Medical Examiner's office in Fort Worth. She stated that she did DNA testing on the "two pieces of teeth [from a hair clip found at the crime scene] . . . and this particular DNA profile . . . was consistent with having originated from both Susana Toledano and Rick Wamsley."

"Did you also test hairs that were forwarded to you from Patricia Eddings or from the trace department?"

"Yes."

On the roots of two hairs, she said they "were able to determine a major DNA profile." It was the "same as the DNA profile from Susana Toledano." She stated that her lab also tested blood samples that they received from the upholstery or carpet cuttings from Andrew Wamsley's Mustang. She said that they were all too weak to determine a DNA profile.

On cross-examination, St. John asked Van Winkle if any of the samples she tested were consistent with Chelsea's DNA profile. Van Winkle said that on a shirt and a spot taken from the car, "Chelsea could not be excluded." Upon further questioning, Van Winkle admitted that the reason she had come to that conclusion was that "the primary component of those stains was from a female."

Phanessa Dawn Hydrick was sworn in next. When asked by Parrish how old she was and where she was currently staying, she said she was twenty-five and staying at "Cold Springs, a jail here in Fort Worth." She was in jail for a parole violation and on probation "for possession of under a gram of dope."

She stated that on April 19, she was arrested and brought to Tarrant County Jail and placed in a cell with Chelsea Richardson. At the time, she stated, she was eight and a half months pregnant. When asked what was the first thing Chelsea said to her, she responded, "She asked me, 'Do you know who I am?' and was real like—like happy about it, like I should know her or something and [she was] proud."

Hydrick told Chelsea that she knew nothing about her, and Chelsea said that "she was on the news and was in jail for murder, a capital murder charge."

Parrish said to Hydrick, "You were in jail for less than a gram of dope and you're in there with someone charged with capital murder. How did that make you feel?"

"A little uneasy."

Hydrick said she spent approximately three days with Chelsea, and Chelsea did most of the talking. At first, Hydrick said, Chelsea claimed she was "innocent and blamed the other girl that was involved. . . . Gradually, she changed her story to being in the house when it happened but not having anything to do with it." Then, said Hydrick, Chelsea admitted that she had some involvement while "her friend was struggling with the father in the hallway." Chelsea told her that the father had the girl by the hair and that the gun was on the floor and she picked it up and shot the father in the shoulder—but said that it didn't kill him and that "her friend finished him off after that." She said that Chelsea didn't feel that she should be charged with capital murder and "thought that her and Andrew should be let out and that they were innocent and that they should still get insurance money and give some to charity."

When Hydrick was asked what happened on June 30, 2004, she stated that she reported to her probation officer. She had arrived early, so she started to read an old newspaper that was lying on a table while she waited. What caught her eye, she said, was an article about a trial that would be coming up sometime in the future in which "they were trying to indict people on capital murder for that same incident that I was told about in jail." She said the newspaper had names and pictures, and she recognized Chelsea Richardson.

"Did something in the article kind of upset you and make you ask a few questions?" asked Parrish.

"Yeah. That Chelsea Richardson wasn't—that her and Andrew weren't gonna be indicted . . . I thought they should be considering they had involvement in it."

"And you were basing this on what Chelsea told you about shooting the father in the back while he had her friend by the hair?"

"Yes, sir," stated Hydrick.

Hydrick said that when she went in to see her probation officer, she told him about it, and subsequently the DA's office was contacted. The next day, she stated she was picked up in Arlington, Texas, and brought to the grand jury, where she gave sworn testimony.

Hydrick reported that not long after she shared a cell with Chelsea, she received a letter from her. It was submitted as State's Exhibit No. 132:

Phanessa, Sunday. Hey girl. It's lonely without you. You forgot to put money on his [Andrew's] books. I hope everything is okay with you and the baby. . . . My mom's waiting to hear from you. . . . Thank you so much for your help and the letters and money you will send us both that you have promised—that you promised. If only you knew how much love as a friend I have for you. . . . And my ex-friend, the murderer's name, is Susana Toledano, so if you want you can write her and tell the 'ho to clear me and Andrew. It's bad enough she murdered his parents, but she shouldn't murder us too. Tell her that for me. . . . You are my only hope and I thank you so very much for being yourself and my friend and helper. . . . Remember you are loved.

Stay strong and keep faith in us and keep believing. God will clear us and free us and I know it will happen. Love always, Chelsea, your friend forever and the person you helped save. Thank you.

The front of the envelope, stated Parrish, read *Chelsea R, 0639756-63D11, 100 North Lamar, Fort Worth, Texas 76102,* addressed to *Phanessa Hydrick, 317 East Mitchell, number 202, Arlington, Texas 76010.* And on the back, *please write back soon, sealed with a prayer.*

Hydrick stated that she was currently back in jail for violating her probation.

On cross-examination, Barlow tried to undermine Hydrick's credibility. He asked, "In fact, there were [a] total of six different times that you were supposed to give urinalysis to be checked for narcotics that you didn't show up?"

"That's true," replied Hydrick.

Barlow asked her if, on the day she spoke to the grand jury, she was asked to take a drug test. She said she didn't give a sample, so they couldn't test her. And, "less than a month after you testified to the grand jury on July the first of two oh oh four, you tested positive for narcotics?"

"Yes, sir."

Hydrick admitted that she was supposed to complete an outpatient treatment for drugs, but didn't, and on August 9, she tested positive for methamphetamine.

Barlow pressed Hydrick about exactly what Chelsea told her while they were cellmates, and reminded her that she told the grand jury that initially Chelsea said she had nothing to do with the murder. Then, suddenly over a three-day period, "Chelsea confesses to you, somebody she hasn't known before. Just out of the blue?"

"Over like three or four different conversations."

"So in the span of three days, you become her best friend and she confesses to capital murder to you?" asked Barlow.

"She confessed to having involvement."

"And you never told anybody other than [your] probation officers sometime later and your lawyer."

Hydrick said she told the grand jury that Chelsea had told her all four of them, "the Hispanic man, [Chelsea's] friend Susana, and her boyfriend Andrew and her were all at the scene." She admitted that she told the grand jury that Chelsea told her that "this Hispanic man, at the end of it, toss[ed] this gun in the dumpster."

"You also remember telling the grand jury that Chelsea shot Mr. Wamsley in the shoulder?" asked Barlow.

"Yes, sir," Hydrick replied.

"Okay. And those are all things that Chelsea told you?"

"Yes, sir."

"And you thought Chelsea was telling you the truth?"

"I would hope so."

"Because you thought you were her friend and she's telling you all about this capital murder that she's in jail for?"

"Yes, sir."

Not masking the disdain he felt for her testimony, Barlow said, "So [Chelsea's] looking at the death penalty and she's telling you—confessing to this capital murder to you?"

"Yes, sir."

Barlow continued to press the witness. "Now this letter that's just been read to this jury doesn't say anything about Chelsea Richardson shooting anybody with a gun, does it?"

"No, sir."

"All it says about anything having to do with this case is Susana Toledano being the murderer, is that right?"

"Yes, sir."

Barlow then passed the witness back to Parrish.

Once again, Chelsea managed a smile. She must have felt that with each witness, her involvement in the murder seemed less and less likely.

Parrish asked Hydrick how Chelsea acted toward her. Hydrick said that Chelsea was overly talkative and "sometimes it's just hard to shut her up." She added that Chelsea "was a little bit proud that she was all over the news. She was kind of famous, I guess . . . Just really, extremely peppy about it." Hydrick also admitted that during those three days in jail together, Chelsea was crying and said that "her lawyer didn't believe her, that he told her she was lying."

"Her own lawyer?" asked Parrish.

"Yes, sir," replied Hydrick.

When Chelsea heard Hydrick's statements, she glared at Hydrick. *How dare you tell those lies!* is what Chelsea seemed to be signaling.

Kathryn Elizabeth Norton, twenty-five, was sworn in next. ADA Simpson asked her how she knew the defendant. "From jail," Norton replied.

Norton admitted that she was in for a drug offense—methamphetamines. She stated that she had violated her probation and was sent to Tarrant County Jail, where she was incarcerated with Chelsea. Around that time, her father contacted her lawyer about Chelsea. "My dad told my lawyer that I was with somebody [in jail] who did something bad, and my lawyer went to you guys."

Norton said that she shared a cell with Chelsea for eleven or twelve days, and that Chelsea was "very talkative." Chelsea told her that she, Andrew, and Susana went to Andrew's house and Susana got a gun out of the car and went back inside and started shooting. She said she heard a shot and realized Andrew's mother fell to the floor "on the couch or something, and then she heard the dad come out, and when she went out she saw them fighting." Norton said that Chelsea told her that Susana screamed to Chelsea, "If you don't help me, your whole family and friends are gonna go down." According to Norton, "Chelsea went back into the kitchen and grabbed a knife and stabbed the dad and then that didn't work so she went and grabbed the gun and shot him."

"Did she say where she shot him?" asked Simpson.

"In the back," replied Norton.

Simpson then read aloud a letter Chelsea wrote to Norton's parents.

Chelsea Richardson 0639756, 63D11, 100 North Lamar, Fort Worth, Texas, 76102, dated 5/5/04. Hello Mr. and Mrs. Norton. Hi, my name is Chelsea Richardson. I'm Kit's [nickname for "Kathryn"] roommate at Tarrant County. She just left tonight and I wanted you all to know she is strong and was saved by God. . . . Please love her and keep her and Caleb Hunter strong. She was the best roommate I could ever have and best friend. . . . Tell Caleb she is the best mommy that little guy could ever have. . . . Please be proud of her and don't judge her. She just cared too much with her heart and not enough with her head. I bet she told you about me so I know you know I'm in here because I believed I could help a friend and she went psycho and now blames me for her actions. So I understand that she thought too much with her head and not enough with her heart. . . . While she was here she was the most kind, generous, loving, faithful, supportive, coolest, most fun, sweetest and bestest friend and person I've ever met. Never let her forget that and never let her think she's fat either. She's not. I wish I looked as good as her. Don't get the wrong idea. I'm not gay or bi, I'm totally straight. . . . Y'all are more than welcome to write me. I only have my family and my mom needs all the support she can get. So if you all could find it in your hearts to be friends with a mother, another parent, please do. Her name is Celia and you can reach her . . . at her work number. I hope to hear from y'all and Kit soon.

After reading the letter, Simpson then asked Norton, "Kathryn, in exchange for what you told us and your agreement to testify truthfully here today, what did the state do for you on your behalf?"

"A recommendation for shock probation," Norton replied. (Shock probation provides defendants with the chance to receive probation after spending a short time in jail or prison. The theory is that immersing a defendant in the penal system for a short time can "shock" him or her into a noncriminal lifestyle.) Norton said that she was currently meeting the conditions of her shock probation, while living with her parents.

Under cross-examination, Barlow tried to show that Norton had lied before and was lying now. He maintained that Norton was saying that Chelsea shot Rick Wamsley only to get time shaved off her own sentence. He said that she had had privileged information on a capital murder (that of the Wamsleys) and didn't disclose it to any law enforcement officials. "Is that true?"

"Yes," Norton admitted.

Frank Shiller was called next. He explained he was a forensic examiner who worked for Forensic Consultant Services in Fort Worth, owned and managed by Max Courtney. He stated he examined four bullets related to the Wamsley crime scene: the bullet from the dining room floor; the bullet from the headboard into the wall in the master bedroom; the bullet from the soffit vent, or attic, of the home; and the bullet from the Jeep in the Burleson shooting. He stated that when there are four different bullets from four different locations, in order to figure out if they came from the same gun, he checks the caliber and the lands and grooves. If those match, he looks at the series of striations or marks imprinted on the bullet as it passes through the barrel. "These are the features that are basically used for identification to a unique source."

"And what was the conclusion as to whether or not they were fired from a single firearm?" asked Parrish.

"Based on my evaluation," stated Shiller, "it's my opinion

that all four of these bullets were fired from the same gun." He came to that conclusion, he said, because they each possessed eight lands and grooves with the right-hand or clockwise twist, along with a particular width of the lands and grooves, as well as ammunition that was the same, based on the construction of the bullet, the jacketed body, and an exposed lead nose.

This was startling. For the first time, someone linked the bullet fired at the Jeep as coming from the same handgun as the one used in the Wamsley murder. After Parrish let this news sink in for a minute, he resumed his questioning.

"Afterwards, did you receive some more bullets?"

"Yes, sir."

Parrish showed Shiller State's Exhibits 75, 76, and 97, which were, respectively, the bullet from Suzy Wamsley, a bullet from Rick Wamsley, and the bullet from the Brustrom pond.

"Do they bear the same marking?" asked Parrish.

"Yes," replied Shiller. "It's my opinion based on the examination that the three bullets mentioned did match the previous four already identified."

"So in total your opinion is all seven bullets were fired from the same handgun?"

"Yes."

Feeling he had scored big, Parrish passed the witness.

St. John asked Shiller, "Now you didn't have a gun to actually test to make a comparison to shoot out of and look at the bullet that came out of that gun and then compare that to the bullets that were retrieved?"

"No, sir. There was no submission of a gun in this case."

St. John hoped—at the very least—to raise a reasonable doubt as to the connection among the bullets.

St. John then passed the witness. Simpson said she had no more questions and that the state would rest.

After the jury recessed, St. John asked the court if he could have a directed verdict for Chelsea Richardson based on the fact "that the state of Texas has failed to prove beyond a reasonable doubt that Chelsea Richardson did then and there intentionally cause the death of an individual, Suzanna Wamsley, by shooting her with a firearm, and did then and there intentionally cause the death of an individual, Rick Wamsley, by shooting him with a firearm and stabbing him with a knife. . . . I would submit that the state has not met its burden of proof and we are entitled to acquittal as a matter of law, and I would ask the court to do so, instruct the jury."

After considering the motion for a directed verdict, the judge denied the motion.

After that little bit of extra drama on the part of the defense, the court then recessed until Monday morning at 10:30.

Chapter Nineteen

Over the weekend, the jurors had plenty of time to think about the case. Of course, they couldn't talk their feelings over with anyone, but they could let all that they had heard percolate in their minds in the hopes that the correct conclusion would rise to the surface.

On May 23, 2005, the trial resumed. Before the jury was brought in, Prosecutor Parrish made a formal request to reopen the case for one witness: "We have advised both the court and the defense of the reason we want to do that and supplied them with a copy of what's been marked as State's Exhibit No. 134."

St. John knew this was coming and stated, "I believe that the state of Texas just found out about it. And I've tried a lot of cases against Mr. Parrish so I believe he has a good faith basis and I have no objection."

The jury was then called into the courtroom. The judge said that the "state has a request to make at this time."

Parrish stated, "Yes, Your Honor. Based on events of the last twenty-four hours, the state requests to reopen their case." Parrish then called Penny Lanell Haynes to the stand. She stated she was currently incarcerated in the Tarrant County Jail for "two possession charges, fraud, and evading arrest." She was housed close to Chelsea.

"What happened last Thursday evening up in the jail between you and Chelsea Richardson?" asked Parrish.

Haynes told the court that Chelsea "came to me and told me she gave her lawyer my name for me to be a witness to where she was at one certain night, December eleventh, I believe it was." Haynes said the purpose was to provide Chelsea with an alibi for the night of the murders. To help Haynes prepare to be a witness, Chelsea armed her with a story about the alibi, which was on "a piece of paper, and about four newspaper clippings." Haynes stated that she was supposed to "memorize it and write it in her own words." Haynes told the court that she had been "around Richardson for about three weeks" and before that time, she hadn't known Chelsea at all. Parrish asked permission for Simpson to read the piece of paper that Chelsea had purportedly handed to Haynes on the previous Thursday. Permission was granted, and Simpson read aloud:

To Whom it may concern: I am Penny Haynes, and on Wednesday, December 10, 2003, I saw Chelsea that night. . . . I was driving with John Napoleon. . . . I was driving because I had nothing to drink. We saw Chelsea and her boyfriend on I-20 headed west into Fort Worth from Arlington and Trig [John Napoleon] said hey, I know her. We waved and followed her to say hi. Her boyfriend was driving. . . . They exited 35 . . . pulled up to a grayish Thunderbird . . . it was almost midnight. . . . Chelsea got out and said hi and said she had to go before she was late for curfew. And we said okay. We followed her so I'd know where she lived. . . . We went back to a friend's where we were staying and I thought nothing of it. I just remember seeing her on the news after that. . . . I don't know the relevance of this but I believe she's innocent. She's a very bubbly, sweet, add what you want, Penny, sincerely Penny Haynes. Put in your words, please. I love you. Thank you. Shorten if you can. These are just the details for you to know in case of testifying. Please include . . .

the date and time and info about my street. What flavor lifesaver you want to be?

Parrish then asked Haynes what she did with the letter after Chelsea handed it to her. Haynes said she put it aside until she saw her lawyer at around 11 p.m. last night, Sunday, May 22, at which time she gave it to him. Haynes said she came to testify today to say she was not going to do what Chelsea was asking her to do.

On cross-examination, St. John did not question the authenticity of this letter, but did try to discredit Haynes by asking, "You're in jail for three pending felonies and a pending misdemeanor?"

"Yes."

"So you're telling this jury that Chelsea Richardson wrote this out and handed it to you?" asked St. John.

"Yes, sir," replied Haynes.

"So you're telling this jury that you weren't with John Napoleon and saw Chelsea and all that stuff. This is stuff she wrote, that she made up?"

"Yes, sir," Haynes said. She went on to say that around the time of the murders, she had been in Ennis on vacation for about a week, "at a drag strip, at car races."

"Before three weeks ago, you never knew Richardson even existed?"

"True," said Haynes.

After Haynes finished her testimony, the state rested, once again. The prosecution believed it had ended the testimony with a bang by showing that yet again, Chelsea was manipulating people to do what she wanted. Only this time, it seemed, the manipulation didn't appear to have worked.

Unlike the other witnesses, Haynes looked over at Chelsea, who shook her head in disbelief at what Haynes was saying.

After a short recess, the judge said, "At this time the defense may proceed."

It was now time for the defense to call its first witness. It would be the defense's strategy to put on witnesses that could testify to the whereabouts of Chelsea on the night of the murder, to show she had nothing to do with the killings, as well as to testify that Chelsea had good character.

St. John called James Alexander Richardson, Chelsea Richardson's brother, to the stand. He stated that he was twenty-six years old and that in December 2003, he had been living at home with his mom, Celia June Richardson; Chelsea; his other sister, Brenda; Susana Toledano; and a couple of dogs. Back then, he had been working at Jack in the Box, where Susana also worked. He stated that he had introduced Andrew to his sister Chelsea. He had known Andrew, he said, from Putt-Putt golf, where he would go with friends and where Andrew worked. At first, the three were all just friends, but after a while, Chelsea and Andrew became boyfriend and girlfriend. Together, the three would often go to IHOP in Arlington, off I-20. He stated that he knew, slightly, the night manager there, named Hilario, but he had never hung out with him.

"Did you ever have any conversation or overhear any conversation at that IHOP regarding the killing of Andrew Wamsley's folks?" asked St. John.

"No, sir."

"Did you ever hear your sister talk about that at all?"

"No."

St. John asked James what time he got off work at Jack in the Box on December 10—the night of the murders. James said it was at 6 p.m. He stated that after that, he hung out with friends at Burger Box (another fast food joint) until they closed at nine, and then he went home. He said he went to bed early, around 10 p.m., because he had to be at work at ten on Thursday, the next morning. He stated that he didn't remember whether or not he saw his sister, Susana, or Andrew in the house that evening. He said he woke up at 8:30 a.m. and worked his shift that day. That evening, Thursday

December 11, he got home around 6:30 and didn't recall seeing his sister at that time. He said the first time he remembered seeing her was around midnight, when she came home very excited because she had won "like a big stereo" while she was at Putt-Putt. He said he went to sleep at 1 a.m., and between 12 midnight and 1 a.m., Chelsea and he were together.

On cross, Parrish asked James about only one thing. "Did your sister ever go to California?"

"No," James replied.

Parrish explained that Jeremy Lavender admitted on the stand that Chelsea told him she went to California. "The going to California story was just a story she told Jeremy Lavender so she could dump him for Andrew, isn't that true?"

James stated that he knew nothing about that story.

"But Chelsea's never been to California, has she?"

"No," answered James.

By showing that Chelsea had lied to Jeremy, Parrish hoped to establish the fact that if she lied to him, she could lie to anyone at any time.

After James left the stand, St. John called James's mother, Celia June Richardson, to testify. Celia stated that she had been an employee for the General Services Administration, a part of the U.S. government, for nineteen years. Since January 2004—about a month after the murders—she had also worked in the federal building from five to nine in the evening cleaning offices. At the time of the murders, she said, aside from working for the government, she had also worked for Brookshire's grocery as a part-time cashier. She stated that Susana had lived at her house because she wanted to finish high school and Susana had said that her mom was moving. Celia said she had wanted to help Susana out. Also, she revealed, she felt guilty about the car accident in which Susana broke her arm.

Celia stated that not long after appearing before the grand jury, she received a letter from Susana Toledano, which she immediately gave to the office of Mike Maloney, Chelsea's original lawyer. Celia stated that she had given Mike Maloney a $3,000 retainer when Chelsea was arrested. Although there was no return address on the envelope, Celia thought the letter looked like it was written in Susana's handwriting. Susana was in jail at that time. The letter was postmarked May 19, 2004, and addressed to Celia R. It read:

CJ *[a nickname for Celia June]*, Hey, I am really sorry about all this but . . . I have to say what Hilario tells me to. . . . Chelsea and Drew . . . had nothing to do with [the murders]. Hilario planned just to rob them but something went wrong. I was high and scared when they woke up and it's all a blur from there. Hilario has the gun and the knives are in a lake. . . . Chelsea will be free soon. Bye, Susana.

When St. John asked Celia about her whereabouts on December 10, 2003, she stated she had been at home studying for a final for an accounting class she was taking at Tarrant County Community College. Then she went to take her test and returned home at around 8:30 p.m. after stopping to do some shopping at Big Lots. When she arrived home, Chelsea, Andrew, and Susana were there. She stated that she went to bed at around midnight and did not hear anyone coming or going after that. Early the next morning, she did not hear anything unusual in her house—no running washing machine, no baths or showers being taken.

In response to St. John's question as to whether or not she saw any blood in the bathrooms, she said she did not. She stated that on the morning of December 11, she got up at 6 a.m. and left for work at 6:45 a.m. At that time, she testified, Chelsea and Andrew were at the house. She stated that she got home from work a little before 5 p.m., and then went to work from 6 p.m. to midnight at Brookshire's as a cashier. After work, she went right home—getting there a little after midnight. When she arrived, Chelsea was excited because she had a gift from Putt-Putt. She "practically dragged me in the door. She wanted me to come see [the stereo]."

On cross, Parrish immediately went back to the letter, which Celia had just testified was in Susana's handwriting and postmarked May 19. He showed her a transcript from her testimony in front of the grand jury on May 21, 2004. He asked if she had brought the letter with her when she testified on May 21.

"No, I didn't."

"Did you think it might be important to call us and say I've got it?"

"I didn't think of that."

"Just didn't think of that?" Parrish asked with derision in his voice.

"No, sir."

Parrish asked her if he had explained to her, both times before she appeared before the grand jury, that if indictments were returned, "your daughter would be charged with capital murder"?

She said yes, and that's why she had taken the letter to Maloney's office.

"But that letter," stated Parrish, "didn't have Susana's return address on it. That could have been written by anybody."

"It looks like Susana's [handwriting] to me."

"It could have been somebody in her cell manipulated to write a letter that says Hilario made Susana do it?"

"I don't know that," she replied.

Then Parrish showed her what he called the "Alex" letter (the letter that was presumably written to Susana by Chelsea in which the writer stated, "Just write a statement saying we had nothing to do with it, only you and Hilario. Tell them he planned it and did it."). He asked Celia if that letter looked like her daughter's handwriting.

"It looks kind of like my daughter's handwriting—as much as the other looks like Susana's."

"Okay, it's the same thing that your daughter is asking Susana to tell in that other letter, right? Hilario made me do it. Hilario wanted to rob the house. Tell them he said he'd kill you. Did you read all that?" asked Parrish.

"Yes, sir."

"Let me show you what was just introduced into evidence as State's Exhibit No. 134. Do you recognize your daughter's handwriting on that?" Parrish showed Celia the letter that Chelsea had allegedly written to fellow inmate Penny Haynes in what seemed to be an effort to get Haynes to provide Chelsea with an alibi for the night of the murders.

"Looks like hers."

"Why would she need an alibi?" asked Parrish.

"I don't know."

On redirect, St. John asked if when she testified in front of the grand jury on May 21, 2004, Chelsea was under arrest.

Celia said no. Susana was already under arrest and Chelsea was just in custody.

"Well, in May your daughter had not been indicted for capital murder, had she?" asked St. John.

"No."

The defense was trying to show that there was nothing unusual or suspicious about Celia's not telling the grand jury in May about the letter Susana supposedly wrote, which would seem to exonerate Chelsea, because Chelsea wasn't the one under indictment at that time.

At the end of Celia Richardson's testimony, the judge called a short recess. When the court was called to order again and the jury returned, the judge announced, "I understand the defense has a witness to recall."

St. John stated, "Yes, we do. We recall Susana Toledano."

St. John showed Susana what was entered as Defendant's

Exhibit No. 16, her written statement given to the Addison, Illinois, police department on April 5, 2004. Susana confirmed that she had been arrested on the fifth and given that written statement the same day.

She was then shown Defendant's Exhibit No. 4, an envelope with a U.S. postmark, dated May 19, 2004.

"The postmark is after the time you gave that statement in Illinois, isn't that right?"

"Yes."

"When you were arrested in Illinois, was Chelsea Richardson up there?"

"No."

St. John wanted the jury to know that Susana had not once—but twice—written that Chelsea had nothing to do with the murders. In neither case had Chelsea been by her side, directly coaxing or influencing her.

After passing the witness to Parrish, Parrish asked Susana about Defendant's Exhibit No. 16, the written statement she had given in Illinois. "Is it the truth or a lie?"

"A lie."

"And I'll show you what's in evidence as Defendant's 3." He showed her the letter that Celia Richardson had testified was in Susana's handwriting. "Did you write that?"

"No." Susana was flatly denying having written the letter to Chelsea's mother.

When Susana stepped down, defense attorney Barlow called Linda James, a forensic document examiner. James explained that her job was to examine "anything that has to do with typewriting, handwriting, that may come under dispute." She stated she had been performing this job for over fourteen years. After establishing her qualifications, Barlow asked what she looked for in trying to determine who wrote something in particular. She stated she looked at "letter form, slants, positioning of the letters, their neighboring letters, proportions, the joining of the letters, division of the letters . . .

and their relationship even to the written line, if there is a written line."

Barlow then showed her Defendant's Exhibit No. 3 and Defendant's Exhibit No. 4—the letter and envelope of May 19, 2004, that Chelsea's mother had received—and purportedly had been written by Susana, plus some additional known writing of Susana's, including her notebook, daily planner, a thank-you card, diary, and written statement to Addison police.

James said that she prepared a chart showing similarities in the writings in all those documents. She began by comparing the e's in the "known Susana Toledano" writings (from the thank-you note and the statement to Addison police) to the e's in the letter and envelope in question. She remarked that she also compared the k's, f's, and i's. All of them in the known and the questionable document, she stated, were done in the same fashion.

What James said she found interesting about this writer is that "she had three distinct writing styles. She had one very small, and then she would have one where she would write very bubbled, and some large writing . . . using more of the arm to write so it frees up and you could use big letters." However, even though the writer, in James's opinion, can "change at will, her e's and her slant, that's just a part of how she writes."

Barlow then asked James to look at the spelling of "Susana" in the original, questionable note, Defendant's Exhibit 3. James replied that "the spelling of Susana wasn't like some of the other signatures of how her name was spelled." In fact, even within the same document—the one Susana wrote to the Addison police, where she signed her name three consecutive times—she spelled and signed her own name in different ways, reported James.

James went on to say that that she compared the known handwriting of Susana to the known handwriting of Chelsea and she stated that she found it "quite different. Chelsea is a finger writer. That means she has to lift the pen and move across the page. She writes with her finger, not the entire arm. And so therefore her writing is going to be smaller."

Barlow then said, "Ma'am, based on your analysis and based on your comparisons of the known handwriting of Susana Toledano, did you reach an opinion as to . . . who wrote the letter which is Defendant's Exhibit 3 and is already in evidence?"

"The document and the envelope, there's just so overwhelming and strong evidence to say that it was written by a Susana Toledano." James went on to say, "It's my opinion that there's no evidence to support that [Chelsea Richardson] wrote it and she can be eliminated as the writer of the note and the envelope."

And with that definitive statement, Barlow felt satisfied that he had shown the jury a professional's analysis—a person who "proved" that Susana did, in fact, write the letter stating that Chelsea and Andrew had nothing to do with the murder and that she and Hilario were responsible.

It was then Parrish's turn to cross-examine James, and, he hoped, call into question the authenticity of the professional's analysis. Parrish began, "Who peer reviewed these for you?"

"These have not been peer reviewed."

"Okay, so right now, all we have is your opinion?"

"That is why I am here, to give you my opinion, yes."

"And let's get to that. Handwriting analysis is an opinion science, it's not like DNA where it could be scientifically tested, correct?" asked Parrish.

"It's an accurate science, yes, but it is an opinion," replied James.

"Because often in cases you've testified in there's been an examiner on the other side that has had the exact opposite opinion, isn't that true?"

"That is true."

Citing the different spellings of "Susana," Parrish asked, "Is one possibility that the person that wrote this just didn't know how to spell Susana's name and was just trying to implicate Susana?"

"It's possible, but the evidence doesn't support that."

Parrish then pointed out that the name "Chelsea" was spelled correctly in the statement Susana gave in her own handwriting to the police in Illinois, yet in Defendant's Exhibit No. 3, it was spelled incorrectly, C-H-E-L-E-S-A.

"She had a lot of misspellings," James replied.

"So are you sure you want to continue to say that Susana Toledano wrote this?"

"I have confidence in my opinion, yes, sir, I do."

"But you will concede Chelsea is spelled absolutely correctly in Defendant's 16 and absolutely wrong in Defendant's 3?"

"I will concede that they are different. . . ."

"One is correct and one is wrong?" Parrish said adamantly.

"Yes," stated James reluctantly.

And with that, Parrish felt he had made his point and passed the witness back to Barlow for redirect.

Barlow asked James if there is always a peer review.

"No. There is no requirement. Lay opinion," she said, "doesn't matter much either." In response to Barlow's question about whether or not she was sticking by her opinion, she said that she was.

Barlow passed the witness back to Parrish, who asked, "Does it bother you that the two personal names supposedly written by Susana Toledano, who knows how to write her own name and her best friend['s] . . . were misspelled? Didn't that bother you just a little?"

"I cannot be influenced by the story or the happening that is around the case. In fact, I do not even know what this case is about, other than it is a capital murder case. . . . I can't explain the misspelling. I can only tell you that I am convinced that this writing is that of Susana and the evidence strongly supports that."

After the feisty exchanges between the prosecutor and the defense's handwriting expert were over, St. John called Molly Lyn Donald, who was Chelsea's world history teacher in her sophomore year, from the fall of the year 2000 through the spring of 2001, at Everman High School. Donald said that Chelsea and Susana were often together, but she never saw "Chelsea try to influence Susana or vice-versa." Donald stated that she saw Chelsea and Susana together "as friends, for two years."

St. John called Gary Schulte next. He, too, was a teacher at Everman. Chelsea Richardson, he stated, was one of his chemistry students and Susana was in his chemistry class two years after that. He saw that their relationship was one of a "good friendship." "Was one dominant over the other?" asked St. John.

"No, sir."

John Andrew Napoleon was called next by St. John. Napoleon stated that he was currently in Tarrant County Jail for manufacturing methamphetamine and possession of a firearm. For those offenses, he said, he had received fifteen years. When asked if he knew a Penny Haynes, he stated he did. He said they had been boyfriend and girlfriend in December 2003. (Recall that Penny Haynes had come forward with the letter she said was written by Chelsea in which Chelsea gave Haynes a story to memorize, an alibi, in case Haynes was called as a witness.) On December 10 of that year, Napoleon said that he saw Andrew Wamsley in a parking lot by a McDonald's. He knew the date because it was his son's birthday. On that day, he hadn't known Andrew, but when Andrew was brought into his pod, he recognized him as the guy who was with the defendant that night, sometime between 11:30 and two in the morning. That night, he had gone out to collect money from dealing drugs and while

Andrew Wamsley grew up in an upper middle-class home in Mansfield, Texas, with his mother Suzy, his father Rick, and his sister Sarah.

Author's collection

Chelsea Richardson began dating Andrew in 2003. She came from the working-class town of Everman, Texas. The two spent as much of their time together as possible.

Author's collection

The luxurious Walnut Estate home of the Wamsleys, with Christmas decorations on proud display. It was here that Rick and Suzy were viciously murdered.

Author's collection

Andrew Wamsley graduated from Mansfield High School in 2002. His sister Sarah had been a cheerleader there.

Author's collection

The IHOP in Arlington was considered the home-away-from-home for Andrew, Chelsea, and Susana Toledano. They would spend hours there, playing card games and plotting. Hilario Cardenas was the night manager.

Author's collection

The Wamsley home, at 820 Turnberry Drive, had two garage doors. One was a double door, the other a single. The doors were open the night the officers came upon the two bodies inside the house.   Author's collection

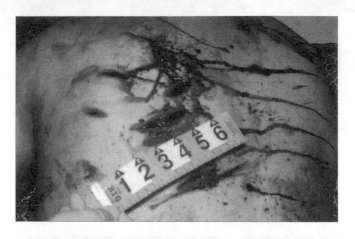

Rick Wamsley's back with stab wounds.

After the murder, an intruder went into the Wamsley kitchen, dialed 911, and left the phone off the hook. It was after the police investigated the call that they first discovered the bodies of Rick and Suzy Wamsley.

As the officers were investigating the crime scene, they came upon a large pool of blood near the formal dining room. Within the blood they saw a knife blade, with no handle attached.

Author's collection

An aerial view of Ruth Brustrom's house and lake, where Andrew, Chelsea, and Susana practiced shooting with a .38 caliber.

Author's collection

Offender Information

Photograph of Offender

Name	Richardson, Chelsea Lea
TDCJ Number	999499
Date of Birth	03/26/1984
Date Received	08/10/2005
Age (when Received)	21
Education Level (Highest Grade Completed)	12
Date of Offense	12/11/2003
Age (at the time of Offense)	19
County	Tarrant
Race	White
Gender	Female
Hair Color	Blonde
Height	5' 06"
Weight	172
Eye Color	Blue
Native County	Tarrant
Native State	Texas

The Texas Department of Justice keeps a criminal file on record of all offenders. This is Chelsea Richardson's file.

Author's collection

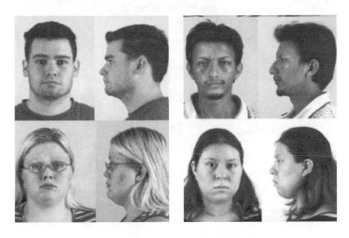

Mug shots of Andrew, Hilario, Chelsea, and Susana.

Ralph Standefer, detective with the Mansfield, Texas, Police Department, was lead detective investigating the Wamsley murders. Later, recalling this case, Standefer said: "This was one I automatically knew I would never forget."

Detective Mark Malcom of the Mansfield Police Department assisted in the recovery of bullets from the pond of Ruth Brustrom. Malcom also interviewed Hilario, ultimately leading to his arrest. Author's collection

Jeff Ambreit, police officer in the Mansfield Police Department, was among the first officers to enter the Wamsley home and discover the bloody victims. Author's collection

coming down Interstate 20 he and his girlfriend saw Chelsea in a vehicle that was right beside them that followed them to the Felix Street exit.

"So when you saw Chelsea and Andrew, you didn't know who the heck they were, is that right?"

"No, I didn't."

St. John asked, "Did you see any Hispanic girl with them or Hispanic guy?"

"No, there was only two people in the vehicle."

"Just two Anglos in the vehicle?"

"Yes, sir."

St. John passed the witness. On cross-examination, Parrish said almost mockingly, "And when was it that you just came upon this revelation that you knew something about the night of the capital murder?"

"Because I've been questioned by a police officer over the telephone."

"I asked when," Parrish stated firmly.

"Just twice. Detective Montgomery, or I'm not sure if it was detective or officer, Deputy Montgomery from Ellis County tried to contact me on the telephone . . . sometime in either the end of December or the first part of January of 2004. . . . They wanted to question me about two possible homicides that happened in Mansfield, a husband and wife."

"And you got some proof of this?"

"Yeah, I assume you could contact Detective or Deputy Montgomery."

"That's your job," said Parrish with anger in his voice, "that's not mine. You got some proof of this?"

Then he showed Napoleon the letter Chelsea supposedly wrote to Penny, giving her an alibi to say, if needed—State's 134.

"Why did Chelsea write this for Penny to say?"

"I have no idea."

On redirect, St. John tried to establish that Napoleon was telling the truth about having seen Andrew and Chelsea on the night the murders took place. "Mr. Parrish just showed you State's 134. Well, the weird thing is it says 'Felix' and 'I-20,' and that's where you and this lady saw them and that's what you just testified to, isn't it?"

"Yes, sir, it is."

St. John pointed out that Napoleon had never seen the letter that Chelsea supposedly wrote to Haynes, had he?

"No."

Pass the witness.

To sway the jury into not believing Napoleon, Parrish said, "You're an habitual criminal under the laws of the state of Texas, correct?"

"Yes, sir."

On redirect, St. John then asked, "Are you gaining any benefit by testifying today? The state of Texas gonna cut you a magic deal that would reduce your sentence?"

"No, sir."

St. John hoped he had shown the authenticity of Napoleon's testimony, thus establishing that Chelsea was nowhere near the Wamsley home on the night of the murders. St. John also hoped that he had thwarted the prosecution's theory that Chelsea was a master manipulator by demonstrating that Haynes was lying about Chelsea manufacturing another alibi—just as he hoped he had done with the letter he believed Susana had written Chelsea's mother from prison, exonerating Chelsea.

Jana Webb was called next. She stated that she met Chelsea in March 2004, while they both were in jail. She said she had been in and out of jail for prostitution for about eleven months and spent a lot of time with Chelsea while incarcerated. St. John asked her if Chelsea ever talked about her case. Webb stated that Chelsea never did. "I got the newspaper every day and she was real adamant about me cutting out the articles about her and giving it to her so nobody else sees it. So I always did and it wasn't none of my business."

When the defense finished, Parrish tried to establish that Webb was a friend of Chelsea's and that's why she was saying Chelsea never discussed her case. Other fellow inmates had testified for the prosecution that she couldn't shut up about it.

"You're a friend of Chelsea's, aren't you?" asked Parrish.

"There are no friends in jail," Webb answered. "I'm here to do my time so I can go home to my family."

Next, St. John called Nicole Lee Morris, who was twenty-three and currently housed in the Gatesville state jail facility of the Texas Department of Criminal Justice, serving a two-year sentence for forgery. Morris admitted that she knew Chelsea "from out in the world, and then I ran into her just here recently back in December. We were . . . housed in the same dorm together and we recognized each other." She knew Chelsea, she stated, through her mother and Chelsea's mother, both of whom had attended Everman High School. Morris said she and Chelsea were housed together for four months and during that time, Chelsea never talked about her case, never mentioned what she was charged with, and never wrote her any letters stating her position on the allegations. She admitted that inmates generally do not talk about their cases with each other. When asked why that was, she replied, "Because it starts gossip and rumors and it causes like a conflict of interest in the pods. And it could cause fights and stuff like that."

Darissa Humphries, called on next by St. John, stated that she was twenty-six and was currently housed in the Gatesville state jail. She said that she had been housed with Chelsea Richardson for about a month. When asked if, at that time, she knew what Chelsea had been charged with, she said, "No, sir, I did not." Then she was asked if she knew Susana Toledano. She said yes.

"Where did you meet Susana Toledano?" asked St. John.

"At a crack house, sir," replied Humphries.

". . . When you use that term 'crack,' what is that exactly?"

"That's a drug that we use, that I used to smoke."

"What is it? Is it a type of cocaine?"

"Yes, rocked up," said Humphries.

"Okay. And does it give you a high?" asked St. John.

"Yeah, for about five, ten minutes, yes, sir."

"Okay. How—is that where you met her, at the crack houses?"

"Yes, sir, and through her boyfriend who sold me dope. I can't remember his name right now."

"Was he Anglo or Mexican?"

"He was Mexican. . . . He went by a nickname, Carlos or something like that."

"Now, did you ever see Susana with a gun?" asked St. John.

Humphries replied that she had, around December 2003. "It was during the night. . . . I was sitting on a log and I seen her shoot the gun." At that time, she stated, she was smoking in a friend's car on a dead-end street and it was on a trail leading behind a house where Humphries stated she saw Susana shoot the gun.

"What kind of gun did she have?"

"A nine. I seen it, I guess."

After St. John passed the witness to the prosecution, Simpson asked, "You distinctly remember seeing Susana at all these crack houses?"

"Yes. Because I used to talk to her and buy crack from her and her boyfriend."

"When you would smoke at these crack houses, what time of day would you smoke there?"

"All day long, if I could."

Humphries admitted that when she was in jail with Chelsea, Chelsea used to rub her feet, but they never talked about Chelsea's case—"No, ma'am." After Simpson showed her a picture of Hilario, Humphries stated, "He was [the one who was] with [Susana] when she was shooting the gun. Yes, ma'am, he was."

Andrea Parsons was called next. Defense attorney Barlow asked her how she knew Chelsea, and Parsons stated she was on the same floor in jail with Chelsea from November 19, 2004, until toward the end of January 2005, but in different cells. Parsons said she was incarcerated for arson and was serving four years. During the time she was housed with Chelsea, she said she never heard Chelsea talk about her case.

When Parsons finished testifying, it was already a quarter to six and the judge said he didn't anticipate keeping the jury much longer, but asked them to go to the jury room briefly and then he would bring them back in shortly.

After the jury was dismissed, St. John told the judge that it was important at this juncture to have his client testify as to her knowledge of her rights. The judge concurred, and to that end, Chelsea was sworn in.

St. John then said, "Ms. Richardson, according to the court's jacket, I was appointed to represent you back on October the first of oh four, and I believe I came just to talk to you at the jail very shortly thereafter. And needless to say, you understand you have a constitutional right to testify in this case. You understand that?"

"Yes sir," responded Chelsea.

"And you know the law clearly states that you have a right to testify in each phase of the trial, should we have to go to the second phase in this trial, but at this phase of the trial, are you telling me and Mr. Barlow, based on many, many, many, many hours of conversations, that you do not want to testify at this portion of the trial?"

"Yes, sir, I choose not to testify," stated Chelsea.

"No further questions," said St. John.

When the jury was called back into the courtroom, the judge said, "All right. Thank you again, ladies and gentlemen. The defense may proceed further."

St. John then stated, "Judge, at this time, the defense would rest."

The judge then dismissed the jury and called a recess until the next morning at 9:30.

At this point, the defense felt confident that it had done an excellent job for their client. After all, in all the days of testimony, not one bit of physical evidence had surfaced that linked Chelsea to the crime. Furthermore, in their minds, Susana hadn't fared so well, having been portrayed as a liar and a crack addict, and having been seen with a gun. But would all of that be enough to convince a jury?

Chapter Twenty

On May 24, 2005, the trial continued. The judge began, "Thank you again, ladies and gentlemen. We're ready to proceed at this time. And the state may proceed with any rebuttal at this time."

Parrish called Ellis County Deputy Ketchum to the stand. He stated he was a detective with the Ellis County Sheriff's office. Parrish asked him if he was familiar with all the detectives "down there." He said, "yes, all the detectives and officers."

In an effort to portray John Napoleon as a liar when he testified the previous day that a Detective Montgomery had tried to get in touch with him about the Wamsley case, Parrish asked Ketchum, "Have you ever heard of a Detective Montgomery down there?"

"No. Never."

"Did you have one back in September, October, November of 2003?"

"No, we did not."

"How about an Officer Montgomery, have one of those?" asked Parrish sarcastically.

"No, we did not," replied Ketchum.

"With regard to Ellis County, do you know all of the city police officers?"

"Most of them."

"Do they have a Detective Montgomery?"

"No they don't."

"And I'm asking about the time frame back in 2003."

"No they did not at that time."

On cross-examination, St. John tried to discredit Parrish's questioning by asking Ketchum if Hill County touches his jurisdictional county. Ketchum said that it did.

"You know Dan Dent in the Hill County's D.A.'s office?" asked Parrish.

"No I don't."

"He's the D.A. of Hill County. You don't know Mr. Dent?" asked Parrish with forced incredulity.

"No, I don't," replied Ketchum.

When Ketchum stepped down, St. John said, "Close, Judge."

"All right," stated the judge.

But then St. John quickly said, "Excuse me. Excuse me. I'm sorry I apologize. I remember this now. Judge, I do have something I'd like to get marked real quick. Judge, it's marked as Defendant's 23. It's a certified copy of an indictment pending in the 297th District Court of Hilario Cardenas."

Parrish said, "No objection."

"Very well," said the judge. "Defense Exhibit No. 23 will be admitted. May I publish [read aloud] to the jury, Judge?"

"You may."

St. John then read the following:

Hilario Cardenas, Indictment No. 0928126D styled the State of Texas vs. Hilario Cardenas in Tarrant County, Texas, herein called the defendant and the state of Texas.

On the 11th day of December 2003, Hilario Cardenas did then and there with intent that a felony of capital murder be committed agree with Andrew Wamsley, Chelsea Richardson and Susana Toledano that they would engage in conduct that would constitute said offense, to-wit, cause the deaths of Suzana Wamsley and

Rick Wamsley during the same criminal transaction by shooting them with a firearm and said defendant performed an overt act in pursuance of said agreement, to-wit, provided the firearm that was used to shoot Suzana Wamsley and Rick Wamsley. It's filed July the 1st, 2004, signed by the Honorable Tim Curry and the foreman of the grand jury.

It appeared that the defense was trying to plant a seed of doubt in the jury's mind about Chelsea's involvement in the murder. Here, in the indictment, it alleged that Hilario supplied the gun. Previously, testimony by Susana determined that she shot the Wamsleys. Therefore, Chelsea's involvement was minimal—and possibly even nonexistent.

Following the introduction of the indictment against Hilario Cardenas, the judge asked if there was anything else.

St. John replied, "No, Your Honor. Close."

"The state rests and closes," said Parrish.

After both sides rested, the judge told the jury that that was all the evidence they were going to hear. He then dismissed the jury into the jury room "while the attorneys and I have a chance to review the proposed jury charge." After the attorneys looked over the charge, the judge asked if either attorney had an objection to it. Parrish said he did not. St. John said that he did.

Outside the presence of the jury, St. John began to state his objections to the jury charge. His goal was to reduce the charges against Chelsea, thus giving the jury the option of convicting her of a lesser charge.

He told the court that his client was "legally entitled to two lesser included charges, that of murder and that of conspiracy to commit capital murder—and specifically if the court remembers the testimony of Kathryn Norton that will raise the inference that . . . according to what Chelsea allegedly told her that Chelsea and Andrew were outside, Susana picks up a gun, runs inside the house, they hear shooting, they

go inside, and apparently Mrs. Wamsley had been shot. . . .
There's no indication based on that scenario that my client
had any knowledge that anybody was going to be killed specifically." St. John stated that to him, "it sounded like Susana
picked up the gun which came loose and ran inside the house
and did it on her own. Therefore," continued St. John, "I think
we're entitled to a lesser included charge of murder as a matter
of law."

After considering this motion, the judge said, "The court
at this time is going to deny that requested lesser offense of
murder."

St. John then requested a lesser charge of conspiracy to
commit capital murder, based on testimony about Celia Richardson's receiving a letter from Susana Toledano. "It clearly
states that the actors, the parties, in that offense were Susana
Toledano and Hilario Cardenas." That, along with the testimony of Darissa Humphries indicating that Susana was a habitual crack smoker and shot a nine-millimeter firearm, "goes
in line with exactly what the letter indicates that Susana Toledano initially tells the authorities in Addison, Illinois, that it's
her and Hilario Cardenas. . . . Based on those reasons . . . we
are legally entitled to have a lesser-included instruction of
conspiracy to commit capital murder."

After thinking that over for a few moments, the judge
stated, "The court denies the request."

The judge had decided there would be no middle ground
in this case. The jury would be left with two starkly different choices: Convict Chelsea Richardson of capital murder
with a death sentence hanging over her head . . . or declare
her innocent and set her free.

Chapter Twenty-one

After less than five days of testimony, the trial of Chelsea Richardson was winding down to its final hours. The judge called the jury back in and told them, "I've allowed each side a total of an hour per side for final arguments." The prosecution, he mentioned, "has the right to open and then to close the argument with the defense proceeding in between."

Parrish began the closing arguments for the state. "You're left with a simple task," he said. "Who tells the truth? One side does, one side does not. Y'all get to determine what the true facts are. . . . You heard Dr. Sisler say Suzy [Wamsley] was killed by a gunshot wound to the head. You've heard Dr. Peerwani say Rick had two almost simultaneous causes of death. . . . And the way these people were butchered, can you even doubt this is not an intentional act, an intentional killing?"

He then got right to the question of the handwriting expert. He stated that Susana spelled "Chelsea" correctly in the longhand confession she wrote in Illinois and she also signed her own name correctly. But in a letter submitted into evidence, in which "Susana" is misspelled and "Chelsea" is spelled "completely wrong," the handwriting expert, Linda James, contended that the writing was the same—that it was Susana's writing in both cases. "She is wrong," Parrish stated emphatically. Her opinion was "just wrong." Even when Susana looked at the letter, she said it wasn't her writing. "If it was hers," he asked the jury, "why wouldn't she admit to it? . . . She admitted hundreds of things worse than writing this." Parrish then reiterated his belief that Susana had told the truth during the trial.

Parrish pointed out that Jeremy Lavender testified that Chelsea asked him to get her a gun and that Chelsea called Jeremy within twenty minutes of the capital murders. "Why? She wants an alibi. She got in some trouble, I need an alibi." And Jeremy did it, but then when he, Parrish, said he would prosecute Jeremy for perjury if he lied to the grand jury, Jeremy corrected himself. "But they deserve a chance to correct it when they've been used and abused by someone like her, and I gave it to him."

And what about Ruth Brustrom's testimony, asked Parrish, who said that she was with Chelsea and Andrew when they got the call on their cell phone that Susana was arrested. What did Chelsea say? According to Ruth herself, Chelsea said, "This wouldn't have happened if she would have gone to Mexico."

Parrish then pointed out that Napoleon "just pulled the name Montgomery out of the air. There is no Deputy Montgomery down there and there's not even a City of Ennis police officer named Montgomery. He's just lying to you. Remember the letter? He's telling you the lie that Penny Haynes would not." Chelsea was not where Napoleon said she was on the night of the murder.

If Susana were going to lie, Parrish stated, she would say, "'I saw Chelsea shoot him in the back and I saw Andrew stab him.' But she doesn't know. She doesn't know. She comes back over here and stabs Suzy and she can't tell you who did what with regard to the fatal stabbings and the shooting. She doesn't know. If she were gonna lie to you, wouldn't she just add something in like that 'cause it's not contradicted? I mean, she just doesn't know." In other words, according to Parrish, Susana should be believed in all that she testified to, and in particular, that Chelsea and Andrew were involved every step of the way in this murder.

Regarding Chelsea, Parrish told the jury, she was guilty according to the law, if she did any one of the following: "shoot [Rick] in the back, and it is fatal; help, encourage with Suzy's part [with murdering Suzy]; help Susana; encourage her; direct her; aid her." If she did any of those things, "she's guilty of capital murder. If you help do the crime, if you do one little piece and help the rest of it, you're guilty of capital murder. . . . And when you examine the evidence, you'll find that [Chelsea Richardson] is guilty beyond any reasonable doubt of capital murder."

With that definitive statement ringing in the jury's ears, Parrish passed the baton to the defense.

"Ladies and gentlemen of the jury," began Barlow. "Everyone knows when you make a deal with the devil, the devil wins. The prosecution has made their deal with the devil, and the devil's name is Susana Toledano. Susana has got her deal. She's already won. You know that she murdered two people in cold blood and she's getting murder [with] life. . . . [The prosecution] struck a deal with someone who has lied numerous times and they've tailored the case to fit those lies. . . . But that doesn't mean that this lady over here is guilty of anything."

He remarked that Susana was arrested because they had a rock-solid case against her with the DNA evidence. "And they ask [her] this question: Tell us who else was involved and maybe you won't get the death penalty. So what are [her] choices?" He went on to say that one choice was to admit that she killed the Wamsleys on her own, to say "give me the death sentence because no one else was involved."

Another choice was to say that sure, others were involved. "And can I have my lesser included murder life charge, please? Let me tell you all about it." He said that the entire prosecution case was built around Toledano. "You take Susana Toledano out, they have no case. There is no case."

To discredit Toledano further, Barlow stated that on February 17, 2004, Toledano spoke to the grand jury in Tarrant County. "She doesn't tell them anything then, but right after that, she runs up to Illinois. Then in April, April the fifth of two oh oh four, she's arrested, she gives a statement to the police up in Illinois. . . . She tells them that she was with Hilario and Hilario did it. . . . That's the story that she gives when she's first arrested for the offense of capital murder. . . . Then in July of two oh oh four . . . the story suddenly changes. Now it's not her and Hilario Cardenas. Now it's Chelsea and Andrew and all these other people that are involved. . . . Then in April of two oh oh five, she goes over the testimony [with the defense team] and then she testifies in front of you in May of this year, just a few days ago. When was the first time that she told the story of the closet? . . . A year and a half after the murder at this trial, she comes up with a whole second story. Now why would somebody do that? . . . Because she's talked to us and she's starting to get worried about her deal. She's starting to think, *Gee, the case might be crumbling against Chelsea, so I've got to come up with something else that's gonna bolster my case.* So she tells you and tells us for the first time from the witness stand about this ridiculousness—they're running all over the house, hiding in closets and the Wamsleys don't have a clue, there's two—three people in their house that are messing around. For the first time, that's when we hear it. Does that make any sense?"

Barlow continued, "You don't find someone guilty of the offense of capital murder based on the testimony of a co-defendant who has lied." He said that when Susana was asked how Chelsea and Andrew could get her to do the act, she said, 'I don't know.' Susana declared she just murdered two people in their home . . . killed them, shot them, stabbed them, and she says, 'I just don't know why I did that'? They made a deal with that person. That person gets life. Murder life. Chelsea Richardson, if you convict her, she's already getting more than anyone else in this case. But you can't do that because she's not guilty. The state of Texas has not, has not"—he repeated emphatically—"proved its case. . . . Chelsea Richardson is not guilty."

And with that, St. John stood up and took over from Barlow, to begin his final argument for the defense. He stated to the members of the jury that they had been responsible members of the community and would follow the law, "and when you follow the law, you will acquit my client. She is innocent. . . . We don't have a burden of proof."

St. John stated that Susana was the manipulator. Jeremy Lavender stated that he was afraid of her. She "cursed him, was mean to him. If Chelsea is such a great commander at manipulation, is she up there in Addison, Illinois, on April the fifth of two oh oh four [trying to persuade Susana]? No. She's not in command of any manipulation."

According to St. John, "Two people with extensive drug histories took it upon themselves to gain a financial benefit because they knew the Wamsleys had money. Hilario had the gun. Hilario and Susana went up there. Hilario and Susana killed those people, not my client." According to St. John, Susana is a "crackhead, she smokes crack cocaine." To help her cause, St. John said, Chelsea gave a DNA swab voluntarily because she "ain't afraid of [a] swab, she ain't afraid of nothing, because she wasn't there. She knows she wasn't there and she'll cooperate with whatever they need. . . . Use your common sense. She wasn't there." According to St. John, "the only legal, reasonable conclusion that can be made is Chelsea Richardson is innocent. Therefore, you must vote not guilty."

After the weight of this declaration had time to sink in, prosecuting attorney Simpson stood up and began her counterattack. Contradicting Barlow and St. John, she began by saying that Andrew—Chelsea's boyfriend—had the most to gain from the deaths of Rick and Suzy Wamsley. Simpson said that Chelsea was a "wolf in sheep's clothing. It should be frightening how young she is and all of the manipulation that she's capable of." She pointed out that Chelsea had said she and Jeremy had spoken for hours on the phone. "That was a lie."

Simpson continued, "Susana had the biggest physical part in this crime. . . . But why does she do it? You might not understand it. Why would anybody kill another person? But she did it because Chelsea told her to and because Chelsea promised her, 'You get to chill with me in a big house that we'll buy' and fix up this old Mustang [of yours]. To a normal, reasonable person, that sounds crazy. But who had the most to gain by killing the Wamsleys? It wasn't Susana and it wasn't Hilario, who is not even there. It was Chelsea. . . . Find her guilty. Hold her responsible."

And with that, all the testimony and all the arguments that the jury would hear had come to a close. The judge told the jury that they would now be sent to the jury room to consider their verdict. "When you've received a unanimous decision, you may ring the buzzer that's available and the bailiff will respond."

At 11:44 a.m. the jury left the court.

The trial on the guilt or innocence of Chelsea had come to a close. The Richardson family silently prayed that the jury would find their daughter, their sister, their loved one, not guilty. *They just had to!* The Wamsley family and friends, on the other hand, wanted the jury to hand down a guilty verdict. To them, Chelsea Richardson was the mastermind. *She was the killer!*

Chapter Twenty-two

After the jury left to consider their verdict, most spectators walked out of the courtroom, but didn't go far. They stayed outside in the hall. The buzz was that a verdict would be reached quickly.

At 3:08 p.m.—less than four hours after beginning deliberations—the jury informed the judge that it had reached a verdict. The word went out. *A verdict! After only four hours!*

St. John and Barlow felt that they had given it their all. They had planted a huge seed of doubt in the jurors' minds: Susana was not to be trusted, and on her word alone the entire case rested. Further, they felt that because there was no evidence of Chelsea's presence found at the scene, there was *certainly* a reasonable doubt.

Parrish and Simpson, on the other hand, felt that they had portrayed Chelsea as a manipulative personality who was able to get others to do her dirty work. They felt they had portrayed Susana as a credible person and had shown that Chelsea was involved in this murder to a huge extent.

But what would the jurors think?

The jury walked back into the courtroom, and the attorneys from both sides scanned the jurors' faces for any sign of their decision. The jurors did not look at Chelsea. Often, that signaled a negative result for the defendant. However, as lawyers know, there is absolutely no way to read a jury.

The judge asked the foreman of the jury if the jury had reached a decision.

"Yes. That's correct," he responded.

The judge asked, "And is the verdict of the jury unanimous?"

The foreman replied, "Yes, sir."

The judge then asked for the verdict to be handed to the bailiff and stated that he, the judge, would read it in open court.

When the verdict had been handed up, the judge began, "This is Case No. 0929234A styled the State of Texas vs. Chelsea Lea Richardson. The verdict of the jury is as follows."

In the momentary pause before the judge read the verdict, the courtroom was totally silent. It seemed as if everyone was afraid even to breathe.

The judge continued, "We, the jury, find the defendant, Chelsea Lea Richardson, guilty of the offense of capital murder as charged in the indictment."

"Yes!" came a muffled sound from the audience as people from the Wamsley family allowed themselves a moment to smile—amid their deeper sorrow.

A soft wail came from the lips of Chelsea's mother. "Nooooo." It couldn't be.

The judge then told the jury that, as required by law, the court would conduct a poll and the jurors should indicate whether or not this was their verdict. He then called the jurors' names, one after the next, and each juror indicated that this was, in fact, his or her verdict.

As each name was read and the reality of the verdict began to sink in, Chelsea looked down at the floor, hands covering her eyes, and sobbed.

The judge stated that it was about 3:15 p.m. They were going to recess and would reconvene following a short break. Then, with barely a pause, the sentencing phase of the trial would commence. The same jury that had found Chelsea guilty of capital murder would have the responsibility of determining whether or not she deserved to receive the death penalty.

It had been quite a heavy day of courtroom drama already—closing arguments and a verdict. But more was to come.

Chapter Twenty-three

Twenty minutes after the guilty verdict was read, the sentencing phase of the trial began.

The prosecution would not be pulling any punches. They were seeking the death penalty, and Parrish was ready with their first witness, Elizabeth A. Tovar. After being sworn in, Tovar stated that she knew Chelsea Richardson through her brother, John Burroughs. Burroughs had been Chelsea's "boyfriend on and off, here and there." Tovar also knew Andrew Wamsley through Chelsea. She said they would hang out together, from time to time, and one time went to a place called Kelly's in October 2003. It was a little country bar, and they went there just to play pool after her brother was no longer Chelsea's boyfriend. "[Andrew] just talked about [his parents] having a lot of money and that he would be set. . . . Yeah, he was just bragging that his parents had a lot of money, and that's pretty much it. . . . They were joking around, so I thought . . . about getting married . . . having money to go on vacation . . . and Drew was talking about . . . we don't have any money, we have to wait until I get my money from my parents, until my parents, you know, die. Chelsea said, Well, why don't we just knock them off? You know, I mean they were laughing, though, so I thought they were joking. I really didn't know they were serious about doing it."

On cross-examination, St. John asked Tovar, "And you said that [Chelsea] said it in a kind of a teasing jest?"

Tovar replied, "It seemed to me that she was joking about it. Yeah, they were just playing." She said that Andrew and Chelsea didn't seem like the kind of people who would do that, so she didn't take it seriously.

John Burroughs was called next by the prosecution. Simpson questioned him about his relationship with Chelsea. He stated he dated Chelsea for about a year several years ago, and he had met Andrew Wamsley a couple of times through Chelsea. Simpson asked him if he also knew Susana Toledano, and he stated that he did. Although he had never heard them talk about how much money Andrew's parents had, he did see Andrew and Chelsea "attempt to or actually sell marijuana."

According to Burroughs, Chelsea was the "weigher . . . weigh it up, bag it up." It was "her duty to package it for Andrew."

On cross-examination, however, Burroughs admitted that Chelsea and Andrew were not that good at selling dope. He also admitted he had only seen them doing this once.

When Burroughs stepped down, the judge said, "I understand the next witness to be called will be available at nine o'clock tomorrow morning?"

Parrish replied, "Yes sir. We have one other piece of evidence."

"You may continue then."

Simpson rose and said, "At this time, the state will offer State's Exhibit 113." She asked the bailiff to pass out photocopies of the evidence to the jurors. The evidence being introduced was a letter, allegedly written by Chelsea to Andrew. The letter was dated about a month before the murder of Andrew's parents—and just one day after the failed attempt to kill Rick, Suzy, and Sarah Wamsley as they were driving home after going horseback riding. Parrish stated that he had planned to introduce it earlier but decided against it.

Simpson proceeded to read the letter aloud.

November ten, two oh oh three. Drew, hey what's up?
It's pretty fucked up you're being followed. . . . Your
family treats you like shit. They don't seem to love or
care for you at all. . . . They just don't understand a
genius like you needs to see how the world works too.
Just know that we are your friends and we will be here
for you. If your family just tried and love you and
trusted you, they would see how much you could help
them and love them. They would see how you could
benefit them. All theirs and your days would be happy.
Signed by the defendant.

Following the reading of the letter, the judge ended the
proceedings for the day—and it had been a very long one.
The sentencing phase would continue the very next morning.

On May 25, 2005, the jury was reconvened and the state had
the opportunity to call several witnesses.

Simpson first called Sarah Wamsley and asked her to tell
the court about her parents. Sarah stated right off that they
were loving parents who took care of her and Andrew.
"They were best friends to me, and any time I needed anything I could go to them for support, for guidance." Sarah
stopped speaking and told the court she needed to take
some time to compose herself before talking about her
daughter, Brittany. After she gathered herself together, she
recalled how her parents would pick up Brittany from school
every Wednesday and take her to ride their horse, Toby. On
December 10, 2003, they did that, and then went back to the
Wamsleys' to play Candy Land. After the murders, Sarah
stated, she went back to the house to collect the game, which
she now had, along with some Christmas presents that were
in the house. One of the gifts, she said, was from "Mom and
Dad to me. That's still wrapped."

After the murders, Sarah said she was "always watching
[her] back. I would have nightmares that I was next." She said

she hired bodyguards to make sure nothing happened to her. She related how after the murders, she moved five times in one year because she was afraid "they would find out where I was."

She stated that when she wants to hear her parents' voices, she turns on their old answering machine and plays the message. She said that to this day she couldn't sing "that 'Old Susana' song, she's coming around the mountain," because as a family, they used to love to sing it. Sarah broke down again when talking about how hard the extended family was taking the death and how everyone just wanted to see her parents again. "It is especially hard for Brittany," she said, "who is in counseling and is afraid whenever I leave that I, like Mama and Papa, will never come back." Several jurors had tears in their eyes when Sarah described making a phone call to her grandparents in Oklahoma to tell them the news. "It's really hard seeing Grandma and Grandpa crying," Sarah testified. "It's hard on everybody."

Simpson asked Sarah what she would miss about her parents in the future. "They don't get to see me grow up. I don't get to see them grow older. They don't get to see my daughter grow up either. They've already missed her first day of school. . . . They don't get to meet my boyfriend. They don't get to plan a wedding if I ever get married. Dad can't give me away."

Then Sarah recalled the last time she celebrated her birthday when her parents were still alive—February 14, 2003. It was Valentine's Day as well as her birthday, and her parents brought twenty-four balloons to her workplace, along with one more for good luck with her name on it. It was a great surprise. She told them that for her next birthday, when she would turn twenty-five, *her* gift to *them* would be that they would get to spend Valentine's Day alone, since every other year they had spent it with her. Then she dropped her head and said, "Sadly, they never had the chance."

Simpson passed the witness, but St. John said, "We have no questions, Your Honor."

Sarah Wamsley was the very last witness for the prosecution. "The state rests, Your Honor," said Simpson.

It was now the defense's turn—and their last chance to save Chelsea from a death sentence. To begin, they called several of Chelsea's teachers to the witness stand. The first, Gary Edward Schulte, was Chelsea's chemistry teacher, and he stated that Chelsea was a "pretty hard worker" and a "B, C student." He affirmed that he saw Chelsea help Susana at various times. He mentioned that she was "one of the kids that actually took the time to let the teachers know that she appreciated what we were doing for them, which in the school I teach in it's pretty rare." Chelsea, he said, was on the yearbook committee and that was considered an honor, because teachers needed to recommend the student and then the student needed approval by the teacher who is in charge of the yearbook.

Molly Lyn Donald, Chelsea's world history teacher, was the next witness. She stated that Chelsea was an A student in her class. To Donald, Chelsea seemed very bright. "She was outspoken, always very sweet, very helpful in class." She said they became more like friends, "not just a student-teacher relationship."

Patricia Monople was called next. When asked what she did for a living, she responded that she worked at the General Services Administration, "which pays the government's bills, in a nutshell." She stated that she had known Celia Richardson, the defendant's mother, for eighteen years and had known Chelsea since the girl was two. Over the years, Chelsea would come around once a month to see her mother at work. Monople stated that Chelsea was "always friendly, bubbly, affectionate. Always giving hugs to everyone she met." She said she never saw Chelsea in a bad mood. "I never saw any problems [between mother and child]." She said she was "very surprised, shocked" when she heard that Chelsea was charged with capital murder.

Another witness, Harold Booth, who was a friend of the defendant's mother, stated that he hired Chelsea ten or fifteen times over the years to help with some events he put on. He said she always did a very good job and "she was better than some of our older employees." He said he was in "disbelief" when he heard Chelsea had been charged with capital murder.

Annie Moore, who worked with Celia and also with Chelsea when Chelsea was a cashier at Wynn Dixie, testified that Chelsea would come and check on her after she had "a lot of surgeries." Chelsea would call Moore before coming and ask if she needed anything. Chelsea "would always give a hug. She was always friendly." She said she never saw any hints or indications of aberrant behavior as she watched Chelsea grow up, over nineteen years.

Chelsea's brother James was sworn in next. He said he never saw either Andrew or his sister "possess, sell, package, or smoke marijuana." He talked about his family, saying that they were close. He stated that Chelsea was about fifteen when her father passed away, and he was about twenty. He said the death affected everyone in the family. "Chelsea was sad for a long time," said James.

St. John called Celia Richardson next. He asked her to tell the court about Chelsea's childhood. Celia said that Chelsea always seemed happy. She loved everyone in the family, and she was always helpful. "She used to sit and talk to some of the elderly people in the neighborhood, check on them." She stated that when Chelsea was in the eighth grade, her husband passed away. "We were close in our family and [Chelsea] was kind of upset about it. She asked me to spend more time with her. I was working two jobs. So I did quit my second job for over a year and just spent more time with her in the evenings and [with] the kids." She stated she was shocked when she heard Chelsea was arrested because "it's just not her personality." She stated that Susana lived with her family from November 2002 until "this happened." She said she would take Susana and her sister Jessica places. "I treated other people the same as my kids," Celia stated. She noted that Chelsea "has been in jail since she's nineteen, and now she's twenty-one, so it's close to two years." Since the beginning of her incarceration, Celia had visited Chelsea every week. Chelsea's brother visited her, too. Celia said she would visit Chelsea no matter what the sentence was, but she said firmly, "I don't believe she did this."

Next, Barlow called Andrea Parsons—one of the inmates who had served time with Chelsea. She repeated the testimony she had given earlier, saying that she was housed with Chelsea in January for two weeks and they became friendly. They participated in Bible study groups together. She said Chelsea went to Bible classes "almost every time I turned around." Parsons said Chelsea was respectful, so they got along well. She said Chelsea had a good relationship with both inmates and guards. She never knew Chelsea to have any discipline problems, never saw her being disrespectful.

Barlow stated, "We pass the witness."

"No questions," responded Parrish.

The final witness called by the defense was S. O. Woods, Jr. He stated that he lived in Huntsville, Texas, the headquarters for the Texas prison system, and was currently retired from the Texas Department of Criminal Justice, Institutional Division. He stated, however, that he worked part-time as a criminal justice consultant. He said that since being retired, he had been contacted by both prosecution and defense lawyers to testify in capital murder cases. He researched records, particularly on appeals. He said he had testified in court hundreds of times.

In order to give the jurors an idea of what life was like inside the Texas prisons, St. John asked Woods if he ever worked inside a women's unit in Huntsville. He said he had.

He stated he was in charge of the intake of those prisoners and processing them. St. John asked him where females on death row are housed. "The female death row is on the Mountain View Unit in Gatesville." He stated that currently, there were seven women on death row. In response to St. John's question about security in the prison, he said, "They usually have double fencing, an outside fence, a chain link fence, which is usually eight foot tall, and it has razor ribbon wire and it's usually across the top and across the bottom. And then they have a space usually around six to eight feet between that and a second fence with more razor ribbon wire at the bottom and more razor ribbon at the top. So escaping from a state facility in this state is very challenging. . . . Females don't have, in my opinion, the physical strength to [escape]."

St. John then asked Woods to explain the jail records of Chelsea, which had been sent to him previously. He stated, "She's on medium-custody-type status and basically has freedom of movement around the facility for various reasons. She's not confined, hasn't had any problems."

If the jury were to sentence "that woman who's on trial to death," asked St. John, "how is that person housed?"

"She is placed in a cell on death row . . . which at Mountain View has single cells for the death row inmates and they're allowed out one hour a day for recreation on a rotation between inside and outside the building. They're not allowed to work. They don't have any in-cell programs. They are allowed access to religious materials." Woods stated that the execution chamber, for both men and women, is located in Huntsville, Texas, at the Huntsville unit.

After he was satisfied that Woods had painted a clear picture of what it would be like for Chelsea on death row, St. John passed the witness.

Parrish tried to show that by being in the prison system—and not on death row—inmates could be susceptible to a manipulator. "In the women's units as in the men's unit, are there some people in there that are just kind of slow?" asked Parrish.

"Certainly," said Woods.

"Lots of them are M.H.M.R. [Mental Health Mental Retardation]?"

"Yes, sir."

"And are you aware of situations where people who are manipulators use those people to do their dirty work?"

"I'm sure that's happened. . . ."

Parrish said, "That's all we have. Thank you."

On redirect, St. John asked about the manipulation of women inmates, and Woods stated that "manipulation is gonna happen [in] male or female prisons. I don't think it's quite as easy to manipulate inmates as it is to manipulate civilians. Inmates are experienced. They know those games. They know the consequences of those games."

The defense hoped it had ended the sentencing phase by first offering witnesses who testified to the character of the defendant, and then by bringing in an expert to paint a picture of the jail system: Chelsea was doing all right in medium security; she had not gotten into any trouble and had a low classification of danger; if she were put on death row, it would be a horrific fate, with twenty-three hours of the day spent in confinement. Further, Woods disagreed with the prosecution that if Chelsea was not on death row, she could manipulate inmates into doing whatever she wanted them to do—like she did in the "outside" world.

At that point, both sides rested and closed their cases.

The judge said, "All right, ladies and gentlemen. Both sides have rested and closed in this phase of that trial, so that's all the evidence you're gonna hear in this case. It's now necessary that the court finish preparation of its jury charge containing your instructions for your deliberations in this case. And following delivery of the jury charge, the attorneys will have an opportunity to make final arguments to you and then you'll begin your deliberations." He then dismissed the jurors, advising them to return after lunch, at 1:30 p.m.

With the jury out of the courtroom, Judge Young asked if there were any objections to the charge. Once again, Parrish said, "None from the state." St. John said he would like to "reiterate that it's our position that the Texas death penalty statute is unconstitutional as a matter of law, that it's clearly arbitrary and capricious and in direct violation to the Eighth Amendment to the United States Constitution and it violates the prohibition against cruel and unusual punishment. So I would ask the court to declare that statute unconstitutional."

The judge immediately responded, "The court at this time is gonna deny your requests to declare the statute unconstitutional."

It was now time for the final arguments before a sentence of life in prison or death was issued. Each side was allotted a maximum of thirty minutes in which to make its case. The jury was then brought back in.

The judge then read the charge. "All right. Ladies and gentlemen, at this time, both sides will have an opportunity to make final arguments to you and then you'll begin your deliberations. The state has the right to open and then to close the argument with the defense proceeding in between. And I've allowed each side a total of thirty minutes for their argument. So if you can, give your attention back to the attorneys. The state may proceed at this time."

Simpson began, speaking directly to the jurors. "This is it. You've heard all the evidence in this case. [The jury charge is] number one, is the defendant a future danger? Number two, did the defendant kill, intend to kill, or anticipate that human lives would be taken? Number three, does the defendant deserve a life sentence rather than the death penalty? . . . The judge's instructions to you will be to answer questions one and two, and only if you answer questions one and two unanimously yes, then you'll move on to question number three."

Simpson said that Parrish would speak to the jurors concerning question one. As for question two, she said, "From all the evidence in the case, this planning for the killings began long before December 10. Did the defendant Chelsea Richardson actually kill? Well, there's evidence that she actually killed. Is there evidence that she intended for them to be killed? There's a bunch of evidence that she intended for them to be killed. Could she have anticipated that human lives would be taken? Absolutely. Because if nobody died, there was no way for her to share the money with Andrew.

"Issue number three. Does the defendant deserve a life sentence rather than the death penalty?" Simpson continued, "While Suzy is meticulously decorating the house and planning the events of the season, the defendant and Andrew Wamsley and Susana Toledano were planning their deaths. . . . When Suzy is wrapping presents . . . they're getting the gun back from Hilario. . . . While the victims' families are planning their funerals, the defendant is orchestrating the clean up. . . . And it continues. They lie to the grand jury. They lie to the police. They continue to lie, still expecting that they're gonna get the money."

To emphasize her case for Chelsea to receive the death penalty, Simpson said, "This defendant here and her co-defendants gave this family out here the gift that keeps on going. Every holiday, every birthday two people are going to be missing. They will never be the same." Simpson recounted some of the many things the Wamsleys would never get to see—birthdays, weddings, and their granddaughter grow up. Furthermore, Simpson said, while the defendant is behind bars, she "continues to work on someone to convince them to come up here and give a false alibi and to lie about one of the co-defendants. Is this someone that has something redeeming about her life? You heard from all the witnesses that came in and testified today that the defendant never had any psychological problems, never any emotional problems, which in some way [if she had problems] might explain why someone could do something so brutal and something so horrible. But there isn't anything. . . . When she met Andrew Wamsley and began conspiring with him to kill not only Andrew Wamsley's parents but his sister, those were her choices."

Simpson continued to portray Chelsea as a manipulator, citing her attempt to get an alibi in jail and the letter she wrote Andrew the day after they tried to kill his parents in Burleson, about how his parents didn't love or trust him.

In concluding her remarks, Simpson said, "There is nothing redeeming about any of the facts of this case. And the law recognizes that there are some cases that are so brutal and so heinous that nothing else is required to prove future danger. . . . Cutting the brakes wasn't gonna be feasible. Let's try shooting at the car. How about a robbery? Well, if that's not going to work, then we'll sneak in and slaughter them in their own home and partially with their own kitchen utensils."

Simpson paused a moment and then walked close to the jury. "You've had a very difficult job and we appreciate it. I'm gonna ask you to go back there and answer questions one and two unanimously yes, and then you move on to question number three. And I think from all the evidence it's pretty clear what the answer to that should be. Thank you for your service." And with that, Simpson passed to Barlow.

Barlow slowly rose and with solemnity, he began, "You've delivered your verdict and we accept that as we must. . . . We ask you, we beg you very respectfully and humbly, to spare this young woman's life. She's just twenty-one years of age. She was nineteen when these acts were committed. And up to this point, up to the facts of this case, she led an exemplary life. Witness after witness was shocked to even know that this young woman was involved with anything like this." He went on to say that it had already been decided that Susana Toledano, "the one that bears most of the responsibility and culpability," is getting life, with a thirty-year minimum. Barlow stated that part of our judiciary system is that people who commit the same crime should get the same punishment. "And you already know that the least you can do to Chelsea is give her ten more flat years than Susana Toledano will get. And we know that Hilario Cardenas isn't even facing capital murder charges, the one who provided the gun. So I ask you to search your hearts and ask you if that's fair . . . that some people are getting less time or are not even facing the death penalty when only Chelsea Richardson [is]."

Barlow pointed out that Chelsea was not a danger to society, since no witness brought any evidence to support that. On the contrary, many witnesses reported that Chelsea was helpful and friendly. Her teachers reported that she was a bright, hardworking student. Neighbors said she helped them when they were in need. Chelsea made friends easily. She was outgoing. According to Barlow, Chelsea was a child any parent could be proud of.

Barlow admitted that Chelsea had a poisonous relationship with Andrew, Susana, and Hilario. "Up until October, November, December of two oh oh three, she led a good life. We ask you to keep that in mind and take that into consideration."

"And," he continued, "we've brought an expert witness to actually tell you what the women's prison system is like. Mr. Woods told you that there was only one escape in thirty-one years; and there were no assaults on guards or prison personnel that he could remember in thirty-one years. . . . And this woman, if you sentence her to life in the penitentiary, she's not gonna be a future danger to other inmates, to guards, to herself. She's gonna live the rest of her years, at least until she's sixty years old, in that prison system, going to work every day, five days a week, spending her time in her cell."

Barlow said he was about to finish up, and he urged the jurors to listen carefully to his last words. "If she's a master manipulator," he said, "she's done a mighty poor job. She's manipulated herself right into a capital murder case." Everyone brought from jail, he continued, stated that she was not violent; she was nice; she got along with the guards; she didn't cause any problems. "And that's the way she's gonna act in any jail that the prison system puts her in, if you give her that opportunity.

"The last few words I want to leave you with is that, with time, Chelsea can reflect, she can learn, she can read, she can work, she can move her life towards redemption. If she dies, she may not get that chance. There's always a chance for salvation, for sorrow, for reflection. Give her that chance. It's not like we're asking you to set her free . . . we're talking about at least until she's sixty in the penitentiary. . . . There's no need to take her life. Allow Celia and James, her co-workers, allow them the chance to at least visit her, speak with her, at least watch her grow old. And no, the Wamsleys' family do not have that chance. But you folks are not killers. . . . We're asking you to look at all of Chelsea's life, the good and the bad, the evil and the good. Take all of that and decide what should be done. She may not deserve that chance, but we're begging you for that chance for her to reflect and reform herself. And we submit to you what should be done is a life sentence rather than the death penalty. Thank you."

Barlow sat down, exhausted. It was his last attempt to save his client, and he could only pray that he had succeeded.

With still some time remaining, St. John continued for the defense. He stated that the jury should be faithful to its obligations and to their oath to hold the state to its burden of proof. "Is Chelsea a future danger to society?" he asked. The answer, St. John said, was no. "There is zero evidence that Chelsea Richardson is a threat to society. She had no prior arrests or convictions." Furthermore, he continued, no one ever called Chelsea rude, not even people in the jail. In fact, she attended Bible classes.

St. John pointed out that only two testimonies even hinted at any criminal acts committed by Chelsea: one witness said "he believes on one occasion he saw Chelsea weigh some marijuana for Andrew," and another witness overheard Chelsea talking at a bar about killing the Wamsleys and she thought Chelsea was kidding. "Those are your big extraneous criminal acts that the state wants you to take into consideration regarding her future dangerousness.

"You have to make a decision based on the law and the evidence and based on your common sense and emotion," St. John continued. "But the decision the twelve of you make will rest with you the rest of your lives. . . . I don't want the twelve of y'all to ever be in the position when you leave here today, six, seven years from now, you're leaving work, going home to see your family, I don't want y'all to ever be in a position to turn on the radio and hear that Chelsea Richardson has been put to death at Huntsville, Texas, if that's not the right decision. Don't ever be in that position. Because the state has not proved its case. I know the twelve of y'all will make the correct decision."

St. John, emotional and spent, took his seat and the defense rested.

It was now Parrish's final attempt to persuade the jurors to give Chelsea death. He began his closing arguments by stating that he would not "guilt trip" the jury, like the defense had. He said the defense was begging for mercy, whereas he was asking for justice. Parrish stated that Chelsea was not emotionally disturbed or psychologically flawed. No, he said, she is "greedy and has no conscience." He stated that Rick begged for mercy and asked, "Why?" and what did Chelsea do? She lied, saying she was pregnant. Rick said he would help. But Chelsea would not hear of it. "She's the mover and shaker," said Parrish. "She's the bus driver." There were some capital murders, he told the jury, that "demand the death penalty. This was such a case." He stated that "a manipulator like that . . . she is a future danger." He stated that this was not a random drive-by shooting or a murder in which the killers are high on drugs. It was a thought-out murder, "talked about for over two months by four people, all normal . . . just sitting there in a public restaurant, the IHOP, talking about ways to kill, methods to kill." They even went to a pond to get proficient in using the weapon they would use to do the killing. Chelsea wrote to Andrew, telling him his parents didn't love or appreciate him, on the day after they failed to kill his parents by shooting their Jeep, on November 9.

The motive, said Parrish, "is greed. Money. Chelsea is a future danger because she wants money and has to kill people to get it. Although she may not have had a police record, in November oh three, she became the mastermind of the plot to kill the Wamsleys. She got Susana to do the killing. She uses people to her advantage. Susana is not a born killer. She's a naïve girl with zero self-confidence just looking for acceptance. And if she had fallen in with somebody whose goal it was to sell more Girl Scout cookies in the world than anybody else, I guess she would be out there doing that, if that had been her mentor. But her mentor sits there. The person that made her the killer that she is . . . Is that a future danger? You bet. If you decide Chelsea should spend her life in prison, [Chelsea] will use people like Jeremy Lavender. . . . As Mr. Woods said, is there manipulation in prison? You bet. Convicts know that game. Chelsea's already a pro at it; she'll only get better."

Parrish ended on an emotional note. He recalled how devastated Lewis and Marjean Wamsley were when they received the phone call in which they learned that their second born and his wife were dead. "Their hearts were broken, their worlds and lives shattered. That deserves the death penalty. . . . Follow the law. Base your verdict on the evidence. I thank you."

With Parrish's time up, the sentencing phase of the trial was over. It was 2:20 p.m., and the jurors were told they should retire to the jury room and when "you've reached a verdict in this case, you may ring the buzzer and the bailiff will respond."

Had the defense done enough to convince just one juror to answer either issue number one or issue number two with a "no"? If he had, his client would not face the death penalty. At this point, there was nothing more the defense could do. Twelve men and women would be deciding the young woman's fate.

Chapter Twenty-four

The buzz inside the courtroom was that a verdict would be coming soon. No one could say exactly why they felt that way, but nearly everyone was convinced that they would know the answer to whether Chelsea would get life in prison or death before the day was done. Most courtroom attendees in this trial felt that it was a clear-cut case: *definitely,* Chelsea Richardson deserved death; *definitely,* Chelsea Richardson did not deserve a death sentence. Passions ran high.

Around three hours after the jury began their deliberations, at 5:12 p.m., the judge was informed that a verdict had been reached. Indeed, the courtroom spectators were right. Considering that this was a capital murder case, the verdict was quick. Whichever way the jury went, they seemed to have been close to a unanimous decision from the start.

The judge called the court back in session and the spectators returned to their seats. The twelve jurors solemnly filed in. As they took their seats, they looked at neither the defendant nor the lawyers.

The judge addressed the foreperson. "Has the jury reached a verdict?"

"Yes, sir," he replied.

"Please hand the charge to the bailiff," said the judge. The foreman handed the verdict to the bailiff, who passed it on to the judge. The judge glanced it over. An obvious expression of surprise crossed his face. But what did it suggest?

Had the young woman, whom the prosecutors believed was the mastermind behind the brutal slaying of two people, been sentenced to death, or had she received life in prison because there was still doubt in the jurors' minds?

Judge Young asked Chelsea to stand to hear the verdict. Then, he began to read aloud:

"On the special issue number one: Do you find from the evidence beyond a reasonable doubt that there is a probability that the defendant would commit criminal acts of violence that would constitute a continuing threat to society?

"The answer: We the jury, unanimously find from the evidence beyond a reasonable doubt that the answer to special issue number one is yes. And it's signed by the foreman of the jury."

As soon as Chelsea heard the word "yes," her knees buckled, but she remained standing. She knew, as did everyone else in the courtroom, that if the answer was *not* unanimous to special issue number two, then Chelsea would have a chance at life in prison. However, if the answer was yes, it was possible for Chelsea to receive death.

"Special issue number two: Do you find from the evidence beyond a reasonable doubt that the defendant actually caused the death of the deceased, or did not actually cause the death of the deceased but intended to kill the deceased or another or anticipated that a human life would be taken?

"Answer: We, the jury, unanimously find from the evidence beyond a reasonable doubt that the answer to special issue number two is yes. And it's signed by the foreman of the jury."

Chelsea looked down at the floor. She seemed stunned. Without wasting a moment, the judge continued.

"Special issue number three: Taking into consideration all of the evidence including the circumstance of the offense, the defendant's character and background, and the personal moral culpability of the defendant, do you find that there is a sufficient mitigating circumstance or circumstances to warrant that a sentence of life imprisonment rather than a death sentence be imposed?

"Answer: We, the jury, unanimously find that the answer to special issue number three is no. And it's signed by the foreman of the jury."

By the time the judge completed reading the verdict, Chelsea had collapsed into her chair, her head in her hands on the defense table. Her shoulders shuddered, and she sobbed. She had just heard that the jury believed that there was no reason to spare her life. *What worse news could any person ever hear?*

In the courtroom, James Richardson looked at his mother in disbelief. Did he hear correctly that his sister was just sentenced to die? Did Celia hear correctly that her daughter— bubbly, friendly, and outgoing—was going to *die!* It was unreal. James put his arm around his mother, and they both wept.

On the other side of the room, relatives and friends of the Wamsleys smiled, wept, and hugged one another. Although it was a cheerless victory—after all, they would never see Rick and Suzy again—at least someone was going to pay for the murders.

The judge then asked the foreman if the responses he had just read were the unanimous answers to the special issues.

"Yes," he replied.

The defense then asked for a poll of the jurors. The judge called each juror by name. Each in turn said that those were, in fact, the answers they gave to the three special issues.

The judge then spoke directly to Chelsea. "Ms. Richardson, upon your plea of not guilty in this case, the jury having found you guilty of the offense of capital murder as charged in the indictment, the jury having answered special issues one and two both yes, the jury having answered special issue number three no, it being mandatory that your punishment be death, the court now assesses your punishment as death . . . and that after the hour of six o'clock p.m. on a date to be determined by this court . . . that you be caused to die by intravenous injection of a substance or substances in a lethal quantity sufficient to cause your death, and until you, the said Chelsea Lea Richardson, are dead. . . .

"At this time, Ms. Richardson, I'll remand you to the custody of the sheriff for transportation to the Institutional Division of the Texas Department of Criminal Justice for execution of this sentence. And Ms. Richardson, the law does provide for an automatic appeal to the Texas Court of Criminal Appeals. Do you understand your automatic appeal?"

Chelsea responded haltingly, "Yes, Your Honor."

After ascertaining that Chelsea was "too poor to afford an attorney," the court appointed David Richards as Chelsea's attorney for the direct appeal of her case. Judge Young went on to say that in a criminal case, after the sentence is pronounced, the relatives of the victim are allowed to make a statement regarding their feelings. He asked both the state and the defense if they had anyone who wished to speak. Both responded that no one wished to address the court.

The judge then thanked the jurors for their faithful service. He told them, "So at this time I'll discharge you as a jury and recess you back to the jury room. Thank you again."

After the jury was excused, the judge said, "All right. We'll be in recess at this time."

The ultimate verdict had been handed down. Chelsea was to be executed by lethal injection. The jurors would have to live with this decision in the days, months, and years to follow. And the judge's words—"your punishment as death"— would resonate in Chelsea's ears in the long years she would wait on death row for the verdict to be fulfilled.

Chapter Twenty-five

After the death sentence was handed down, the media immediately spread the word. Headlines in the *Star-Telegram* screamed, "First Woman Sentenced to Death in [Tarrant] County." Another headline read: "Woman, 21, Sentenced to Die." The *Star-Telegram*'s article began, "Even the judge appeared stunned reading the verdict—lethal injection for a young woman."

The prosecutors were more sober. They felt they had presented a strong case in favor of death for Chelsea, and they believed justice had been served by the verdict.

Parrish held firm to his belief that Chelsea had a manipulative personality. She was able, he said, to organize a group of her friends to kill the Wamsleys so her boyfriend could inherit his parents' $1.65 million estate. Both Parrish and Simpson felt that four letters written by Chelsea—and introduced as evidence—had solidified their argument that she was a master manipulator: the letter she sent to Susana the preceding summer, in which she made up the fact that she was pregnant and begged Susana to clear her name; the pleading letters to Hydrick's and Norton's families, in which Chelsea begged them to help her while promising lifelong friendship with their daughters; and the letter she sent to Andrew the day after he tried to kill his parents, telling him that his family didn't love or respect him.

The prosecutors believed that Susana's testimony helped

seal the case, especially when she described how she, Chelsea, and Andrew attempted to murder Rick and Suzy two times before they actually succeeded. They also thought that the testimony of the two inmates who had been housed with Chelsea while she was awaiting trial had been very helpful—after all, Chelsea had admitted to them that she was in the Wamsleys' home on the night of the murders, and that she took part in the killing of Rick Wamsley.

Commenting on Chelsea, Parrish said, "You see, she accepts no responsibility for her actions and shows no remorse. Some capital cases deserve the death penalty. This case deserves the death penalty." Although he felt the sentence was appropriate, Parrish stated that he was nevertheless surprised by the outcome. He had felt that because of Chelsea's age and sex, the jury would give her life in prison. "But," he added, "[the Wamsleys] are very relieved by what the jury decided."

The defense, on the other hand, was shocked and outraged by the verdict. They firmly believed that justice had not been served. After all, there was no physical evidence linking Chelsea to the crime scene—not one bit. They felt that Susana had a drug problem and had lied to save her life. They recalled how she had changed her story several times—in Illinois, in front of the grand jury, and then in front of the trial jury. "It's hard to memorize a lie," said St. John, in a phone interview. "It's real tough."

Another important element in the defense's belief that Chelsea was not guilty was the letter Celia Richardson received around a month after Susana was arrested. In it, Susana stated that she accompanied Hilario to the Wamsleys' home—while both were high—and killed the Wamsleys. Further, Susana stated that Chelsea was *not* involved. "She was writing to Chelsea's mom because she felt bad," said St. John. "She's apologizing to [Chelsea's] mom and saying that Chelsea will be free soon." Although Susana testified that she never wrote the letter, the defense attorneys maintained that she did write it. As their handwriting expert testified, they believed "overwhelmingly" that the letter was written by Susana.

Chelsea's defense team felt that witnesses Hydrick and Norton, cellmates of Chelsea's, should not have been credited with telling the truth. St. John and Barlow pointed out that both women made deals to lessen their own sentences in exchange for their testimony. On the other hand, said St. John, "We put on four or five [former cellmates] who said that Chelsea never talked about her case."

Furthermore, St. John stated, Celia Richardson and her son James testified that they didn't hear anyone enter or exit their home on the night of the murder. "These are not people who get into trouble," stated St. John.

When asked how Chelsea felt about the sentence, St. John stated, "She was beyond upset. She's twenty-one years old, and she's never been arrested in her life, and now she's sentenced to death."

And this is what Chelsea would be facing. A lethal injection consists of a combination of three drugs: sodium thiopental, to sedate the person; pancuronium bromide, to relax muscles and collapse the diaphragm and lungs; and potassium chloride, to stop the heartbeat. It usually takes about seven minutes for the person to die once the injection has been given. The cost for drugs for each execution: $86.08.

When Chelsea Lea Richardson was received onto death row, her profile appeared on the Texas Department of Criminal Justice website, along with her photograph:

TDCJ Number: 999499
Date of Birth: 3/26/84
Date Received: 8/10/2005
Age When Received: 21
Education Level (highest grade completed): 12
Date of Offense: 12/11/2003

Age at Time of Offense: 19
County: Tarrant
Race: White
Gender: Female
Hair Color: Blonde
Height: 5' 6"
Weight: 172
Eye Color: Blue
Native County: Tarrant
Native State: Texas
Prior Occupation: Laborer
Prior Prison Record: None
Summary of Incident: On 12/11/2003 in Tarrant County, Texas, Richardson and three co-defendants entered the residence of a 46-year-old white male and a 46-year-old white female. Richardson and co-defendants fatally shot and stabbed both victims.
Co-defendants: Andrew W. Wamsley, Hilario Cardenas, Susana Toledano
Race and Gender of Victim[s]: White Male & White Female

Now, the trial for the first of the four people indicted for the murders of Suzy and Rick Wamsley was over. Next, Andrew Wamsley would go on trial. Would he, too, be convicted of capital murder? And, if so, would he, also, be sentenced to death by lethal injection?

Andrew would not learn his fate until March 9, 2006—ten months after Chelsea's death sentence. Meanwhile, he would wait in a jail cell, ever more fearful that he would receive the same sentence as Chelsea.

Chapter Twenty-six

On September 21, 2005, four months after Chelsea Richardson was sentenced to death, an article in the *Fort Worth Star-Telegram* read, "Suspect can't get a fair trial, lawyers say." The story went on to report that Andrew Wamsley's attorneys felt that pretrial publicity about their client's case had made it impossible for an unbiased jury to be selected in Tarrant County.

On September 22, 2005, during a hearing before Judge Young, the defense formally asked for a change of venue, citing television accounts aired on WFAA, CBS 11, KDFW Fox 4, KDAF-WB33, and KXAS, the NBC affiliate. Videos from the stations were given to the judge to help him determine whether or not the media exposure warranted a change.

After reviewing the tapes, the judge stated that he did not feel the publicity alone warranted a change of venue. However, he continued, he wanted to wait to see if a jury could be selected—acceptable to both the defense team and the prosecution—before making his final decision.

On January 12, 150 prospective jurors were brought before Judge Young. The judge told the assembled group that they could be selected as jurors in a case where the alleged offense was capital murder. He then went over the qualifications they would need to serve as jurors. A juror must be at least eighteen years of age, be a citizen of Texas and of Tarrant County, be qualified to vote in Tarrant County, be of sound mind and good moral character, be able to read and write, not have served as a juror for six days in the preceding three months in county court or the preceding six months in district court, not have been convicted of theft or any felony, and not be under indictment or other legal accusation for misdemeanor or felony theft or any other felony.

In a capital case, he told the prospective jurors, the law required that where the state is seeking the death penalty, the jurors must be examined individually outside the presence of all other jurors. He continued, "Each of you will be given a date and time to return for that questioning." The process would begin on January 17, he said, and continue through February 24, 2006. After twelve jurors and two alternates had been chosen, the case would begin on February 27. The judge estimated that the case would take one to two weeks.

At the end of this recitation, the judge dismissed the panel of prospective jurors and advised them to return for examination on the date they would be assigned.

Several weeks later, after the jury pool had been extensively questioned, Judge Young made his decision on the defense's change of venue motion. He stated, "We have a large pool to choose from, so I formally deny the motion." Despite heavy coverage of the case in the local media, it was his opinion that a Tarrant County jury was capable of hearing the case without partiality or prejudice.

On February 27, 2006, the trial of Andrew Wamsley began. For some courtroom watchers, his trial promised to be even more fascinating than Chelsea's. After all, here was a young man from an upper-middle-class home being tried for capital murder in the deaths of his *own* parents. It doesn't get much darker than that.

Michael D. Parrish and Catherine Page Simpson were once again the attorneys for the state. Larry Moore and David A. Pearson IV were representing the defendant. According to savvy Tarrant County courtroom watchers, Andrew was lucky to have two such capable and outstanding lawyers representing him.

Moore represented Wamsley at the plea hearing. After graduating from Texas Law School, he had been in practice for over two decades, having tried more than seventy-five murder cases. Most of his work was devoted to murder and capital murder cases.

Pearson, a 1990 graduate of Baylor University School of Law, had handled over twenty-five hundred criminal cases, including death penalty cases, and over 150 criminal appeals, including death penalty appeals. In his appellate practice, he successfully reversed convictions and sentences out of several different courts and counties.

The two men couldn't be more unlike physically. Moore was over six feet tall and weighed in the low three hundreds. Pearson was around five feet four inches and weighed a slight 130. Moore preferred dark blue or gray suits unless he was directly addressing the jury. Then, he favored brown or beige. He always wore a white button-down shirt and a "power" tie, with a lot of reds or maroons, and regimental stripes. Moore preferred oxblood dress shoes and matched his socks to the color of his suit. With white hair at his temples and "Paul Newman" blue eyes, he was an unforgettable presence in the courtroom. Pearson wore conservative suits along with dress black or brown cowboy boots. With brown moderately graying hair, blue eyes, and glasses, he looked nothing if not genuine and earnest. A person might gratefully put his or her life in his hands.

Moore believed that it was important to dress in the manner in which most people expect lawyers to dress so that they can match jurors' expectations when they come to court. He found that it helped him establish credibility with the jury more quickly. He felt that it was more difficult for the jury to accept and trust a lawyer if his or her manner of dress was unorthodox or distracting. "I want the jury to concentrate on what I am saying, and not on what I am wearing."

Now twenty-one years old, Andrew cut a smart figure in the courtroom. Six feet tall, around 165 pounds—he had lost some seventy pounds in prison—with glasses and brown hair and eyes, he wore a smart-looking navy blue suit with gold plastic buttons, a light blue shirt, a striped tie, and brown shoes. He hardly looked like the kind of person the news had portrayed him to be: a heartless son; a cold-blooded murderer; and the mastermind behind the killing of his parents.

The jury was composed of eight men and four women, plus two alternates, one male and one female. The trial began with Parrish reading aloud the indictment, in which the defendant, Andrew Wamsley, was charged with intentionally causing the deaths of Suzanna and Rick Wamsley.

Asked how he pleaded, Andrew, standing with shoulders bent, stated softly, "Not guilty."

After Andrew took his seat, Simpson rose and began the prosecution's opening argument with a bang. "This case is about the ultimate betrayal," she said forcefully. "It's about the betrayal of trust and the sanctity of one's home."

Simpson reviewed the details of the case, emphasizing what for her was the most important element: Andrew; his girlfriend, Chelsea; her friend Susana; and IHOP manager Hilario Cardenas attempted to kill Andrew's parents not once, not twice, but several times—for a $1 million life insurance policy and money connected to the Wamsley estate—until they finally succeeded in murdering both Suzy and Rick Wamsley. After describing each murder attempt, Simpson closed her remarks by standing directly in front of the jurors, looking intently at each, and stating, "At the end of all the evidence, I will stand back up here before you and ask you to find the defendant guilty of the capital murder of his parents, Rick and Suzy Wamsley. Thank you."

Simpson took her seat, and it was then the defense team's turn. Larry Moore stood up, faced the jury, and said, "Surprisingly, I agree with the prosecution. Yes, this case is about the ultimate betrayal. But," he added, "the ultimate betrayer was Susana Toledano."

As he moved around the room, Moore stated, in his customary soft yet confident tone, that they would hear from Susana Toledano, but, he added, she should not be believed. She changed her story several times, each time accusing a different person of the crime, until finally—after her DNA was identified on the hairs found in Rick Wamsley's hand— she admitted that *she* had committed murders, that she alone pulled the trigger.

According to Moore, it was three months after Susana gave her first statement that she implicated Andrew and Chelsea— three long months. "And why did it take her so long?" Moore wondered aloud. He suggested an answer. When Susana realized that she was facing a possible death sentence, she decided to give a statement to the district attorney—a statement implicating Andrew. But, Moore added forcefully, "her statement was not true. There is not one bit of DNA of Andrew's at the scene. No blood evidence either. Not a lick to tie Andrew Wamsley to the death of Rick and Suzy Wamsley." Moore remarked that to find Andrew Wamsley guilty because of the testimony of "somebody who has been bought and paid for" is not only blatantly ridiculous, but a travesty that would have dire consequences. "You don't come into a court and ask a jury to find somebody guilty of capital murder on the testimony of a liar. You don't do that."

With that strong admonition, Moore took his seat and the trial got underway.

Several witnesses were called to the stand that day, including Lewis Wamsley; Jeff Ambreit, Daniel Sherwin, and Mark Kelly of the Mansfield Police Department; and forensic specialist Max Courtney. The officers and specialists recalled the day of the murder and their role in the investigation, while Lewis Wamsley reminisced about the tenacious personality of his murdered son. All the information the witnesses presented was consistent with what they had said at Chelsea's trial. Of course, one significant difference was that, in this trial, Lewis Wamsley was testifying against his own grandson.

During the entire court session, which lasted from 9 a.m. until 5:45 p.m., Andrew Wamsley sat with eyes downcast, pencil in hand and a pad of paper in front of him. As he listened to the witnesses, he took voluminous notes. When Lewis came to the stand, Andrew looked at him, but Lewis did not look back. Wearing tan slacks, black turtleneck and a dark blue sports jacket, the dignified older gentleman cut a sympathetic figure. What Andrew was thinking was anybody's guess, but it couldn't be far from his mind that in this jury's hands, in the hands of these twelve strangers, rested the answer to whether he would live or die. The stakes didn't get any higher than that.

Chapter Twenty-seven

On the second day of the trial, February 28, Susana Toledano was called to the stand. Without wasting a second, Parrish walked right up to her and said, "Are you one of the folks that went in and murdered Rick and Suzy Wamsley . . . in the early morning hours of December the eleventh of two oh oh three?"

"Yes," Susana replied softly.

"Who was with you?"

"Andrew and Chelsea."

He asked her to "tell the jury what offer we have made to you for your testimony in this trial."

"A life sentence in prison," Susana replied, nearly breaking down in tears.

Seeing that Susana was extremely upset, Parrish said, "Okay. Just calm down." He gave her a moment to collect herself. Then he asked, "And for getting a life sentence in prison, what do you have to do?"

"Serve thirty years," she replied.

"And the deal I made with you," stated Parrish, "is that you're going down for just murder, not capital murder."

"Correct," replied Susana.

Parrish reminded her that if she did not tell the truth today, she would still face the death penalty. Susana stated that she was aware of that.

When asked if Andrew Wamsley ever said why he wanted to kill his parents, Susana replied, "To get insurance money."

Parrish continued, "And when was the first time you ever shot a gun?"

"At the pond . . . it's in Burleson. And it was me, Chelsea, and Andrew," Susana replied.

"And how did y'all get there?" asked Parrish.

"With the Mustang. Andrew's."

"Did the defendant, Andrew Wamsley, shoot the gun?"

"Yes."

Parrish then asked Susana about shooting at the Jeep. "So, how did this plan work out? What was the final result of the plan?"

"He [Andrew] was going to drive and I was going to shoot the car."

"And did that happen?"

"Yes," Susana stated.

Parrish went on to ask Susana what took place after she was not successful at shooting the Jeep. Susana said that Chelsea "started bitching me out and [Andrew] was chiming in."

Parrish then asked, "Two weeks later, did you, Andrew, and Chelsea go to Andrew's house?"

"Yes."

"Where did you go in the house?"

"We went straight to Andrew's room."

"And all three of you back there?" asked Parrish.

"No. It was me and Andrew in his bedroom, and I don't know where Chelsea was at," replied Susana.

"And who's got the gun?"

"Me."

"And why you?"

"Because I was the one that messed up with the shooting of the car and I had missed."

"And who was telling you this?" asked Parrish.

"Both Chelsea and Andrew," stated Susana.

"While you've got the gun and you're in Andrew's room, what is Andrew saying to you?"

"Just coaching me, telling me to take my time, that there's no rush in doing this, that basically the sooner we do it, the sooner we get this done and go home."

"And what was Andrew's mood after you told him you just couldn't go through it?"

"He was just mad and really didn't talk to me," said Susana.

Moving ahead in time, Parrish asked, "Who drove over there the night you did the murders?"

"Andrew."

"And who was in the right front seat?"

"Chelsea."

"Who had the gun?"

"I did."

After Parrish went over the details of Chelsea pushing Susana into the living room, where she shot Suzy Wamsley, and how she then went into the bedroom to shoot the dad and ended up wrestling with him, Parrish asked, "How did you get free from him?"

"Andrew helped me grab a hold of him and we both came up in the living room, wrestling."

"You're talking about the defendant, Andrew Wamsley?" asked Parrish.

"Yes," said Susana.

"At this point, where was the gun?"

"I had lost it at first when we went down. Then somehow Andrew got a hold of it and then gave it to me."

"I want to ask you this question," said Parrish. "Between Andrew and Chelsea, do you know who shot Rick Wamsley in the back?"

"No."

"Between Andrew and Chelsea do you know who stabbed Rick Wamsley all in the front?"

"No," replied Susana.

When asked how the knives came into play, Susana said that Chelsea brought in some knives and Andrew had a knife. Susana said that at that time, Rick was "sitting down Indian style kind of" by the front door, "which is when he asked 'Why?' and Chelsea said, 'Because I'm pregnant,'" and then she told him to "shut up."

"What did Rick do?" asked Parrish.

"He said he could help," stated Susana. Then, she continued, "That's when me and her switched from me having the gun to her having the gun and me having the knife."

"And Andrew still had his knife?" asked Parrish.

"Right."

Susana said she then went to stab the mom, following the orders given to her by Chelsea. She admitted she didn't know at the time that the mom was already dead. Susana stated that when she left the front door area to go to the living room, Rick was sitting up. When she came back, he was lying facedown. It was then, she stated, that she stabbed him in the back.

After pausing for a moment, Parrish went back to the beginning of the rampage. "What did you do after Chelsea pushed you into the living room, where Suzy Wamsley was sleeping?"

"I shot her in the head," replied Susana.

"Why?"

"I don't know."

"How could they get you to do this?"

"I can't actually answer that," replied Susana.

"Have you ever been in trouble before?" asked Parrish.

"No," said Susana.

"Ever been arrested before?"

"No."

"Why did you do it?"

"I don't know."

"Tell them what you were supposed to get out of it," said Parrish.

"I was supposed to go to school, not have to work. They were going to fix up my Mustang, and I was going to switch Mustangs with Andrew, and then I was going to just be at the house and chill."

Parrish asked her how old she was when she committed the murders.

"Nineteen."

"And how old are you now?"

"Twenty-one."

Parrish asked her if jail had been a good thing for her.

"I have realized so many things go on in the world that I wasn't aware of."

"Do you have anything you want to say to the Wamsley family?" he asked.

"Yes. I would like to say I'm sorry. There's nothing I can really do to go back and change things. I wish I could go back and change everything from the beginning, none of this would ever have happened. I wouldn't be here in front of y'all, you wouldn't have lost two of your loved ones, and everything would have been just fine. I'm sorry."

Parrish hoped he had successfully shown that Andrew was in on the plans from the beginning and was a participant—at the very least, by driving the car—and at the most, by possibly shooting or knifing his own father. After all, if Susana admitted to shooting the mother and shooting at the father, *if* she had shot or knifed the father in the back, why wouldn't she admit to that, too?

On cross-examination, Moore tried again, as he did in his opening statement, to discredit Susana. He stood right next to the witness box, so the jury would be looking directly at the witness and at him. He believed that "invading the witness space," especially when he was trying to impeach the witness, was a necessary tactic. It made the witness uneasy and thus helped him in his cross-examination. Moore began, and immediately got Susana to admit that she lied to the grand jury when she said she didn't know who had done the

killings. "So all your testimony on February the seventeenth
of 2004 before the Tarrant County grand jury was a lie?"

"Yes."

Then, he brought up the fact that when Susana was arrested in Illinois, the officers had told her they had evidence
against her and that she "couldn't get out of it and that they
knew it was [her]." Still, she lied, said Moore, who then
showed Susana the copy of the statement she had given the
police in Illinois. After looking it over, Susana stated that yes,
that was the statement she had written. The statement, Moore
said, was taken on April 5, 2004, at 10:12 p.m., six hours after
she was arrested and interrogated in Illinois. Moore read the
statement aloud:

> My name is Susana Toledano. I'm 19 years old and my
> date of birth is 9/28/84. I presently reside at 7417 Lea
> Place, Fort Worth, Texas, 76140. . . .
>
> I have twelve years of education, and I do read,
> write, and understand the English language. I was
> picked up by Hilario to get something to eat but didn't
> know where. We were at the [Wamsley] house and he
> had gotten out of the car, walked to the house, and the
> garage door was open. We walked in and I somewhat
> followed him in. But it was dark except for the front
> light of the garage door. . . .
>
> I heard a gunshot, backed up, and had bumped the
> table. I quickly turned around, bumped into it again,
> and quickly went towards the truck. Got in real quick
> and panicked until he came back, got in and all I heard
> was him telling, don't tell no one, not Chelsea, not An-
> drew, about anything. I just agreed, with stuttering
> and confusion. I kind of just panicked, couldn't say
> anything.
>
> The officer asked me when I got my hair pulled and
> I told him twice. One by him brushing with his hand

when I asked him about how it was, and by another in the dark by the table. I was panicking when I had bumped into the table and heard two more shots on my way out after the first one. I couldn't do anything because I was afraid of him doing something to me.

I have read each page of this statement consisting of three pages . . . And I certify that the facts contained herein are true and correct. Taken at the Addison, Illinois PD on the fifth day of April of 2004 at 22:30 hours ending time. Signed: Susana Toledano.

After reading the confession aloud to the court, Moore asked Susana, "When you gave the statement in Addison, you told them that basically you and Hilario were the ones that went out to the house and committed the crime, is that right?"

"Yes."

"And now you're indicating to the jury that's not true."

"Correct," stated Susana.

When asked why she told the police that she and Hilario committed the murders, Susana responded, "Because I was trying to protect Chelsea."

"Because Chelsea meant that much to you?" Moore asked.

"Yes," said Susana softly, clearly holding back tears.

"You pretty well knew that you were cooked at that point, didn't you?"

"Yes."

"Why did you decide to put Hilario in the deal?"

"Because he was a part of the plan from the beginning and I thought in my head that he was guilty as much as I was," Susana replied.

"Now, when you were originally charged in this case, you were charged with the offense of capital murder, is that right?" asked Moore.

"Yes," replied Susana.

Moore showed her the plea agreement she signed, in which

she was offered life for the offense of murder—*not* capital murder—and would not face the death penalty if she gave testimony against Chelsea and Andrew.

Susana admitted that she made an arrangement to accept the plea-bargain agreement sometime in June 2004, after the prosecuting attorneys told her the state had linked her DNA to the murder. She said they told her she could take the plea deal or they would take her case to trial. "And that's when I decided to take it," she added.

As part of the agreement, Susana said, she was required to make a "statement to the district attorney's office at that point regarding what had happened." She said she actually made that statement in the DA's office in mid-July 2004. In it, she said, she was supposed to describe what happened from beginning to end, and Celeste Rogers, an investigator for the DA's office, would type it.

"Did you [tell the truth]?"

"Yes," Susana stated.

Recounting what she said in that statement, which she swore was the truth, Susana said that on the day of the murders, she was picked up from work, went to Chelsea's house, changed her clothes, went to Putt-Putt golf, and then went to the Wamsley house. She wore her Nike black sweater with a black tank top, a pair of jeans, and Nike shoes with an arrow pattern on the bottom. She said that she shot both Suzy and Rick and then stabbed Suzy. She said she never saw Chelsea or Andrew shoot the gun. She said she never saw Andrew or Chelsea stab or shoot anyone. As far as she knew, "the only person that that did any shooting was [me]."

To continue to try to cast doubt on Susana, Moore asked her what she did after the murder. Susana stated that she went back to the Richardson house, but then later, she and Andrew returned to the Wamsley home to get a CD and jeans.

"Did you tell that to Rogers [in the statement] in 2004?"

"No."

"Did you tell Rogers about Chelsea using your cell phone [to call Jeremy Lavender]?"

"No."

After Moore felt satisfied that he had gotten Susana to admit to withholding information and outright lying, he thanked her for her testimony and passed the witness.

Parrish then asked Susana if she liked remembering the events of November and December 2003. She said no, she tried to block them out. Parrish asked if she had a "clear memory of this or some of it, you're guessing?"

"I don't have a clear memory of it," replied Susana.

Parrish then asked again if she knew who had stabbed and shot Rick Wamsley. She said, "To this day, I do not know who shot Rick in the back," nor did she know who stabbed Rick in the front.

Parrish hoped the jurors would see that it *could have been* Andrew who killed his father.

Several more witnesses were called by the prosecution that day, including the Wamsleys' neighbor Keith Cowand and Jeremy Lavender. The state drew out much of the same testimony the two had presented during Chelsea's trial. Specifically, Parrish got Jeremy to say he was speaking to Chelsea at approximately 3:42 a.m. on December 11, 2003, and in a series of phone calls that followed.

"And what did she want?" asked Parrish.

"Asked me if I could be an alibi for her."

Jeremy said that Chelsea told him she had gotten into some trouble, but she wouldn't offer any other details.

"What story did Chelsea want you to tell?" asked Parrish.

"She asked me if I could go out to Putt-Putt to meet them and I told her no, I didn't have any gas to go out there. And then she said, well, all right, we'll come over there. And they're like if anybody says that we came over, tell them yes."

"And when you say *we* came over there, who was she saying that *we* should be?" asked Parrish.

"Her, Andrew, and Susana," replied Jeremy.

"And was that the truth or was it a lie?"

"That was a lie."

Jeremy admitted that he lied in front of the Tarrant County grand jury on February 23, 2004—even though he had sworn to tell the truth—by telling the story that Chelsea wanted him to tell. Jeremy said he did, however, tell the truth to the grand jury on May 19, 2004, after Parrish showed him his phone records from that night. Jeremy stated that on December 11, Chelsea called not only his cell phone many times, but also his landline. Parrish then passed the witness.

Defense attorney David Pearson began his cross-examination in a polite, measured, and reserved way. He believed that making logical, credible points kept the jury's attention and that was just what he planned to do. Influenced by years of listening to preachers in church, where the minister never raised his voice, Pearson believed that his message, not his personality, should be what was compelling. His first job, he felt, was to raise new doubts about Andrew's involvement.

"Mr. Lavender, do you mind if I call you Jeremy?" he asked.

"Go ahead."

"On the night of the murder, you got a call from Chelsea Richardson?"

"Yes," Jeremy replied.

"You got about five or six calls, right?"

"Yes."

"And you're telling us that the only person you talked to was Chelsea Richardson, right?" asked Pearson.

"Yes," responded Jeremy.

Pearson then went on to try to portray Chelsea as a person who could not be trusted. He asked Jeremy, "When were Chelsea and you boyfriend and girlfriend?"

Jeremy replied, "Until she went away."

"When she came back, was she your girlfriend again?"

"No."

"Did she start hanging out with Andrew Wamsley?"

"Yes."

A little later in the testimony, in an effort to cast doubt on the idea that Andrew was with Chelsea on the night of the murder, Pearson asked Jeremy, "Andrew Wamsley didn't talk to you on the phone about an alibi?"

"Right."

"And before [Chelsea] was arrested, a month after this night that she called you, were you over there at her house?"

"Yes."

"And in front of Andrew, did Chelsea say anything else about an alibi?"

"No, she did not."

"Jeremy, you can't look at the jury and tell them you know anything about where Andrew was on the night that those records show that Chelsea called you, right?"

"Right."

"You don't even know if he was with Chelsea, right?"

"No, I do not. I have no idea."

"And that's the truth?" asked Pearson.

"Yes," replied Jeremy.

"Jeremy, what you told the grand jury in May of 2004 was that Chelsea said to you that she got into trouble, right?"

"Right."

"She just said it was her in some trouble?" asked Pearson.

"Right," responded Jeremy. "She had said, I got into some kind of trouble. What kind of trouble did you get into? I just got into some trouble. I need you to be an alibi. At that time, I was stupid enough to say yes because I didn't know what she did."

"And that's how she left it, it was *her* problem, the trouble that *she* was in, would you be an alibi for *her*?"

"Right."

And that's what you told the grand jury the second time when you had learned to not lie to the grand jury?" asked Pearson.

"The second time, I told them the truth," said Jeremy definitively.

Believing he had planted a seed of doubt as to Andrew's involvement, Pearson said politely, "All right. Thank you, Jeremy. Pass the witness."

"Nothing further," stated Parrish.

As the judge closed the proceedings for the day, spectators reflected on something slightly odd about Andrew Wamsley's demeanor. During this, the second day of the trial, Andrew continued to stare down at the table, rarely looking up to see the face of anyone testifying either in his favor or against him, or to scan the courtroom to see who, if anyone, had come to support him. Some in the courtroom believed that he felt so guilty that he simply couldn't look any of his previous friends and family in the eyes. Others felt that he was so overcome with sadness at his parents' deaths that he could barely hold his head up.

Andrew later stated that his lawyers had advised him not to make eye contact with anyone in the courtroom.

Chapter Twenty-eight

When court reconvened on March 1, ten witnesses were called to testify, including Ruth Brustrom, Sarah Wamsley, Mansfield police detective Mark Malcom, deputy medical examiner Gary Sisler, trace analyst Patricia Eddings, and FBI agent Ann-Margaret Hinkle. They each provided details similar to those they offered during Chelsea's trial.

When Ruth Brustrom was on the stand, she told the jury about the times Chelsea, Susana, and Andrew came to her house to practice shooting a gun into her pond. When Pearson cross-examined her, he reminded her that in May 2005, when she was asked about Chelsea in terms of her relationship with Andrew, "You said that if there was a dominant one, it was Chelsea, is that right?"

"Yes."

"And you were telling the truth, obviously, that day?"

"Yes."

As he cross-examined each witness, Pearson was slowly drawing a picture that Chelsea was the mastermind behind this bloody operation. Maybe Andrew had nothing to do with it. And if he did, maybe he was just Chelsea's pawn.

Detective Malcom was called next. He stated that he was present during the search of Ruth Brustrom's pond and had participated in searching the Wamsley house on December 11 and 12. He said he was also present when Andrew was brought into custody at the Mansfield Police Department. In response to defense attorney Moore's question about how Andrew acted, he stated, "Andrew was always cooperative."

Sarah Wamsley followed Hinkle on the stand. After giving details about her seven-year-old daughter's past close relationship with her grandparents, she was asked about the day the Wamsley family Jeep was shot at. She recalled her surprise when she heard a "big old boom," and shortly after that, she said, she remembered her mother using her father's cell phone to call Andrew. Sarah stated that her mother was extremely upset. "She actually said the F word, which is something she never or rarely did."

When asked by Simpson who she had originally suspected might have shot at the Jeep, Sarah stated that she felt it was her ex-boyfriend, Todd Cleveland. Sarah admitted that she was involved in a rancorous custody battle at that time and her parents were helping her financially.

Sarah gave information about being a patient at a mental hospital and about her being a "wild child" from the age of thirteen. She stated that her parents were supportive of her most of the time, in spite of her wild ways. Sarah concluded her testimony by giving the jury information about the day after the murders, when she and Andrew were both called down to the police station—and how Andrew told her that the police would probably find the blood of both their parents in his car.

On cross-examination by Pearson, Sarah stated that on December 12, 2003, she voluntarily went to the Mansfield Police Department after finding out about her parents' murders. She said Andrew went there voluntarily, also. She reiterated that at that time, she believed Cleveland might have some involvement in the murders because the night before the Jeep incident, she had filed a CPS report on him because she suspected that while her daughter was in his care, "she had been harmed or endangered in some way."

Pearson asked her if she understood that "you do stand to inherit [your parents'] estate and if you are the sole beneficiary [and] you would benefit more than you otherwise might, correct?"

"Correct."

Sarah admitted that her parents told her a few months before they died that the "money that they were giving [her] for the legal fees and the custody fight, it was like [her] money anyway because it was coming out of [her] inheritance."

"And the custody battle continued for several years, is that correct?" asked Pearson.

"Correct."

"And the legal fees that you incurred were pretty substantial?"

"Yes," admitted Sarah.

"And, now since your parents have died, you have received disbursements of their estate, right?"

"Correct."

"And you have been able to purchase a house . . . and a new pickup?"

"Yes."

Hoping to at least have hinted that Sarah might have had more interest in the money than had come to light before, Pearson passed the witness.

To discredit Pearson, Simpson asked, "All the money in the world, would you just give it back if you could have your parents back?"

"Even more, yeah," replied Sarah in tears.

Throughout Sarah's testimony, Andrew looked directly at her. Occasionally, Sarah would glance his way, and according to Andrew many months after the trial, she had a slight smile on her face every time she looked at him. Exactly what that meant was anyone's guess—including Andrew's. When asked a year later about Sarah's testimony, Andrew said he was surprised she got away with some of the things she said. He felt that a lot of what she said was

"B.S." Obviously, bad blood existed between them, as it had from their teen years.

The last witness of the day was William Wesley Bates. When he was called to the stand, he stated that he was currently serving time in Tarrant County Jail and admitted to having a criminal history, including delivery of marijuana; burglary; and possession of a controlled substance, among other offenses.

In response to Simpson's question as to how he knew Andrew, Bates said he met Andrew in jail in 2005. "I came in contact with Andrew running card games. I was running blackjack and stuff like that. Poker too." After that, Bates said, the two began to talk. In particular, stated Bates, Andrew asked him "to sneak some nitroglycerine up to the thirteenth floor and have one of my friends give it to Susana and put it in her food."

Simpson asked how it would be possible to sneak stuff into the jail.

Bates replied that he had a good friend who worked in the commissary and that he "could have probably gotten it done." However, Bates added, Andrew told him that he already had the nitroglycerine. Bates asked Andrew what it was supposed to do to the person who consumed it. According to Bates, Andrew replied, "If it was put in the food and if she ate it, it could bust her heart if she ate enough of it."

"Do you know why Andrew wanted this person, Susana, harmed?" asked Simpson.

Bates said that Andrew told him that the only thing the prosecutors had on him was this witness Susana "and if for some reason she didn't show up in court, they couldn't find him guilty." Bates said he then contacted "y'all [the state] because my heart went out for the parents, really." He said he had only another month and a half before he would have been released when he wrote the letter to the state.

When asked if he was given a deal in return for his telling

the story, Bates said no. He stated that he only came forward because Andrew's case had to do with killing parents. He said he never "gave up information" before and "wouldn't tell on you unless you killed your parents." Bates stated that he sent the letter and underlined the name Susana Toledano, writing that he sincerely hoped to hear from the DA and promised that he would testify against Andrew in court.

After Simpson passed the witness to the defense team, Pearson tried to discredit him.

Bates said he was in prison for a misdemeanor, but Pearson got him to admit that it was actually enhanced to a felony after he pled guilty to a felony charge. Asked about how he conducted himself in jail, Bates boasted that he was known in the jail as being very good at cards. "I am the best in cards," he said, adding that Andrew wanted to work for him as a blackjack dealer. He stated that he could make a hundred dollars a day while in jail playing cards and by gambling. He said he was also a good card cheat. "[I] can deal off the bottom of the deck better than anybody else can deal off the top of the deck."

As Bates was giving his testimony, Pearson walked back and forth in front of the jurors and looked at them, as if to say, *Are you going to believe this guy? Give me a break!*

Chapter Twenty-nine

On March 2, 2006, several forensic witnesses were called to testify for the prosecution.

Dr. Daniel J. Konzelmann was the first witness. He stated that he had performed the autopsy on Rick Wamsley. He then detailed all the wounds he found on the body, including two gunshot wounds, one "of the back." He stated that the cause of death was a dual one: "multiple gunshot wounds and sharp-force wounds."

Carolyn Van Winkle, specialist in the DNA section of the Tarrant County Medical Examiner's office, was sworn in next. She told the jurors that the hairs she received—originally discovered on Rick Wamsley's left hand—matched the DNA profile of Susana Toledano.

Ron Van Fleet, firearms and toolmark examiner for the Fort Worth Police Department crime laboratory, also took the stand. He stated that he examined seven bullets in all—from the Wamsleys' dining room; from the headboard in their master bedroom; from the soffit, or attic area, in their master bedroom; from Suzanna Wamsley's body; from Rick Wamsley's autopsy; from the Wamsley family Jeep; and from Ruth Brustrom's pond, where Andrew, Susana, and Chelsea had practiced shooting. He concluded that all of the bullets were fired from the same gun, a .38 caliber.

After Van Fleet, the state rested.

The state felt they had presented a strong case against

Andrew. They had clearly established that Andrew drove the Mustang during three attempts at murdering the Wamsleys. It had also been established that the bullet fired at the Jeep matched the bullets that killed the Wamsleys. Brustrom had testified that the three of them—Andrew, Chelsea, and Susana—had come to her house to practice shooting a gun into her pond. Susana had admitted to shooting Suzy in the head and to shooting Rick in the front, but she didn't admit to shooting Rick in the back or stabbing him in the front. Surely someone else had done that, and why couldn't that have been Andrew?

It was now the defense's turn to bring in witnesses to cast doubt on Andrew's involvement in the murders. To that end, they planned to show that Andrew might not even have been at the Wamsleys' on the night of the murders and that Hilario and Susana might alone have done the murders—and certainly not Andrew.

The first witness for the defense was James Richardson. He stated that he first met Andrew at Putt-Putt golf and that he knew him for six months before Chelsea met him. James said that Andrew worked at Putt-Putt and he, James, went there a lot.

Pearson asked him about Wednesday, December 10, 2003. James stated he went to one of his favorite hangouts, More Than Cards, after work at Jack in the Box. When More Than Cards closed at around 6:30 p.m., he headed over to the Burger Box "right there in the same parking lot." He stated he hung out there until 9 p.m. and then went home to sleep. He said he arrived home at 9:30 p.m. and didn't think anyone else was there. He went to bed around 10:30 p.m.

When asked about what he observed on December 11, he stated he got up and went to work, but he didn't see anyone at home. He said he "threw on clothes and ran." He said he got off work at around 5 p.m. and went home. Again, no one was there. Later that evening, around midnight, his sister and

Andrew came in. Chelsea, he said, had been really excited. She had been to Putt-Putt and was given a stereo with redemptions. Redemptions, he stated, "are while you play the games for a while, you collect tickets, and then you turn them in at the redemption counter for various prizes." He said he went to bed at around 1 a.m. and that Chelsea and Andrew were still there.

Celia Richardson—Chelsea's mother—was called next. She stated that during the first part of 2003, Andrew would come over with some friends of James's and play video games. She got to know Andrew better as the year went on "when some of the nights [I] didn't work, he would be there."

On December 10, 2003, Celia recalled that she stayed home to study for an accounting final. Later in the day, she took her daughter Brenna to her job, and then she went to take the test. Afterward, when she arrived at home around 8 p.m., Andrew and Chelsea asked her if she wanted to go out for waffles. She said she had to pick up Brenna at ten, so she couldn't.

At around 12:30 a.m., in the early morning of December 11, Celia recounted that Chelsea came into her bedroom to say goodnight. After she went to bed, Celia stated that she didn't hear anyone leave the house, nor did she hear water running in the bathtub, in the shower, or in the washing machine.

Celia testified that she woke up before 6 a.m. and turned off the outside light, signaling the people in her carpool to stop and pick her up. Passing through the living room, she saw a head of blond hair peeking out from under the covers where her daughter was sleeping on the floor, so she knew Chelsea was home. At 6:40 a.m., after getting dressed, she went back into the living room and saw Chelsea and Andrew watching TV. She thought Susana was probably in a bedroom getting dressed. Once in the carpool, her friends commented that Andrew's car was still there, and they were surprised because they thought the kids were going camping. Celia told them that they had decided not to go, due to the weather.

On the night of December 11, after she came home from her regular job at 5 p.m., she changed. Before 6 p.m., Brenna picked her up and she went to work at her second job. At midnight, she got off. They got home at 12:30 a.m. Chelsea and Andrew were at the front door, and Chelsea said, "Mom, Mom, you've got to see my stereo." It was in the living room when Celia walked in. It was a triple CD player, with detachable speakers. Chelsea told her mother she had gotten it from redemptions at Putt-Putt.

Celia stated that she stayed up late that night playing solitaire on the computer because Friday was her day off. Friday morning, Celia testified, a friend of James's and the kids, Peter Nguyen, called, and as a result of what he said, she woke up James and "was waiting to hear if I needed to go" to the Mansfield Police Department. Andrew and Chelsea were already there.

At that point, Celia said, she called the school and asked if Susana could be dismissed early. She and James picked her up, and they all went down to the Mansfield Police Department. They got there around 1 p.m. and stayed until 3 p.m. At around three, Andrew came out and "everyone was going to the car, but Andrew said he wanted to go back in and check on his sister." Andrew told them the police had taken the keys to his Mustang, and he was really upset. Celia said she replied that he shouldn't worry. "Forget it," she had told him, and then they all left.

During the weeks after the murder, Celia stated, Andrew stayed at her house. In fact, she said, Andrew stayed there until he was arrested. She learned that Susana had been arrested on April 5, when someone at work told her. Two days or so later, Chelsea and Andrew were arrested. Later, she heard that Hilario had been arrested, also.

Celia admitted that she testified in front of the Tarrant County grand jury twice. After the second time, sometime in May 2004, she received a letter, which she recognized as coming from Susana [Exhibits 51 and 52: envelope and letter]. She knew the handwriting, she stated, because it was the same as that which was in the day planner and notebook that Susana had left at her house. When defense attorney Moore asked her who the letter was addressed to, she said, "Celia R." She said it had no return address on it. In the letter, Susana, or whoever actually wrote it, stated, "I have to say what Hilario tells me to. I just want to say I am very sorry to do this to Chelsea and Drew. They had nothing to do with [the murders]. . . ."

Moore asked, "What did you do with it?"

"I took it to Chelsea's attorney, who was Mike Maloney."

On cross-examination, Parrish again showed Celia the envelope and letter that Susana *supposedly* wrote from jail to Celia. Then he showed her the handwritten statement Susana made in Illinois and asked, "Does that look, I mean, do you want the jury to believe that the same person wrote both of these documents, correct?"

"Yeah. This looks like her handwriting," replied Celia.

Parrish suggested that anyone—including Chelsea—could have written that letter. "Isn't that correct?"

"Possibly, but it looks like Susana's," said Celia.

"Well, did Susana spell Chelsea's name right? Look in Defendant's 52 at the fourth line down. Isn't *Chelsea* misspelled in what you think is Susana's handwriting?"

"Yes."

"And let's look on down just for a minute at the signature on the bottom line. You want this jury to believe that Susana misspelled her own name, put an extra 's' in Susana? And I guess it's debatable whether there's an extra 'n' in there also, is that correct?" asked Parrish disdainfully.

"I suppose."

"Let's look at what's in evidence as Defendant's 53 [the handwritten confession Susana made in Illinois when she was arrested]. Do you see the way that Susana spelled *Chelsea* there, right about here?"

"Yes."

"She sure knows how to spell her name, doesn't she?"

"I guess, but I have spelled people's name wrong before and I know them. I mean you could say that."

"Say what?"

". . . I'm just saying that I spell people's names wrong when I'm in a hurry."

"Your opinion is that this is Susana's handwriting on Defendant's Exhibit No. 52?"

"Looks like it, in my opinion."

"If that were true, it would be good for your daughter, Chelsea, wouldn't it?"

"Possibly. Isn't it a little late? But possibly."

"Are you a handwriting expert?" asked Parrish belligerently.

"No."

"At the time this letter was written," stated Parrish, "Chelsea was in jail around a lot of other inmates, and she was trying to figure a way not to go to prison."

"Yeah. But that doesn't prove she did it or anybody else did it."

Parrish switched gears and stated, "You don't like me very much, do you?"

"Not really," replied Celia.

"I'm going to get right to the bottom line," said Parrish. "You went to bed on Wednesday the tenth of December, 2003, at about midnight, correct?"

"Midnight, twelve thirty."

"And you slept through the night and did not get up in the middle of the night, and you got up about six to six-thirty a.m., correct?"

"Six a.m., yes."

"Do you know where—You don't know where Andrew,

Chelsea, and Susana were at 3:23 a.m. on the eleventh, do you?"

"I guess not."

Changing the topic once again, Parrish said, "So you worked two jobs [then]?"

"Yes, sir."

"But Chelsea hadn't worked any?"

"No," replied Celia.

Parrish asked Celia to read aloud a statement she made in May 2005, in which she said, "Andrew, Susana, and Chelsea were at home" on the night of Wednesday, after her test. And in the morning, they, all three, were there, too, according to her statement in May 2005. "And you don't know where they were in between?"

"No, sir."

"However, in court today, you said you weren't sure [you] saw Susana in those times."

Celia conceded that was true.

If true, that would mean that Susana could have been up to no good, but Chelsea and Andrew were accounted for. Parrish was trying to get the jury to believe that Celia was setting up Susana as the possible murderer, but *not* Chelsea or Andrew.

After Celia Richardson's testimony, court was dismissed for the day.

Chapter Thirty

On the fifth day of the trial, March 3, 2006, handwriting expert Linda James was called to the stand. Asked by Moore about her qualifications, James gave a long list of credentials, including having been a forensic document examiner for fifteen years; having more than eight hundred study hours and more than two hundred hours of lab work; and having been apprenticed to two experienced examiners. Also, she stated, she had testified in more than sixty cases as an expert witness in the area of handwriting verification.

She stated that she examined Defendant's Exhibits Nos. 51, 52, 53, 54, and 55—which included the letter and envelope *supposedly* written by Susana; Susana's handwritten confession in Illinois; and a note and a day planner left at Celia's home after Susana was arrested. James stated that it was her conclusion that they were all written by the same person. Moore pressed her, pointing out that the signatures were different and that certain words were spelled one way in one exhibit and another way in another. But James continued to hold firm to the belief that although the spellings varied, the person who wrote the exhibits did not. In response to Moore's specific question about the letter Susana supposedly wrote from prison, James concluded that Susana absolutely *did* write the letter, which stated that Chelsea and Andrew had nothing to do with the murder, and that she, Susana, was the guilty one.

On cross, Parrish tried to discredit James. He said, "Ms. James, we've done this before, haven't we?"

"Yes, we have."

"We did it last May?"

"Yes."

"And I caught you flat-footed when I stood up there and cross-examined you. You didn't realize Chelsea was misspelled, did you?"

"No, sir, I did not."

"Yeah. That just floored you, didn't it?"

"It didn't floor me."

"Okay. But you had prepared all these charts and all these handouts and all of that, and you never caught that *Chelsea* was misspelled along with *Susana* in the questioned document, did you?"

"No. I was concentrating on what I did best, what I am supposed to do, and looking at the handwriting characteristics."

Parrish continued trying to cast doubt on James's expertise by saying she did a sloppy job and that her conclusion was not necessarily correct. He pointed out that she never had a peer review of her work and she never had an exemplar (a representative sample from which to make a comparison). He asked her if it bothered her—just a little bit—that the letter Susana supposedly wrote to Celia had both Chelsea's and Susana's names misspelled.

James said, "No, it didn't bother me. Basically, people do that."

"And," asked Parrish, "did it bother you just a little bit that this letter that allegedly confesses to capital murder misspells Chelsea and Susana?"

"It did not bother me, not even a bit," responded James.

Disgusted, Parrish said he had no more questions.

Following James's testimony, both the state and the defense rested, and the judge spoke directly to the jurors. "That's all the evidence that you will hear," he told them.

The judge told the attorneys that they could now make their final arguments.

Parrish began by saying, "If you help do the crime, you're guilty of the crime—the law of parties." (The law of parties states that a person is criminally responsible for an offense committed by the conduct of another if "acting with intent to promote or assist the commission of the offense he solicits, encourages, directs, aids or attempts to aid the other persons to commit the offense" or "if, in the attempt to carry out a conspiracy to commit one felony, another felony is committed by one of the conspirators, all conspirators are guilty of the felony actually committed, though having no intent to commit it, if the offense was committed in furtherance of the unlawful purpose and was one that should have been anticipated as a result of the carrying out of the conspiracy.")

Parrish then stated that the accomplice rule applied here (an accomplice is "any person connected with the crime charged as a party thereto and includes all persons who are connected with the crime by unlawful act or omission on their part, transpiring either before or during the time of the commission of the offense") and "Susana is an accomplice." But, he continued, "you cannot convict [Andrew] strictly on what Susana says. There must be other evidence that tends to connect him to the crime. And you have a bunch of it in this case."

He reminded the jury that because of Susana, the entire case was solved. Parrish stated, "I want to go back and talk about Susana for a moment in terms of the deal she got from us and how this case really got solved. Susana got subpoenaed to the grand jury and we swabbed the inside of her mouth with her consent. And that's the thing that started breaking this case down. And once we learned the entire facts of the case, I made a deal with her attorney, Mr. Tim Moore, and told him I would give Susana a life sentence for the charge of murder—thirty years, flat time, day for day. She was nineteen, and she's going to do it. She's got twenty-eight more years to do before she can ask to come out. And I thought that it was fair to get Chelsea Richardson and Andrew Wamsley, the real culprits, here. It was fair. Because without Susana Toledano's testimony, you don't get him and you don't get her."

Then he asked the jury to consider this: "Did Susana tell you the truth? Of course she did. She told you . . . about going down to Ruth's pond and they're all shooting the gun. Sure she [told the truth]. Absolutely. Ruth told you that, too. And the ballistics man told you that. . . . Did [Susana] tell you the truth about the Jeep? Of course she did. She admits it . . . and the ballistics man tells you [that all the bullets match]. . . . Did she tell you the truth about Chelsea using her cell phone nineteen minutes after Mr. Cowand hears the shots?" Of course. "And the one thing that ought to really tell you that Susana is telling the truth is when I asked her the question, 'Do you know between Andrew and Chelsea who shot Rick in the back?' What was her answer? No. Do you know for sure between Chelsea and Andrew who stabbed the fatal stabs to Rick's front? No. Why? Because I was over doing what I was told, which was stabbing the already dead Suzy Wamsley." Parrish continued, "Everything she told you that happened in that house is absolutely consistent with the evidence, the physical evidence and the photographs we've shown you. . . . And it would be easy for her to say either one, Andrew shot or Andrew stabbed, or Chelsea did that or that. She's telling you the truth. That ought to be a glean right there where you can see how truthful she is."

Continuing on, Parrish stated, "The defense, on the other hand, relies on one witness, Linda James . . . with the letter matching. . . . She went all the way through that examination and never realized the document . . . had Chelsea's name misspelled. . . . But dadgum it, she had already done her work. . . . She just dug her heels in and said, I ain't changing. . . . The law in Texas is a layman can look at handwriting and decide for themselves. I think y'all have.

You saw Susana's handwriting from that statement she gave up in Illinois. She knows how to spell Chelsea and she knows how to spell her own name. That letter is a hope and a prayer from jail somewhere trying to get Chelsea off. And Celia would do anything to get Chelsea off."

Parrish ended his statement by saying, "And when you look at the law and the facts and apply the law of parties and the accomplice, you will find Andrew Wamsley is guilty as a party to capital murder. Thank you."

It was then the defense's turn. Pearson began calmly yet assertively. "Ladies and gentlemen of the jury. I would remind you again of the oath that you're under, which is to render a true verdict according to the law and according to the evidence. . . . If something is not shown to you, then if you're going to uphold the law, you're going to say it's not shown, not guilty. And if you uphold the law in this case, you will acquit Andrew Wamsley."

Pearson continued, "There are only a couple of things that are clear in this case. There are too many gaps in the evidence to say that you know what happened. About the only thing that is clear from the evidence is Susana Toledano was in the house. You know that from the scientific evidence. And that she took a part in killing Rick and Suzy Wamsley. But beyond that, you don't really know, you don't have enough evidence, and it's not your job to provide that evidence."

Pearson continued, "There is no evidence that Andrew Wamsley killed his parents. There is just no evidence whatsoever according to everything that you have heard that as a principal, by himself, that he had anything to do by himself with the death of Rick and Suzy Wamsley. There is just no evidence for that.

"Now, the rest of [the charge] goes into the law of parties, to find out any of it, if you can, it must rely upon, it sets on the shoulders of Susana Toledano. And that is exactly right there where it craters.

"Susana Toledano is an admitted liar. She is a liar that was caught lying right before your very eyes when she testified. She admitted to telling you that she was lying. And, of course, the thing with a liar is you don't know when they're lying and when they're not lying. But if you know they're a liar, you have got to take that into consideration. She said some of the written statements she made to the police officers are lies. . . . When she gave a statement to the DA's investigator, she left things out. . . . Important details, according to her, that are true yet they were left out."

Pearson stated that Susana had to come up with a story to give the state what they wanted. "She has to come up with a story with somehow two other people helping her, Chelsea Richardson and Andrew Wamsley. . . . That's the story she created after she's had some time to think about it. But it is not shown by the hard evidence in this case."

When Pearson finished smearing Susana, he moved on to William Wesley Bates. "Now, while we're on the subject of liars such as Susana Toledano, let's talk about Mr. Bates, Wesley Bates, I don't think it's comic relief. I don't think there can be comic relief or comedy in a capital murder case. It is not funny to put a liar on the witness stand to try to put a young man in prison or kill him based upon the word of a liar." He said that Bates was a liar when he said he wouldn't set anybody up or do deals, except in this one special case. "Sure!" said Pearson sarcastically. Both Bates and Toledano had great motivation to lie—"for Bates, it was to get time out of jail; for Susana it was to save herself from a possible death penalty."

Pearson, slowly and methodically, got to the DNA evidence. He said there was a huge gap there, "and you don't fill gaps in with suspicion, you don't fill gaps any other way but with the evidence. . . . It [DNA] doesn't tell you that Andrew Wamsley had anything to do with the physical evidence or what occurred with Mr. and Mrs. Wamsley, and it doesn't put any of their blood standards or their samples out in the car."

Pearson concluded by saying, "There's the presumption of innocence as to the elements. The presumption of innocence, if it's not overcome, then you must acquit. Susana Toledano is a liar and beyond—without her, there is no way that this case can rest on Andrew. There is just no way. And I would ask you to find him not guilty."

Pearson had given it everything he had before passing the baton to his colleague. Moore reiterated that the only thing that linked Andrew to the murder was Susana Toledano, a liar. "Her footprints were all over the house. She told five different versions of what happened. She told her story to get a deal," Moore said.

"You've got Susana and you've got Mr. Bates, and that's it. Is that the kind and character of evidence that you in your heart can say convinces you beyond a reasonable doubt to make a life and death decision? Can you say that?"

Continuing to discredit Susana, he stated, "In the statement she gave in Illinois, she said Hilario went over there. In the statement that she gave to the police in July, they pick her up from work and it's a big surprise to her that they're going over there to do the killings. And the testimony in May of 2005, she . . . got a text message at school, and that's how she knew that the killings were going to be done that day. And in the testimony that she gave you here, well, she worked until ten thirty at night, then they picked her up, then they went to Putt-Putt, and then they went to do the murders. Which one of those is the truth?"

And concluding, Moore said, "Reasonable doubt is not a word on a page. Reasonable doubt is what lets you and I go home and sleep at night. It protects us from people like Susana Toledano and Wesley Bates. Thank you."

And with those words, the defense rested its case and the state had the opportunity to conclude the closing argument.

Simpson immediately tried to negate all that Moore and Pearson had said. She stated that Jeremy had no reason to lie, and the cell phone records corroborated that. "Why would they need an alibi if they had not done something?" She stated that Susana was not very bright and certainly could not have been the mastermind behind the murder. "She's not even smart enough to think that, wait, I've been arrested for capital murder and I don't need an attorney?" So who, in Simpson's mind, was the mastermind? Andrew, of course, and he got Susana to carry out his plan. Simpson pointed out that in spite of what the defense said, William Wesley Bates did not get a plea deal out of this. She said, "We've brought you enough evidence here to prove beyond a reasonable doubt that the defendant acted as a party in the killing of his parents."

In wrapping up her argument, Simpson stated: "When I talked to you in my opening argument about what this case was about, I told you it was about the ultimate betrayal. The ultimate betrayal, a son participating in the killing of his parents and his father actually knew before his death who was responsible. . . . He was tortured in his own home and died behind the front door to his residence in his underwear. Killed by his own son with knives out of his own kitchen. . . . This defendant is responsible, and I'm asking you to hold him responsible and find him guilty of capital murder. Thank you."

The closing arguments were now over. There were no more witnesses to testify, and no more evidence to see. Everything that would help the jurors decide guilt or innocence had been presented to them. All that was left was to go to the jury room and come to a unanimous decision. An easy task? That remained to be seen.

The judge told the jury that when they reached their decision, they should ring the buzzer and the bailiff would respond. It was 2:10 p.m.

Chapter Thirty-one

Around two hours later, at 4:59 p.m., the jury sent the judge a note saying that they had reached a verdict. Some felt that such a quick decision meant that the jurors had been convinced—even before beginning their deliberations—that the defendant was guilty. Others felt just the opposite.

The courtroom filled again as all parties returned to their seats and sat quietly, tensely, waiting to hear Andrew's fate. The judge spoke sternly to those in the courtroom. "The court expects for everyone in the audience to maintain order during the receiving of the verdict. The trial had been one with some emotion" so that "if someone feels that they cannot keep control, I give you an opportunity to leave at this time, but otherwise, the court expects order to be maintained."

After a few moments, the jurors entered the courtroom. With faces averted from the defendant, they took their seats. The judge spoke directly to the foreman. "Mr. Morgan, has the jury reached a verdict?"

"Yes, sir."

"Is the verdict unanimous?" asked the judge.

"Yes, sir."

Sarah Wamsley could hardly breathe. The extended Wamsley family, too, waited breathlessly to hear the judge's pronouncement. They knew what they felt. And they knew they were right. But the jury? What did they believe? Now that was another story.

The foreman handed the verdict to the bailiff, who handed it to the judge. Judge Young then turned to Andrew. Andrew had a premonition. Since no jury member would look at him, he felt that the word "guilty" would soon be coming.

"Mr. Wamsley," said Judge Young, "please stand while I read the verdict." Andrew and his lawyers stood and the judge began:

"This is the state of Texas versus Andrew Wamsley. The verdict is as follows: We, the jury, find the defendant, Andrew Wamsley, guilty of the offense of capital murder as charged in the indictment. And it's signed by the foreman of the jury."

Andrew showed no visible reaction when he heard the guilty verdict. However, others in the courtroom were not so restrained. Lewis and Marjean Wamsley smiled and hugged each other. This was the verdict they were hoping for. Neighbors of the Wamsleys who had attended the trial also showed emotion. Some wept, while others simply shook their heads. Regardless of who they felt had actually committed the crime, a son—someone they had known for many years as a good young man—had been found guilty of capital murder. It was a harsh dose of reality.

Andrew briefly thanked his lawyers and then put his hands behind his back, ready to be handcuffed. He was taken back to the holding cell, where the private investigator and a mitigation specialist followed him. While he sat on the bench with his head tilted back against the wall, both of the professionals started crying. One said to Andrew, "Oh, sweetie, I'm so sorry." At that point, tears started rolling down Andrew's cheeks. He didn't get up and talk with them. He just sat there, unable to move a muscle. Within minutes, he was led away.

Once again, a person was convicted of capital murder in

the deaths of Suzy and Rick Wamsley. The only question that remained now was, Would Andrew face the same fate as Chelsea in the sentencing phase of the trial—death by lethal injection?

Chapter Thirty-two

On March 6, 2006, the sentencing, or punishment, phase of the trial began. The same jurors would be hearing testimony. The same jurors who ruled on Andrew's guilt would now be in charge of deciding his ultimate fate.

During the sentencing phase, the defense had the opportunity to call witnesses to speak on behalf of the defendant. The hope was that these witnesses would sway the jury to spare Andrew's life. But before the defense called its witnesses, the state called three witnesses of its own: Elizabeth Johnson-Tovar, John Burroughs, and William Wesley Bates.

Johnson-Tovar stated that she knew Andrew Wamsley through her brother, John Burroughs, because Chelsea was her brother's girlfriend at one time. She admitted that she heard Andrew talk about his parents' money while they were at the bar at Kelly's. She said Chelsea and her brother were no longer dating at that time but Andrew and Chelsea were. Johnson-Tovar said she heard Andrew and Chelsea make plans about getting married and taking trips.

"And at that time, how were they going to finance that?" asked Parrish.

"Well, they said they would have to wait until Drew got the money from his parents. And then they were joking, from what I understood they were joking because they were laughing. They said we'll just, you know, knock 'em off and get it over with and get the money." When asked who said that, she replied, "Drew."

On redirect, Pearson asked if when they were laughing about how Andrew could get money, "was it just Chelsea talking about something or being involved in a conversation that was just, you know, loose talk or just silly talk or just talk that didn't amount to much?"

"Yeah, for that, yes," she admitted.

John Burroughs was sworn in next. He gave testimony similar to that which he gave during Andrew's trial. He saw Andrew selling "weed" while Chelsea "bagged it up."

When Tarrant County Jail inmate William Wesley Bates was called to testify, he not only stated that Andrew wanted to put nitroglycerin into Susana's food, but he also said there was a second part to the conversation he had had with Andrew. The second part was, said Bates, "[Andrew] said at one point that after the charges had been dropped and he got out, after I succeeded in that, that we might have to kill his sister."

"And when he was talking about his sister, did he seem to have any good feelings towards her?" asked Simpson.

"At that time," said Bates, "I said, 'Not your sister, man, that's your blood, you got to be kidding me.' And he said, 'Fuck the bitch, she don't care nothing about me, all she cares about is the money.'"

Simpson asked, "And did he tell you why he wanted to have his sister killed?"

"Something about the contesting of the will, if one of them fought over the will and not to get it or something like that, she was, I don't know, she was already contesting it or something like that."

"Did he discuss with you what you could get in return for helping him out?"

"Yeah. I was told I was going to get two hundred and fifty

thousand dollars once everything was taken care of," said Bates.

"Would you get it all in one payment?" asked Simpson.

"No. He said they would be watching him . . . and that he would have to do that under the table some way."

On redirect, Pearson asked, "Mr. Bates, you just said that in the letter you wrote to the DA's office, you put in you're no killer, right?"

"I'm a flimflammer, a short-changer, a thief, but I will never take nobody's life for no amount of money."

"You have your morals, don't you?"

"Yeah."

"And you've been a thief since what age?"

"Shit, I can't remember."

After Pearson passed the witness, the state said that it rested its case. It hoped it had shown, through these three witnesses, that Andrew had spoken, even if it was in jest, about killing his parents; that Andrew had sold marijuana; and that Andrew wanted not only to kill Susana, but also to kill his own sister.

A short lunch break was taken and then the jury returned to see how the defense would try to save their client's life. The defense's tactic would be to present witnesses who could speak to the character of Andrew—that he was an upstanding member of the community, that he came from an extremely dysfunctional home, and that he was not hotheaded or violent in any way.

To that end, Moore called Jimmy Don Thoms first. Thoms stated that as Andrew's teacher in the vocational education department of the Mansfield School District, he found Andrew to be a "nice kid. Always on time, always a gentleman." Thoms stated that he had received job reports on Andrew from Putt-Putt, and "he always did very well." He added that although he got along with the other kids in the class, he didn't have "any close relationships" that he observed. He added, "Sometimes I might be talking to Andrew and I'm not sure he was really connecting." He said he never saw Andrew engage in any violent behavior; in fact, he was "very soft-spoken, very well-mannered." Thoms admitted that he never saw Andrew "angry or depressed . . . but he seemed more insecure than secure."

On cross-examination, Parrish asked him if he was aware that Andrew had graduated early from high school. Thoms said he was aware of that. Thoms admitted that he never saw any signs of Andrew being emotionally troubled or having any psychological problems, nor did Andrew ever complain about any abuse at home. In fact, added Thoms, Andrew spoke well of his father and mother.

Mitchell Kent Myers was called to the stand. Myers, a manager at Putt-Putt, stated that while Andrew worked at Putt-Putt, he did extremely well and "we moved him up to a shift leader . . . which is kind of an assistant to me, someone that I can rely on to make some decisions for me." Myers stated he always gave Andrew a positive evaluation. "He was personable with [customers]. . . . [I] never saw much frustration out of him and felt he was pretty even-keeled with everybody."

The defense then called Cheryl Ann Brookhart. She stated that she knew Andrew because Andrew's mother, Suzy, and she were room mothers at school. Brookhart said that her youngest son and Andrew's sister, Sarah, were in class together. Brookhart stated that she and Suzy had been close friends for about nine or ten years—until about ten years ago—during which time the two families would often have dinners together, and even celebrate Thanksgiving together. She said that she and Suzy also spoke a lot on the telephone.

At one point, Moore surprised practically everyone in the

courtroom by asking Brookhart, "Were you aware of whether or not Suzy Wamsley was accumulating money for the purpose of leaving her husband?"

"I definitely know that. She told me."

Brookhart added further details, stating that Suzy told her on more than one occasion that "the relationship was unbearable." She said that Suzy complained Rick was a disciplinarian and that he would belittle and put down Andrew. In fact, Brookhart said, Suzy told her Rick would tell Andrew he wasn't "worth a—an expletive."

Brookhart recalled that at one point, her son Ryan and Sarah began dating and "Mr. Wamsley began calling Ryan aside, wanting to know what they did on their dates and, you know, are you having sex, are you, you know, leading her down a path that I don't want her to go on. . . . [He would] just hammer at him." She reported that Ryan finally got fed up with Rick's intrusiveness and stopped dating Sarah.

Further, Brookhart said, after seeing Rick over the years and the way he acted, she and her family began to sour on the Wamsleys, and soon, the families stopped seeing each other. She admitted that Rick "scared" her. She felt that Suzy loved her son, but she didn't think Rick's method of discipline showed any love towards his child.

Klinton David Atchley was called next. He stated that he was twenty-two and had known Andrew since they were three years old—they were six months apart. He stated they were best friends throughout childhood and into high school, spending practically every weekend together, even when they went to different schools. He said that he knew Andrew had graduated from high school early because Andrew had told him "he didn't enjoy high school that much and really wanted to get out and get on with things."

When asked about whether or not Andrew had a temper, Klint stated that he had never seen Andrew being violent. He said he loved Andrew "like a brother." When asked to name the good things about Andrew, he said, "He's a strong-willed person that can really get things done and has so much potential and can be a very, very loving person. It just kind of has to be one on one."

Pearson asked him if he was asking the jury to spare Andrew's life.

"Yep."

"Why do you feel that way?"

"Because I know Andrew and I know his heart, and I feel like even if he could have done this, that there is no reason why human life should be sacrificed. He can pay for his crime without having to die and can still contribute to society even from within a prison cell and be productive and get so much done and be able to give back."

Simpson then cross-examined Klint. She asked him if he knew how Rick and Suzy had died.

"Vaguely."

"Do you know they suffered—well, Rick suffered badly?"

"From what I understand."

"They were good people, weren't they?" asked Simpson.

"Yes."

"They didn't deserve to die like that?"

"Probably not."

On redirect, Klinton said that he saw Rick "belittle" Andrew. That was his way of disciplining him. Klinton stated that he rarely saw any hugging or kissing in the family, but if it did happen, it was "more with his mom than his dad."

Andrew tried to make eye contact with the person whom he considered more a brother than a best friend, but Klint would not look back. Later, when Andrew was asked how he felt about Klint being there, Andrew said that he was glad he was there, but sorry that Klint had gotten dragged into the situation.

Karri Atchley, Klint's mother, was called next. She stated that she knew Andrew through Klint. She said she saw Andrew from when he was three until "the summer before Klint went to college . . . in 2002."

Moore asked her if she had ever seen Andrew being violent, and she said no. When asked what she felt about Andrew, she responded, "I feel that Andrew is someone who never found his niche. He never knew what it was that made him feel good about himself. He wasn't really, really good at anything, but he wasn't a bad kid at all and you weren't worried for your child being with him. . . . I think he was a little immature and had some growing up to do." She said he was "consistent. He was easy to be around, easy to entertain, easy to get along with." She admitted that he could be passionate about things he was interested in, but he would lose interest in things quickly. She admitted that he seemed "a little reserved emotionally." Karri said she cared deeply about Andrew.

"Are you asking this jury to spare his life?"

"Yes."

When Parrish began interrogating Karri, he asked, "Do you know how many times Rick Wamsley was shot and stabbed?"

"I don't."

"What do you think of someone who could shoot their father and then hack him to death while they talked with him?"

Moore immediately objected to that line of questioning, stating that there was no evidence that he did that.

The judge overruled the objection.

Parrish continued, "What do you think? Do you remember the question?"

"I cannot imagine that Andrew did that and I have . . . there is no evidence that I know of that Andrew did do that."

"Okay. You realize that this jury has heard all the evidence that you have not heard, correct?"

"Yes."

"And you realize this jury has found Andrew Wamsley

guilty of capital murder, that is, intentionally killing both of his parents?"

"Yes."

"What do you think of someone who could plot, pre-meditate to kill their parents for greed, strictly for money?" asked Parrish.

"I think that there are definite consequences that need to be paid in a situation like that."

"I asked you what you thought of the person, ma'am."

"I think it's a person that has some problems and some issues and I feel badly."

Before ending his questioning, Parrish asked her, "Do you think Rick and Suzy spoiled Andrew?"

"Yes. He never wanted for anything that I knew of."

Moore then questioned Karri again about Andrew's personality. She stated that Andrew was most comfortable around one person, and that one person was her son Klint. She said that Andrew always wanted to spend time with Klint. Andrew, she said, was the kind of kid who would just start out observing things, "and slowly work his way into playing pool or something. But it takes him a while."

Andy Allen Atchley, husband of Karri Atchley, was sworn in next. When Pearson asked Andy if he knew how Andrew felt about his own family, Andy stated he was "very proud of what his dad did. He was always very proud of the homes that they lived in. . . . He just thought that his family was the greatest family around. . . . He was proud of Sarah. He would always tell us about things that she was doing. . . . And he was very proud of the things that [his parents] gave him and the things that they did. I mean, he was very vocal about that."

Andy recalled that whenever his family would go away, there would be fifteen or more calls from Andrew on their caller ID when they returned. That was before cell phones, he said. Andy stated that Andrew was very attached to Klint and the Atchley family. Andy concluded by saying, "With us, Andrew was an ideal little boy. I mean, he was smart, he was personable, he was endearing to us. You know, I mean, there's times I've called Andrew my second son. . . . And I saw the potential in him that I would expect to see somewhat in my own children. You know, I expected great things of Andrew."

"Mr. Atchley, are you asking this jury to spare him, spare his life?"

"Yes, I am, most definitely, as heartfelt as I can."

On cross by Parrish, Andy admitted that he knew the jury had found Andrew guilty of capital murder. He stated that Suzy and Rick were very good people and, he added, "I see a world of potential in Andrew."

"Do you see potential in Andrew to try to get someone else to kill his sister?" asked Parrish.

"No, sir."

"Do you see potential in Andrew to try to get someone to kill the key witness in this case so he can get off?"

"No," said Andy.

Having made his point, Parrish passed the witness.

Next, Moore called Kris Garcia. Garcia stated that he had been friends with Andrew for more than ten years, starting when his family lived in the same apartment complex as Andrew's. He said the two families were very close. He testified that Andrew always seemed to get along well with his parents. Garcia said that there were times when the Wamsleys would bring Andrew to their house because they were having trouble with Sarah and they had to go out and look for her. Andrew, Garcia said, "was very frustrated that she would get all this attention for her bad behavior." He said that Andrew was "very well-mannered. He was never violent. He never had a temper. He was really good."

When Simpson questioned Garcia on behalf of the state,

he said he had visited Andrew in jail. He stated that Andrew never admitted any responsibility for the killings.

"Never showed any remorse for the fact that they were dead?"

"He misses his family a lot. He does miss his parents," said Garcia.

It was nearly 4 p.m. by the time Garcia finished testifying, so the judge told the jurors that they were dismissed for the day. Had the witnesses brought enough mitigation to the fore so that jurors could see that there was reason to spare this young man's life?

Chapter Thirty-three

On the second day of the sentencing phase, two defense witnesses were called to testify about Andrew's psychological makeup.

Dr. Katherine Mary Allen was sworn in first. She stated that she was a clinical social worker "and I am a retired professor, and currently I am a forensic consultant and trainer." Asked what her involvement was with this case, she stated she had been contacted by Larry Moore of the defense team, who had requested she do an assessment of Andrew Wamsley. She said she had spent several hours with Andrew and reviewed documents Moore had sent her, which included medical, school, and jail records. She said she had also reviewed Sarah Wamsley's medical records from the time when Sarah was an inpatient at a psychiatric hospital.

Asked for an analysis of Andrew's personality, she stated that in her opinion, Andrew suffered from a schizoid personality, which, she added, should not be confused with schizophrenia. A schizoid personality, she said, is characterized by the person "preferring to be alone; finding relationships with other people to be stressful; being generally reclusive and isolate; being fairly independent . . . generally not successful in creating bonds or being assured or comforted by others." Allen said it appeared that there were "issues involved in the family dynamics of the Wamsleys that were suggestive or resultive of the impaired attachment situation." Allen stated that Andrew and other people close to the family reported that "there were no signs, absolutely no signs, of affection in the family from any member of the family to any other member of the family." Andrew, Allen stated, exhibited exceptional clinging behavior to the Atchley family, especially when they went away, when Andrew would call up to thirty times, desperately asking, "Are you back yet? Are you back yet?" while he remained at home "isolated and crying." In Allen's opinion, a person who suffers this kind of disorder usually exhibits lower levels of violence compared to others. "The person does not have that emotional energy or engagement," explained Allen.

When it was Simpson's turn to question Allen, Simpson asked her if she was aware that Andrew had broken a glass table, thrown a video at his father, and tossed a bowl of *queso* across the room at a restaurant in public. She wondered, "Don't those exhibit violent tendencies?" Allen replied emphatically that they were impulse control issues, not violent tendencies.

Antoinette Rose McGarrahan was sworn in next. She was a clinical psychologist and professor of psychiatry, teaching forensic psychology. She stated that "for the past four months, I was selected by Dallas County judges to perform their competency-to-stand-trial evaluations, along with some other psychologists in the area." Routinely, she said, she was called to testify. She stated that she was requested by Moore's office to do an assessment of Andrew. In the three personality tests she gave him, she reported that Andrew "showed significant difficulties in social interactions and experience and expression of emotion." It was her conclusion that he suffered from "schizoid personality disorder." She said that he exhibited six of the seven symptoms of the disorder. Four are enough to meet the criteria for the diagnosis, she stated. The six he suffered from were: the individual neither desires nor enjoys close relationships, including those with a family; the individual almost always chooses solitary activity; the individual has little interest, if any, in having sexual experiences with another person; the individual lacks close friends or confidants—even within his family; the individual appears indifferent to praise or criticism; and the individual can often show emotional coldness or detachment, or what is often called a "flat affect." Further, she said, the "quirks and traits have to cause the person significant distress or impairment in their functioning. And that has absolutely been the case with regard to Mr. Wamsley."

In her opinion, Andrew had a low-to-moderate propensity for future acts of violence. Further, McGarrahan added, in the two years that Andrew had been incarcerated, he had never been involved in a fight nor did he even fight back when he was attacked on two different occasions.

Moore ascertained that McGarrahan did not contact Allen or know what diagnosis Allen was going to give. They each arrived at their conclusions independently.

Chapter Thirty-four

On March 9, Dr. Andrew Houtz was sworn in as an expert for the state. Simpson asked him about his credentials, and he stated that he had been the neuropsychologist in the department of psychiatry at John Peter Smith Hospital since 1994. Among other things, he did evaluations of people involved in court cases. As such, he had interviewed the defendant and read the data and test results performed by Dr. McGarrahan. He said the tests appeared to have been performed properly. He said he had interviewed Andrew two days prior to testifying and found him to "be very engaging. I was able to establish rapport with him very, very quickly. We were able to discuss a broad range of interests that he has. He was able to converse fluently with me. He showed a fairly broad range of emotions when he was with me . . . and he became very animated when we were discussing things that he found of interest." The doctor stated that Andrew did not report any difficulties in school or in his work. He "presented most of the things that he experienced as a matter of choice—that he chose not to do certain things or not to participate, or he chose not to have a lot of friends."

The doctor testified that Andrew told him about his interest in auto mechanics, in reading certain books, and in World War II. He said he wasn't interested in girls, nor was he interested in dating. He said he enjoyed driving fast and going to movies. He especially liked the movie *The Fast and the Furious*.

Houtz said he didn't think Andrew suffered from schizoid personality disorder. He said he came to his conclusion based on a variety of reasons, among them, that Andrew interacted with people; he engaged in animated conversation; and he participated in sports. He believed that Andrew simply preferred to be alone; that he didn't need to be with a large group of people; nor did he like to show emotions. Andrew reported that his father had taught him to be self-reliant and independent, and that's the way he chose to live his life. The doctor felt that Andrew thought of himself as smarter than most kids, and that's why he chose to graduate early.

On cross-examination, Moore immediately asked, "Have you ever done an assessment of a criminal defendant to see if they were sane at the time of the commission of the offense?"

"No."

"Have you ever done an assessment of a criminal defendant for purposes of sentencing?"

"No."

"Do you have any particular training in the administration of violent risk assessment measures?"

"No."

When asked about his conclusion about Andrew, Houtz said, "Well, in the end, he didn't present himself as schizoid. Far from it."

Moore then asked, "Did you see any signs of anxiety or depression in Andrew?"

"No."

"He had just been found guilty last Friday of capital murder. You knew that?"

"That's correct."

"And you are the state's expert coming in here to testify in regard to your assessment of the defendant for the purpose of helping the jury decide whether a life sentence or a death sentence is going to be rendered, is that correct?"

"Correct."

"And didn't that strike you as odd," Moore asked, that someone who was just convicted of capital murder and was facing a possible death sentence would not have any "concerns about what was going to happen as a result of that interview or what the circumstances were?"

"It's kind of chilling, isn't it?" said Houtz.

Moore continued hammering at him: "And once again, essentially you're telling me that the evidence that you find of social detachment, emotional alienation, the social discomfort, all that is just not important to you?"

"I'm saying it doesn't reach the degree necessary to be diagnosed with this disorder [schizoid personality]."

"Despite what the results of the tests are?"

"Correct."

Looking disgusted, Moore took his seat.

The state then called Sarah Wamsley. Simpson asked her what effect her parents' murders had had on her.

Sarah responded that it had been particularly hard on her daughter, who was three when the killings took place. She stated that Brittany had had a very close relationship with her grandparents. She told the jury that she had had to tell Brittany that she would never see them again. It was heartbreaking. She said that since her grandparents' deaths, Brittany was afraid whenever she, Sarah, left the house. Brittany was afraid she would never see her mother again.

Sarah continued, "I was really scared [about my own safety]. I would always be watching my back. Whenever I went into my house, I would search under the beds, closets, behind the shower curtain. I didn't feel safe and I still don't." She feared her brother or someone her brother might hire would come after her. "I still fear for my life," she said. She said she had moved four times within a year of her parents' deaths because she was afraid her brother would find her.

She still kept two unopened Christmas presents, which had been under her parents' Christmas tree when they were murdered. One, she said, was "from Mom and Dad to Sarah" and another was from "Suzanna to Rick." She said she will "never be able to unwrap them." She told the jurors, "They were loving parents, and they were best friends to me. Anytime I needed them, they were there for support and guidance." She said she kept an answering machine that still had her parents' voices recorded.

Causing some of the jurors to cry, Sarah said that she had to stop herself from telling her daughter that she'll "see her tomorrow," because that's what her grandparents said to her daughter the last time they saw her. Sarah testified that she believed Andrew had tried to kill her and might continue to try to kill her if he was allowed out of jail—suggesting that she favored the death penalty for her brother.

On cross, Pearson got Sarah to admit that Andrew was a loner. "He didn't interact," she testified, saying that her mother would "yearn" for him to interact and was concerned about him "not having the desire to interact." She admitted that she hadn't seen Andrew date. "He wasn't interested in girls," she said. She also stated that there was not a show of affection in their family, and physical contact was rare. With this information, Pearson was hoping to support the diagnosis of schizoid personality disorder.

After Sarah's testimony, the judge asked if either the defense or prosecution had any other witnesses. Both said they did not, and the testimony in the state of Texas versus Andrew Wamsley had officially ended.

It was 11 a.m. on Thursday, March 9.

The judge said that since there were no more witnesses, it would now be time for closing arguments. The state, he said, had the right to open and close the arguments, and the defense could present their argument in between. Each side would be allowed forty minutes total.

Chapter Thirty-five

This was the most important and crucial part of the trial. The defendant had been found guilty. That much had been established. Now, his attorneys were fighting for his life—and the prosecution was pushing back hard for the death penalty. Who would succeed?

Simpson began by attacking the idea that Andrew suffered from schizoid personality disorder—which would tend to make him unlikely to be violent or to pose a threat to society in future. She stated, "This individual here who sits charged with this crime does not suffer from a personality disorder. Someone who suffers from a personality disorder is going to have a lot of trouble in school, either disciplinary-wise or educationally-wise. . . . We know that he made mostly A's in elementary school. We know he engaged in activities in junior high and high school. We know that he made good grades in high school. And it was only when he got bored with it that he decided he didn't want to go anymore, so he just decided to graduate early. That's not someone who's going to suffer from a schizoid personality disorder. It's just not." One who suffers from schizoid personality disorder, Simpson continued, "has difficulties in social interchanges with other people and at work," yet "his employer said Andrew worked for him for two years. As a matter of fact, [he] even promoted him."

Furthermore, Simpson continued, "What do you know

from the defendant's own mouth [from psychologists' reports of what Andrew told them]? We know that he chose to be alone more than he chose to be in a group. Just because you prefer to be alone more than you prefer to be in a group does not mean that you suffer from a personality disorder."

Simpson stated that the only reason Andrew "killed was to get the money from [his parents'] insurance policy and from the estate. That's not someone who suffers from a personality disorder. That's someone who's filled with hatred and greed." In addition, Simpson stated, someone who suffers from schizoid personality disorder is not going to praise other family members, like he praised Sarah for all her activities. "He's not going to be proud of someone's success, like his father, or grateful for things that his mother does. He's not going to be able to express those kinds of emotions, and he won't be able to have emotional outbursts. He can't break a table. . . . He can't throw a video. . . . He wouldn't be somebody who would be attracted to paintball or racing. He just wouldn't."

When considering mitigation, Simpson added, you must consider whether or not there has been any remorse shown. "After the murders, what is the defendant doing?" she asked. "He's continuing in his deceitful plan to mislead the police and even his own sister. He's coming up with a plan to explain why there might be his parents' blood in his own car. That's not an expression of remorse. . . . Someone who feels remorseful is not going to try to have a hit put out on his sister from jail."

Simpson continued by saying that maybe, just maybe, the family was dysfunctional on some level, "but you could look at every family and point out something that you believe might be dysfunction. But it doesn't explain why the defendant acted the way he did."

The mitigation in this case, Simpson said, did not rise to a level that should cause the jury to consider a life sentence over the death penalty. "I'm asking you," she said, "to give him as much sympathy as he did for his father each time that cold steel blade was plunged into his body and puncturing every living organ he had; to imagine the last moments of Rick Wamsley's life as he had to stare into the eyes of his own son and know that that was his killer."

In concluding her remarks, Simpson stated, once again, "The most reasonable and plausible example of why he did what he did was pure greed and pure hatred. Thank you."

Simpson took her seat. It was now Moore's turn to speak for the very last time for his client. He knew he had to make the strongest argument he could to spare Andrew's life. He had a strategy. "In final arguments, I always tend to approach the jury box and speak somewhat softly so that it is like a conversation between the jury and me. However, I will purposely raise my voice for effect at certain points during the arguments. Jurors have an amazing ability to separate sincerity from theatrics, and a lot of trial lawyers make a serious mistake by failing to recognize that fact, so I always try to be sincere and somewhat emotional in my appeals to the jury."

Moore began by saying, "Ladies and gentlemen. It's very difficult for a lawyer in this situation to come up after we put all the effort that we could into trying to convince you that Andrew is not guilty and to have you return a verdict of guilty. I don't understand it. I don't know how you got there. I don't know what you believe from Susana Toledano's testimony and what you don't believe. And I will probably spend the rest of my life wondering what I could have done different or better. But," he continued solemnly, "punish Andrew based on what you find that he did. Punish him on what you believe from the evidence."

Moore went on to talk about some of the evidence. "You know," he said, "they talk about the knife and the knives and plunging the knife into [Mr. Wamsley's] chest. There's no evidence from anywhere that Andrew Wamsley ever stabbed his father. Susana Toledano said she never saw him stab him. She never saw him shoot him. All she said she saw was that he wrestled with his father, pulled his father off of her during the fight."

Moore said that, despite the state's claims, there *was* something wrong in the Wamsley household. He pointed out that even Sarah admitted that her parents believed that putting a roof over their children's heads and providing for extracurricular activities was love. "And don't we all need more than that? How did it affect Sarah? How did it affect Andrew? Well, it affected them differently, but it affected them both equally." Sarah started acting out at thirteen, running around with boys, engaging in promiscuity. "She is needing and looking for intimacy, and she is needing and looking for love." Andrew, Moore pointed out, reacted differently. "He went within himself and withdrew." The one person in his whole life he bonded with was Klint Atchley, and when Klint went away, "he found Chelsea. And it wasn't sex and it wasn't intimacy, but it was basic human companionship."

Trying to bolster both Dr. Allen and Dr. McGarrahan's testimony of Andrew having a schizoid personality disorder and to discredit Dr. Houtz's, Moore stated that Allen spent nearly four hours with Andrew and looked at every record provided. McGarrahan spent nine and a half hours with him, did twenty-one separate assessments, and read every document provided. Dr. Houtz, on the other hand, spent a mere ninety minutes with Andrew, and based on that mere ninety minutes, Houtz testified—in a life or death case—that "Dr. Allen and Dr. McGarrahan are wrong."

Moore stated, "You have to be convinced beyond a reasonable doubt that [Andrew's] a future danger before you ever consider anything else regarding whether or not mitigation or the death penalty or the life sentence is appropriate. Andrew would be sixty years old before he is even eligible to be released. What do you know about his two years in jail? He's been attacked and he hasn't even fought back. And on this evidence alone, you just can't do it."

Pearson took over from Moore. Later, Pearson stated, "I

gave that closing argument everything I had. I knew what it felt like to stand next to a client sentenced to die, from a previous death penalty case. I knew we had a fighting chance with the jury for life, and I was determined to give it everything I had."

Pearson, in his unaffected and heartfelt manner, pointed out, "If you're trying to identify the manipulator and the leader of this tragic event, of this ruthless act, think about the moment when the dirty deeds are being done. Chelsea pushes Susana . . . And then add to that the fact that when Mr. Wamsley is asking why, the leader, not afraid to speak, Chelsea Richardson . . . says to Rick this thing about, oh, I'm pregnant."

Pearson continued, "We [are] not asking you . . . for the moon and the stars. We're asking you to make him spend, as he must, every day of his life [in prison] with the remote chance after forty years, maybe, he will get out." Pearson pleaded that Andrew, today, is a product of his growing up. He is the boy who "called the Atchleys thirty or forty times because he's clinging to them wondering when Klint would come back. He's the boy that is detached. . . . We brought you Ms. Brookhart, Kris Garcia, the Atchleys. They don't have an axe to grind against Rick and Suzy Wamsley. That's why our witnesses are truth-tellers."

And in his last-ditch attempt to save Andrew's life, Pearson concluded by saying, "If you say that he must die, when they strap him down, when the tie-down team goes in there and straps him down, they're killing not just Andrew in December 2003. They're killing the little boy that a lot of things in life were not his choice. . . . Please do a bold thing. Please give Andrew life in prison."

When the defense concluded its remarks, DA Parrish took his final turn. "Ladies and gentlemen," he said. "That is not a little boy. That's a grown man. Don't let them guilt-trip you. Don't let them plant that seed that you're going to be executing a little boy. That's a grown man."

Parrish stated that two words "premeditated" and "greed" should show the jurors that this crime is one that warrants death. Furthermore, he added, Andrew would be a threat to society if he were allowed to live. "I wonder how many people [in prison] he is going to ask to get out and go kill Sarah. Your decision could affect Sarah Wamsley's life."

The prosecutor stated that Andrew "planned, plotted, discussed theories, changed options, sat in a little booth in an IHOP with Hilario Cardenas, Susana Toledano, Chelsea Richardson and himself, and they talked about ways to kill these two people. And they did it for a couple of months. They got a gun. They didn't rush. I mean, got to find out how to shoot. Who called Ruth [Brustrom] and wanted to come down? Who drove down? Who had the gun? Who had the bullets? Andrew, Andrew, Andrew, Andrew. Andrew. He wanted them dead." In talking about the crime, Parrish stated, "Think about what he did. He drove the three of them over there. . . . He goes in first. . . . He gets Susana and Chelsea in the house. . . . That deserves the death penalty. It does. . . . He goes out and wrestles with his own father, who has a wound here that is pouring into the carpet . . . and he wrestles him backwards. . . . He wished it, he wanted it, and he participated in it. He's a future danger.

"Based on the law," Parrish said, "and evidence and what Andrew did to bring about the death of his parents . . . it won't be easy, but it's what each of you told us you could do if we brought the case to you and told us if there was a case bad enough, you could do it, you could [give the death penalty] on the crime."

After thanking the jurors for their patience and attention, Parrish took his seat. The judge then told the jury that it was now time to retire to the jury room to consider their verdict. Andrew's future lay in their hands. And it was impossible not to wonder, *Would he share the same fate as Chelsea?*

Chapter Thirty-six

The jury retired at 2:12 p.m. At 4:28 p.m., just two and a quarter hours later, the judge was informed that the jury had reached a verdict. Court was called to order, and Judge Young asked the defense and prosecution teams if they were ready to hear the jury's decision.

"Yes, sir," stated Parrish.

"We are," said Moore.

"Okay, let's go ahead and bring the jury in."

The jurors filed back into the courtroom. The judge addressed the court, which was packed with members of both the Wamsley and Richardson families, friends of both families, several reporters, and some young prosecutors who were just there to watch the closing death penalty arguments and sentencing.

Reflecting on the proceedings after the fact, defense attorney Pearson said, "The Wamsley family was not there to support Andrew, but I never perceived that family was bloodthirsty. It seemed to me that they just wanted the ordeal over with more than anything else."

The defense attorneys were clearly nervous. They knew Chelsea had gotten the death penalty, so they were aware of what an uphill battle they had been climbing. They could only pray that the jurors heard their arguments—and were sympathetic towards Andrew.

"All right," the judge began. "Thank you again, ladies

and gentlemen. Has the jury reached a verdict with respect to the special issues in this phase of the trial?"

"They have," said the foreman.

"Very well. If you will hand the jury charge to the bailiff, I will read your verdict here in open court."

After receiving the verdict, the judge paused and glanced over it before he began to read. No expression crossed his face. "All right," he said. "With respect to special issue number one: Do you find from the evidence beyond a reasonable doubt that there is a probability that the defendant would commit criminal acts of violence that would constitute a continuing threat to society?

"The answer is: We the jury, because at least ten jurors agree, find that the answer to special issue number one is no."

The judge then spoke directly to the foreman. "Did at least ten members of the jury answer no to this question?"

"Yes."

That meant that ten jurors felt that Andrew would *not* be a future danger and only two felt otherwise—a clear victory for the defense. Now, regardless of what the answer was to special issue number two, Andrew would not face the same fate as Chelsea. For the defense team, this was a moment to savor.

"All right," the judge continued. "I will go ahead and read special issue number two. Do you find from the evidence beyond a reasonable doubt that the defendant actually caused the death of the deceased or did not actually cause the death of the deceased, but intended to kill the deceased or another or anticipated that human life would be taken?

"The answer is: We the jury unanimously find from the evidence beyond a reasonable doubt that the answer to special issue number two is yes."

The judge asked the foreman if that was the unanimous answer of the jury to special issue number two, and the foreman said yes.

The judge continued. "Special issue number three is not

answered because special issue number one has been answered no." In effect, the judge was saying that in order for the third issue to be of any importance, there had to be a unanimous answer to special issue number one—and there wasn't.

Parrish stated he wanted the court to conduct a poll of the jurors, first with respect to special issue number one.

Of the twelve jurors, ten stated that they did not believe Andrew would be a future threat and two jurors said that they thought he would be a future threat.

Neither attorney wished to poll the jurors on special issue number two.

Then the judge spoke to Andrew. "Mr. Wamsley, will you stand, please, at this time."

Andrew stood up.

"Mr. Wamsley, upon your plea of not guilty in this case and the jury having found you guilty of the offense of capital murder as charged in the indictment and the jury having answered special issue number one as *no* and special issue number two as *yes*, the law under this situation requires that a mandatory sentence of life imprisonment in the Institutional Division of the Texas Department of Criminal Justice be imposed. And the court at this time will now impose your punishment as life confinement in the Institutional Division of the Texas Department of Criminal Justice. . . . And further, it is ordered that you be taken immediately by the sheriff of this county and be delivered to the director of that agency, there to serve your sentence as required by law. . . . And sir, you do have a right to appeal this case if you wish. . . . You do this by filing your written notice of appeal with the clerk of this court within the next thirty days."

As in the guilt phase of the trial, neither Andrew's face nor his body betrayed his feelings. Was he relieved? Most people felt he should have been. After all, he easily could have received the death penalty, as did Chelsea. But many wondered: Is a verdict of death actually a lighter sentence than life in prison?

Andrew's attorney Larry Moore was so affected by the fact that his client's life was spared that he had begun to cry as the verdict was being read. Afterward, he stood up and said, "Judge, we will file notice of appeal this afternoon. . . . At the request of both Mr. Pearson and I, and of Mr. Wamsley, Mr. Pearson will be appointed to do the appeal."

The judge said, "And Mr. Wamsley, you concur in this request? Is that correct?"

"Yes, sir," said Andrew.

"And sir," the judge said to Andrew, "at this time I will remand you to the custody of the sheriff for transportation to the Institutional Division of the Texas Department of Criminal Justice."

Judge Young then thanked the jurors for their service. They had made a judgment. They had chosen to allow Andrew Wamsley to live.

Some felt justice had been served. Others wondered how Andrew's girlfriend, Chelsea, got the death penalty while he got life. And, some wondered, who got the leaner sentence?

But Andrew? How did he view the sentence? Years later, while he sat in his broiling hot concrete cell, he wrote that he would rather be on death row than in prison for life. On death row, he said, he would wait for death for about fifteen years, which he viewed as a better fate than slowly dying in prison for the rest of his life. He wrote, "I won't get out unless I win my appeals, or in a pine box."

After the verdict, Pearson reflected that he felt Andrew's mental health diagnosis—schizoid personality disorder—had been strongly corroborated by the defense witnesses during the punishment phase of the trial. He believed the jury saw that Andrew lived what most people would consider a sad life without the normal human ability to understand warmth and love in relationships. Pearson believed the jury showed Andrew mercy due to his mental condition, a circumstance beyond his ability to control. Pearson said,

"My overwhelming thought was, and still is . . . that it was just a sad case."

Reflecting later about his relationship with Andrew during the trial, defense attorney Moore said, "Andrew was very stoic and emotionless. The only real flashes of emotion that I would ever really see from him would come when he would get angry with me over something that I did, or did not do. He was reserved when each verdict was received, even though I knew he was surprised by the guilty verdict. I don't believe that Andrew has ever considered the life verdict to be a victory, in the way that virtually everyone else connected to the case considers it to be. Throughout the trial, there were members of Andrew's family sitting in the courtroom on the prosecution side, and almost no one (other than members of our defense team) was there to support Andrew, although a few of Andrew's friends did come for parts of the trial. At the conclusion of the trial, after the life verdict was received, some of his family members thanked me for our efforts on Andrew's behalf. Although I was furious at all of them for refusing to even speak with us before trial, I realized that they all had to deal with this in their own way, and to live with the consequences of their decisions, so I did not call them on it. I have often wondered whether I should have handled that differently. . . . I do not believe that any of them actually wanted a death sentence for Andrew, yet their refusal to help me in any way almost precipitated that result. I would be interested in what their attitudes towards Andrew are now."

Moore conceded that the case was difficult from a defense perspective. "I was always concerned about Andrew's case as the evidence against him was so strong. Andrew refused to consider any plea agreements in the case, and rejected a life sentence offer [as did Chelsea] that would have allowed him to avoid a trial. Unfortunately, from the very beginning of the case I felt that Andrew would most likely be convicted, and that we would be fighting to save his life. . . . We fought hard in the guilt/innocence stage, and never conceded that issue, but we had to concentrate a good deal of our efforts on the punishment stage, even though that was not the issue with which Andrew was concerned. I'm not even sure that Andrew ever had a realistic grasp of how dire the circumstances were."

Chelsea's conviction and death sentence—received just a few months before Andrew's trial—had only made the situation more dire. "I think everyone was shocked when she got death, as she had so little prior record, and it really caused me great concern," said Moore, who had literally been sick to his stomach when he heard of Chelsea's fate. "Had she received a life sentence, I had intended to push the state to waive the death penalty in Andrew's case; but her verdict made that impossible."

Although Moore has defended many death penalty cases, he believes every one is a human tragedy and that each has its own unique dynamic. In Andrew's case, he said, "we were severely hampered by the fact that none of his family would help us with obtaining background information on Andrew, or by making an appeal for his life; and thus we worked very hard to develop those things through friends of the family. Unfortunately, Andrew's family was quite dysfunctional, and it affected him in some very profound ways. I think the jury's appreciation of that fact was the key to the life sentence."

Chapter Thirty-seven

Andrew was now serving life in prison. Chelsea was on death row, and Susana Toledano wouldn't be up for parole until the year 2037. And what of the fourth co-conspirator, Hilario Cardenas?

Although Hilario had provided information in exchange for being indicted on the lesser charge of "conspiracy to commit capital murder" in 2004, he and the DA's office had never reached a mutually agreeable sentencing agreement. So Hilario's attorney, Ray Hall, Jr., entered an open plea to Judge Young on May 1, 2006.

On May 6, 2006, Hilario Cardenas signed "a written plea admonishments and a judicial confession acknowledging that he was entering an open plea of guilty to the offense of conspiracy to commit capital murder, a first degree felony."

After receiving Hilario's guilty plea, the judge ordered a pre-sentence investigation so the court could look into Hilario's background. The judge also heard testimony from Hilario's wife and sister-in-law regarding his background and character.

At the end of May, after reviewing the report and the testimony, Judge Young passed sentence: Hilario was given fifty years in prison and will be up for the possibility of parole in 2023 after serving one-third of his sentence. According to Hall, Hilario received the fifty-year sentence, not a life sentence, because his case "was not a 3g offense since it was conspiracy to commit and not a capital murder sentence. Everyone else involved did get 3g offenses," stated Hall, "and they have to do half their sentence before being eligible for parole." (A 3g offense is a crime involving the use of a deadly weapon and other crimes of an assaultive nature.)

Hilario waived his right to appeal at his sentencing hearing.

Looking back, court observers wondered why Hilario was never asked to testify at Chelsea's or Andrew's trials. After all, Hilario had provided the gun that was used to shoot the Wamsleys—and he had been involved in the planning of the murders from the beginning. Hilario's attorney, Ray Hall, said he was never given a definite reason for that decision, except for several statements from the DA's office suggesting that they didn't know for sure what Hilario would say once he got on the stand. Later, when Hall was asked about this, he stated that he thought Hilario would have been a fine witness since he was "remorseful for his part in it and had helped [the DA's office] as much as he could."

Chapter Thirty-eight

In August 2007, two years after Chelsea became the first woman sentenced to death in Tarrant County, Texas, her appellate lawyer, Bob Ford, filed a writ of habeas corpus, stating that Chelsea, now twenty-three, was being held unlawfully. It was his belief that Chelsea deserved either a new trial or her death sentence should be changed to life in prison.

In his writ, Ford suggested many reasons why he felt Chelsea was illegally convicted. Among them, he asserted that Assistant District Attorney Mike Parrish had committed prosecutorial misconduct, that Judge Young was biased towards the state, and that Chelsea's attorneys were ineffective.

Ford alleged that Parrish had never told the judge or the grand jury foreman that he had been indirectly receiving information about Chelsea from the legal assistant of her lawyer at the time—a clear violation of attorney-client privilege. "I never, ever thought I would see a prosecutor go into the grand jury and do what Mike Parrish did and not stop the grand jury proceedings," Ford said. "It is unimaginable." Ford asked that the district attorney's office be taken off the case and a special prosecutor be appointed to handle the writ.

Ford also accused Parrish of not turning over to defense attorneys the results of a psychological examination of Susana Toledano conducted by Dr. Randy Price. "That is a violation," Ford stated, "because prosecutors are required to turn over pertinent evidence to the defense."

Ford claimed that when he tried to subpoena Price's psychological report on Susana, Judge Young denied the subpoena while Ford was on vacation. Ford claimed that both sides should have been present when Young suppressed the subpoena, and he filed a motion to have Young recused.

Ford said that Chelsea's attorneys, J. Warren St. John and Terry Barlow, should have had Chelsea evaluated by a psychologist in order to show the jury that there were mitigating factors that would have warranted her receiving a life sentence instead of a death sentence.

In response to Ford's writ, Judge Young filed a court document in which he stated that he did not "agree with Mr. Ford's evaluation and assessment of my conduct." However, he continued, he would voluntarily recuse himself, saying he "should not be in a position to have to judge my own actions."

After Young recused himself, a new judge was appointed to the case—Steven Herod, a district judge in Eastland County, Texas. Ford asked Herod to hold a hearing to decide whether or not the district attorney's office should also be recused. When notified of this, the district attorney's office refused to recuse itself and asked, instead, that Ford be sanctioned for making false allegations.

Chapter Thirty-nine

On September 11, 2007, Chelsea temporarily left death row—where she was incarcerated with nine other women—and returned to Tarrant County. She was there to attend hearings on the writ submitted by her appellate lawyer, Bob Ford, asking that she receive a new trial or have her death sentence commuted to life in prison. At that time, Chelsea agreed to a jailhouse interview with Melody McDonald of the *Fort Worth Star-Telegram,* as long as the interviewer did not bring up her case.

Since being incarcerated on death row in the Mountain View Prison unit in Gatesville, Texas, Chelsea said, she had been spending her time doing needlepoint, writing poetry, drawing pictures of angels—and praying. She prays for others, and she prays for herself that somehow, something will surface to clear her from the death sentence she's under. Chelsea believes that she is innocent.

In a jumpsuit of bright yellow, the color worn by only the highest-level offenders, Chelsea sat in a tiny interview room—hands cuffed and ankles shackled. In the hour-long interview, Chelsea stated, "It is all horrible. Jail is hell. Prison is hell. Death row is terrifying. You are told, 'They are going to kill you.' There is no moment when you don't know you are under a death sentence. There is no moment of freedom unless you are asleep. . . . And even then, sometimes it seeps in."

Chelsea stated that she was "shocked, depressed, heartbroken, and terrified" when she first arrived on death row. "It destroyed my perspective of the justice system. I used to believe in it. That is why I took it [my case] to trial."

Every morning, with up to four other death row inmates, Chelsea performs some kind of prison work as guards keep a close eye on her. She is permitted two hours of recreation a day—watching TV or walking in the yard—and spends twenty hours in her fourteen-foot-by-six-foot cell with blank walls. No art or photographs are permitted to be taped up.

"I pray to God I never have to go [to the death chamber]," she stated. "You push it out of your mind, but it is never going to leave."

Before returning to her cell after work or recreation, "We have to strip down . . . squat and cough, squat and cough, shake our head. They give us our clothes back after they have checked them for contraband. We get dressed right there in front of them. We never leave their sight."

Chelsea stated that she doesn't socialize much with the other inmates. "You don't have friends in prison," she said. "But we get along. I don't have a problem getting along with people." Chelsea said no one ever talks about what they're in for—or about death. "Nobody asks and nobody is going to talk about it."

Chelsea said she writes poems "about heartbreak," listens to Christian music on the radio, and draws. "I've always drawn angels, but most of the time I just draw what I see—people. I was never good at drawing people until I got down there, I guess. There is more emotion and you can focus better." Chelsea said she gives her artwork to people on their birthdays, so they know that "I'm thinking about them or that their birthdays are not forgotten."

Chelsea told the reporter that she prays a lot. "I pray for everything, the people I see on the TV and the news, the people I hear about—like that bridge collapse and floods. I pray for all of those people because I know what it is like to hurt."

Chelsea's mother, brother, and sister come to visit as often as they can. "They see through the lies," Chelsea said. When asked about Andrew and Susana, she stated she had no idea what either is doing. She is, however, acutely aware that she received the death penalty and they received life sentences, but she didn't comment on that.

Before she arrived on death row, Chelsea said she was a gregarious and trusting person. "I was stupid," she said. "I believed everybody, you know—too happy-and-go-lucky for my own good." Asked if she thought she would ever get off death row, she stated, "I just put my faith in God and trust that he will lead me in victory or not. If he doesn't, then he has a purpose for me." When asked if she thought she would go to heaven when she died, she broke down crying, but was unequivocal. "I know I will," she said.

Chapter Forty

On January 22, 2009, the Texas Court of Appeals turned down Richardson's appeal that challenged whether or not there was sufficient evidence to support her conviction.

In a unanimous ruling, Judge Michael Kaesler wrote: "In the light most favorable to the verdict, the testimony and evidence at trial showed that Richardson participated in the planning of the murders, aided in the two failed attempts to murder the Wamsleys, and was present during, encouraged, and participated in the final attempt during which the Wamsleys were killed."

On June 12, 2009, state district judge Steven Herod heard Chelsea's court-appointed appellate lawyer Bob Ford's allegations that Mike Parrish withheld a report about Susana Toledano's mental health from Chelsea's defense team and interfered with attorney-client privilege. And in a stunning move, Ford introduced two documents outlining problems that Parrish had concerning another death penalty case, that of death row inmate Michael Toney, who had been convicted for the 1985 bombing of a Lake Worth trailer that killed three people. In those documents, it was revealed that the Texas Court of Criminal Appeals overturned the conviction of Toney, after discovering that Parrish failed to turn over to the defense "no less than fourteen documents containing exculpatory or impeaching evidence." In that case, Toney had been sentenced to death basically on the testimony of Toney's ex-wife and former best friend. But the evidence that was withheld cast doubt on their testimony. No physical evidence had ever been found linking Toney to the bombing.

Ford was attempting to show that Parrish had a history of withholding evidence and, at the very least, Parrish should be off the case. At the very most, Ford hoped that Chelsea could have a new trial.

In late August 2009, District Judge Steven Herod revealed his decision. It was faxed to both parties, but he offered no explanation to support the pronouncement. And what did the judge decide? Judge Herod denied Ford's request to recuse DA Parrish from the appellate case of Chelsea Richardson.

To Ford, this was a surprising outcome. Based on what had happened in the Toney case, he thought he had a good chance at getting Parrish off the case. Clearly, he was disappointed. When asked what his next move would be, he said, "I'm in the process of making a decision on what action I'm going to take next. I need to consult with my client, and she is in the penitentiary. We'll move on from there."

Ford could challenge Herod's ruling by filing a writ of mandamus with the Texas Court of Criminal Appeals. A mandamus is an order from a higher court to a lower court to withdraw a ruling if it is found that the lower court made a mistake or ignored the law.

Chapter Forty-one

On March 13, 2008, a hearing was held before Justice Bob McCoy in the Fort Worth Court of Appeals on Andrew Wamsley's conviction of capital murder.

Andrew's appellate attorney David Pearson, who was also his trial attorney, appealed Andrew's conviction, citing twelve points of contention. Several points had to do with jury selection and the contention that the defense was deprived of its use of peremptory challenge (the right to challenge a juror without being required to state a reason for the challenge). Several other points had to do with the court excluding inconsistent statements by Sarah, Andrew's sister, which Pearson felt would have impeached her testimony. A final point alleged that the trial court erred by failing to suppress blood and DNA evidence from Andrew's car "because the repeated search of his vehicle went beyond the temporal scope and authority of the warrant and was therefore unlawful."

After responding to each and every point made by Pearson, Justice Bob McCoy stated, "Having overruled all of the Appellant's points, we affirm the trial court's judgment [of life in prison]."

And with those words, Andrew's direct state appeal process ended. More appeals are possible—habeas corpus in state or federal court—but Andrew is not pursuing any options at the time of this writing.

Chapter Forty-two

Unlike many prisoners, Andrew does not work out. He doesn't play basketball, handball, chess, or checkers. He doesn't drink, smoke, or gamble. He reads when he has books and listens to the radio. At night, he sometimes watches TV for an hour or two. His favorite TV show is *House,* on Fox. If there are enough people, he plays a game of dominoes called 42, or sometimes volleyball—if the ball is not flat. Most of his days, he says, are spent sleeping or listening to the radio. On Sunday through Thursday, he is supposed to get "dayroom" from 6 a.m. to 10:30 p.m. There are four "count times," that take about one and a half hours, at 6:30 a.m., 12:30 p.m., 6:30 p.m., and 8:30 p.m. Prisoners are subject to the whims of the people who work in the prison. According to Andrew, it's part of human nature to adapt so you can survive, "but that does not mean you come to terms with it."

There is no air conditioning in cells, so Texas summers are hot. "Just imagine," he says, "sitting in a concrete box when it's 100°F with just a fan."

Andrew does have a work assignment, but the warden doesn't want any person accused of a 3g offense to work, so he doesn't do that anymore.

Klint, Andrew's childhood friend, sends Andrew a Christmas card with two or three books a year. When Andrew writes to him, Klint doesn't respond. Klint's mother or father writes to Andrew two or three times a year. Those are the only letters Andrew receives—and now those from me, the author of this book. Although Andrew felt Klint was more like a brother than a friend, he wonders why Klint doesn't write him back or write him anything different from what Klint's parents tell him in their letters.

Andrew tries not to think about the murders, or his past friendship with Chelsea. He continues to say he is innocent and doesn't know who did what on the night of December 11, 2003.

Epilogue

When I started researching this crime, I contacted the court reporters, who, in Texas and in many other states, own the rights to the court transcripts. Through Terry Bradshaw and William Shelton, I obtained both Chelsea's and Andrew's entire trial transcripts—thousands of pages of testimony. When people ask me how long the trials lasted, I tell them, "Andrew's was thirteen inches high. How long is that?"

I also researched and read every article written about the case (well over a hundred), but one can gather only so much from media accounts and court documents. I contacted lawyers, detectives, and family members, as well as the convicted parties themselves, in an effort to get a fuller picture of the players in this all-too-real drama.

Three of the four defendants in the case agreed to write to me from prison. I told them in my letters that I was writing a book about the Wamsley murders and wanted to ask them some questions. I wrote that they should answer only those questions they felt comfortable writing about. Surprisingly, all three were forthcoming on just about every question.

I got to know Susana, Andrew, and Hilario in a far different way from how I "knew" them from their testimony and media reports. It's not my job to judge their guilt or innocence. The courts have done that. But I can tell you some things I learned about them through my correspondence.

Susana seems deeply sorry for what happened and for

many other things she did in her past. She is often depressed in prison, thinking back on her life outside. She knows she messed up, big time. As to why she did what she did, she felt that she was too easily led, too trusting, and too needy— which, she points out, is absolutely no excuse for any of her behavior. Susana says she's learned a lot about herself in prison and feels she's a better person for it. When she looks back on her life in 2003—at the time of the murders—it's hard for her to recognize herself.

In her letters to me, Susana can seem like a teenager. She says she dreams of getting married one day and having a family who will "love her unconditionally." Maybe, after all, that was what she was seeking in the first place: someone to love her. She says she's trying to be more discriminating and not to trust people as easily as she once did.

When asked about her thoughts regarding Chelsea, Chelsea's mom, Andrew, and Hilario, Susana has mixed feelings. She says that Chelsea has two distinct sides: the nurturing side, the one who "looks out for others," and the controlling side, which gets people to do whatever she wants. Susana says she still has warm feelings toward the nurturing Chelsea. As for Chelsea's mother, Susana has only praise. She says she could always talk to Celia; she was a fun lady, an understanding person, and a generous soul. Susana said she really didn't know Andrew or Hilario very well. Even though she may have spent time with them, they never talked about anything personal.

Very occasionally, Susana has a visit from her mother or other members of her family. She waits for those visits like she used to wait for her father to come home, praying they come soon. She also prays that the father who left her so long ago doesn't know anything about where she is now.

Andrew and I have been speaking on the telephone and he is sharing many details about life in prison. He calls me collect, about once a week, and we chat about things from the weather to being a vegetarian (which, he says, no self-

respecting Texan would ever *be) to Southern accents. He enjoys reading all kinds of books, even esoteric books on religion. I have sent him many books, and he reads them all and comments on them, offering intelligent critiques. He shares a cell, but he wishes he were alone. He likes solitude. He says he doesn't often go out, even during recreation, preferring to be by himself. He says he lives a "sad and lonely" life. He has no visitors. He writes that Celia was a wonderful lady who always took the time to talk to him and to be kind. He said the Richardson household was the direct opposite of his, and he felt so much more at home at the Richardsons'. The demands that his family put on him to achieve, to dress a certain way, to act a certain way, seemed to have taken a toll on him. He simply couldn't meet their high standards. He preferred a lot less pressure. He also mentioned that he always thought he would go into the Marines after high school, but his parents told him that if he joined, he would be kicked out of the family. He said he didn't want that, so he didn't sign up. Andrew said that had he gone, he would probably be dead now, since whatever he does, he does in a gung-ho way, and he wouldn't have held back in battle. Andrew maintains his innocence. "I was a spoiled rich kid and got almost anything I ever asked for. Why in the world would I want my parents dead?"*

Andrew wants to know a lot about my life: What is New York City like? How do I manage to live among so many people? What do I like to do in my leisure time? He tells me he misses lying in the grass and looking up at the stars. He wonders if I think of him as a country hick. He speaks fondly of his mother and of the many talents she had as a homemaker.

In my correspondence with Hilario, I've learned that he is deeply religious. All of his faith is in Jesus, and he prays that he will soon be able to go back to his family and live a "normal" life. He deeply misses his daughter and his extended family of cousins, uncles, and aunts, all of whom visit him. Before the crime, he says, he was hard-working and always held a job and earned enough money to help his parents and to give his wife and daughter a good life.

Although I sent several letters to Chelsea, she chose not to respond except through a friend who said that she would write to me if she could read what I had written about her in this book before it was published. Of course, I declined. However, in the end, she wrote one sentence at the bottom of my letter to her, which I received in mid-January 2010. It read, "My point of view? I'm innocent & I've been & am are [sic] being screwed by the system. Texas is waiting to Murder me!" Through Chelsea's friend, I learned that Chelsea's opinion is that Susana changed her story so many times that she is totally untrustworthy and should not have been believed. Chelsea firmly believes she is innocent, pointing out that there is not one shred of evidence to show she was at the scene of the crime.

Several detectives went out of their way to add specific details to the book. Ralph Standefer was extremely helpful in describing what took place during the crime scene investigation and the interrogations. He also offered his insights into why he felt the crime was committed and on the character of the perpetrators. For him, this crime stood out—even among murders. "It was not the norm for this kind of crime to happen in an upper-class kind of neighborhood to upper-class kind of people," he told me. "I wouldn't say I have seen it all and done it all, but I have seen and done quite a bit . . . stuff that most people don't even dream of. . . . I can think of at least one case that I was involved in that most would classify as a necrophilia-driven serial killer . . . but Wamsley, like I said, was different in that you knew because of their status in the community, people would be paying attention." Standefer said he still thinks about the crime, and feels an overwhelming sense of sorrow.

Many people, of course, chose not to write or speak to me. I respect their decisions and understand their reason-

ing. I heard through lawyers and news reports that neither Sarah Wamsley nor her grandparents would speak to anyone about the case, so I didn't try to contact them.

One of Chelsea's attorneys, Terry Barlow, politely declined to discuss the case with me. I never heard back from Warren St. John, although I left messages on his machine. Catherine Page Simpson stated she did not wish to correspond with me, and I didn't contact Michael Parrish because I knew Chelsea's appeal was underway, and as a result, he probably wouldn't speak with me either.

Chelsea's appellate lawyer, Bob Ford, is a true Texas character. Willing to talk—but of course only about that which he is able, since Chelsea's case is still pending—he offered tidbits of dirt about the goings-on of the trial, the pleas, and the jockeying for positions. He is quite a raconteur and speaking with him made my work that much more colorful.

When I wrote this book, as in the other true-crime books I've written, I tried to let the facts speak for themselves and not insert my own opinion. After all, I am neither judge nor jury but simply a reporter who wanted to research and tell about a case that I found fascinating. And, no matter how deeply I probed, the "why" of this—or any other murder—never seems to make sense to me. This case seemed particularly senseless. Here were kids—that's what they were, after all—who had their whole lives ahead of them. None had ever been in any trouble before this. How did these young people, who had been relatively functional in both work and school environments, ever reach the conclusion that murder was not only okay, but was also their best option? The question that intrigues—read "haunts"—me is, How did they decide that this was their only choice? What pushes someone over the edge?

As has been said many times before by psychologists and other behavior specialists far more versed in forensic psychology than I, people from horribly dysfunctional *backgrounds can turn out just fine, in spite of their having been subjected to and having witnessed depraved and vile behavior that humans should never have to know about; and people from relatively well-functioning childhoods can turn into murderers. How to account for this? No one seems to have come up with an adequate answer.*

From what I have gleaned, Chelsea's personality seems eerily similar to that of a cult leader. She could be charming, seductive, and charismatic. She, like cult leaders, was able to laser in on the people who would follow her unquestioningly; figure out, or instinctively know, how to exploit the weaknesses; and then seamlessly have them do whatever she wanted. For example, Susana seemed to have been lured into the scheme with the promise that she wouldn't have to work her entire life and that she could chill with friends in a family environment that she never had, and that she would be accepted by someone "better" than she. She had somehow convinced herself that proving her love for Chelsea trumped everything, even rational thought. Hilario seemed to have been dazzled by the idea of a horse for his daughter along with some cash. And Andrew? What was he after? On the most obvious level, it was money. But there must have been either deep, deep anger against his parents, whom it seemed he could never please; or, it could be he had such a great need to please the one person who stuck by him and offered him what seemed a "normal" life, that he, too, gave up whatever rational thought he had. His need for acceptance and a new family seemed to have pushed him over the edge. But then again, if he did have a schizoid personality, as two reputable psychologists attested to, then he probably wouldn't have cared much about a new family. And further—even if he were schizoid, do all schizoid personalities end up as murderers? I don't think so.

Assuming the juries made the correct determinations, it is my belief that none of these four people would have committed the crime alone. They needed the "group mentality" to do the deed. As I mentioned in the book, one lawyer said that if Susana's "mentor" (cult leader) had wanted her to sell the most Girl Scout cookies in the world, Susana probably would have done that. I think the same of Andrew and Hilario. There was something about the group dynamics—herd mentality—that led each of them to do what none of them could have done alone. Andrew appeared to have been so laid-back and uninvolved as a human being that to put this heinous act into motion and to see it through to its execution would have been impossible. Chelsea seemed unwilling to get her hands dirty and needed others to carry out her evil work. She was comfortable using people; she didn't accept responsibility for her actions; she didn't seem to have a life plan and engaged in a parasitic lifestyle (requiring tribute from Susana in the form of killing the Wamsleys for their money, which she'd somehow get from Andrew).

The fact that the four of them were able to keep the plot secret is not only fascinating, but an anomaly among crime-doers. Lying and secrecy—and the trust that none of the others will blab—seemed to have played a role. Also, for their age, the planning was quite detailed. They wore gloves. They did a lot of cleanup. They practiced shooting a gun. There were no pesky witnesses—no one saw them going in and out of the house. And they planned their alibi and had canned statements to give to the police.

The group was at once incredibly cagey and unbelievably stupid. How could they have thought that shooting at a gas tank would actually blow up a car and kill everyone in it—and that they wouldn't get caught, eventually? How could they have thought they would get away with making things look like a robbery gone bad—and shooting Andrew in the arm? They were so naïve that one is left shaking one's head: They couldn't be that dumb!

In speaking to the lawyers, detectives, and convicted parties, a picture emerges of Celia Richardson—who now *must live her life knowing her daughter is on death row—of a person who tried her best. She seemed to have been well liked, conscientious, easy to get along with, capable, and generous. From those qualities, how does a Chelsea form? What role, if any, did she have in it? It is a hard—and heartbreaking—question to answer.*

And although the Wamsleys seemed to have had some cancerous dynamic going on in their lives that resulted in two very flawed human beings—Sarah, by her own admission; Andrew, by the court's determination—one is left wondering, What could have gone on between them and among the four to have caused such dire results? They couldn't have been that *bad!*

So one—at least this one—is left pondering yet again the age-old question of how do we get to be who we are. Luck? Genes? Environment? Nature? Nurture? A combination? None of the above?

If we had the answer, then murder wouldn't hold any lure at all.